DAUGHTERS OF THE
DRAGON
DEEP CUTS

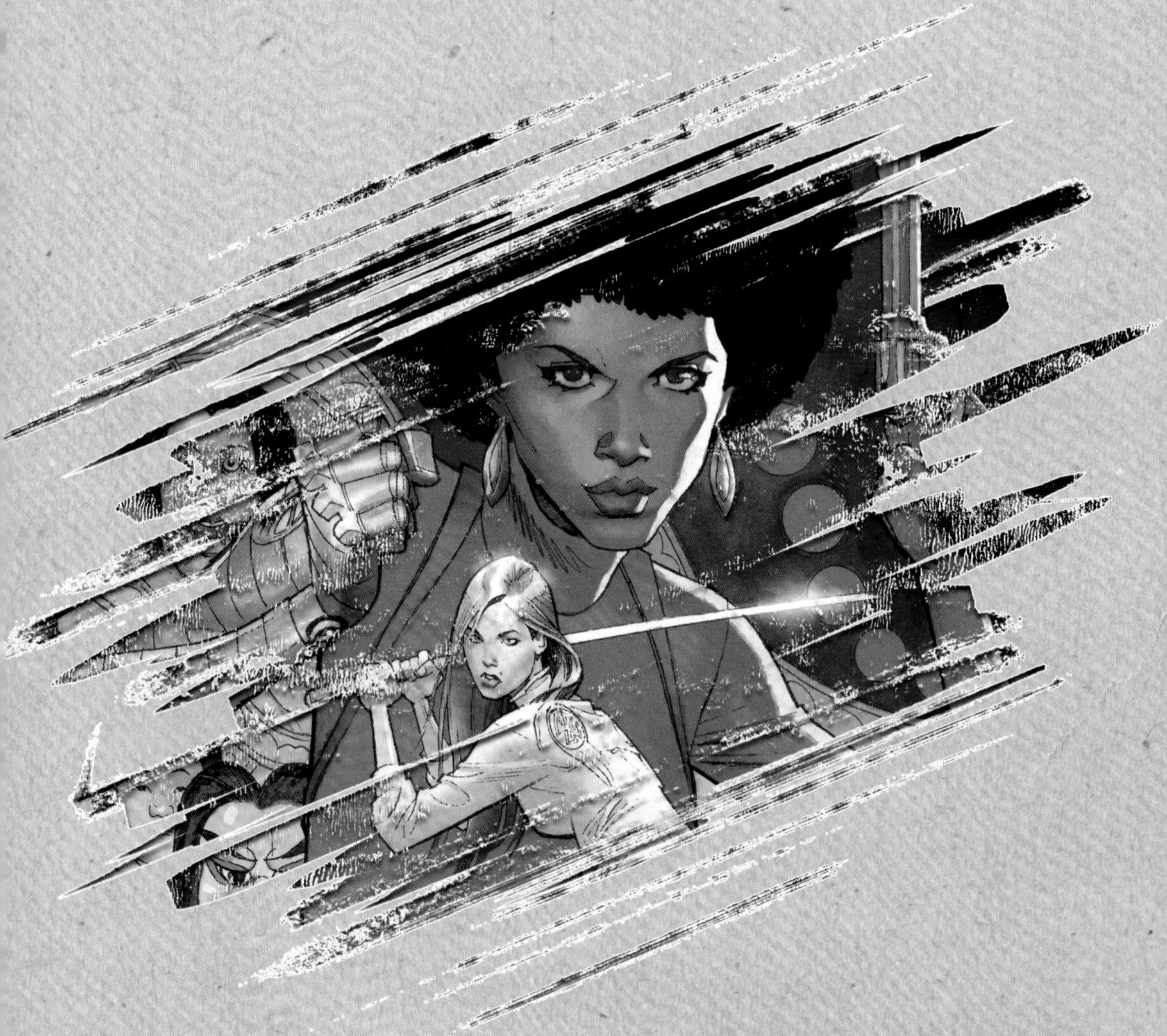

DAUGHTERS OF THE DRAGON

DEEP CUTS

JED MacKAY
WRITER

TRAVEL FOREMAN (CH. 1-2 & 5-6) & JOEY VAZQUEZ (CH. 3-4)
PENCILERS

TRAVEL FOREMAN (CH. 1-2 & 6), JOE SILVER (CH. 1 & 5), JOEY VAZQUEZ (CH. 3) & CRAIG YEUNG (CH. 3-4)
INKERS

JORDAN GIBSON (CH. 1-3), RAIN BEREDO (CH. 3-4) & ANDRES MOSSA (CH. 5-6)
COLORISTS

FERRAN DELGADO
LETTERER

ANDREW C. ROBINSON
COVER ART

KATHLEEN WISNESKI
ASSISTANT EDITOR

NICK LOWE
EDITOR

COLLECTION EDITOR JENNIFER GRÜNWALD
ASSISTANT EDITOR CAITLIN O'CONNELL
ASSOCIATE MANAGING EDITOR KATERI WOODY
EDITOR, SPECIAL PROJECTS MARK D. BEAZLEY
VP PRODUCTION & SPECIAL PROJECTS JEFF YOUNGQUIST
SVP PRINT, SALES & MARKETING DAVID GABRIEL
BOOK DESIGNER ADAM DEL RE

EDITOR IN CHIEF C.B. CEBULSKI
CHIEF CREATIVE OFFICER JOE QUESADA
PRESIDENT DAN BUCKLEY
EXECUTIVE PRODUCER ALAN FINE

DAUGHTERS OF THE DRAGON: DEEP CUTS MPGN. First printing 2018. ISBN 978-1-302-91468-4. Published by MARVEL WORLDWIDE, INC., a subsidiary of MARVEL ENTERTAINMENT, LLC. OFFICE OF PUBLICATION: 135 West 50th Street, New York, NY 10020. Copyright © 2018 MARVEL No similarity between any of the names, characters, persons, and/or institutions in this magazine with those of any living or dead person or institution is intended, and any such similarity which may exist is purely coincidental. **Printed in Canada.** DAN BUCKLEY, President, Marvel Entertainment; JOHN NEE, Publisher; JOE QUESADA, Chief Creative Officer; TOM BREVOORT, SVP of Publishing; DAVID BOGART, SVP of Business Affairs & Operations, Publishing & Partnership; DAVID GABRIEL, SVP of Sales & Marketing, Publishing; JEFF YOUNGQUIST, VP of Production & Special Projects; DAN CARR, Executive Director of Publishing Technology; ALEX MORALES, Director of Publishing Operations; DAN EDINGTON, Managing Editor; SUSAN CRESPI, Production Manager; STAN LEE, Chairman Emeritus. For information regarding advertising in Marvel Comics or on Marvel.com, please contact Vit DeBellis, Custom Solutions & Integrated Advertising Manager, at vdebellis@marvel.com. For Marvel subscription inquiries, please call 888-511-5480. **Manufactured between 12/14/2018 and 1/15/2019 by SOLISCO PRINTERS, SCOTT, QC, CANADA.**

10 9 8 7 6 5 4 3 2 1

CHAPTER 1

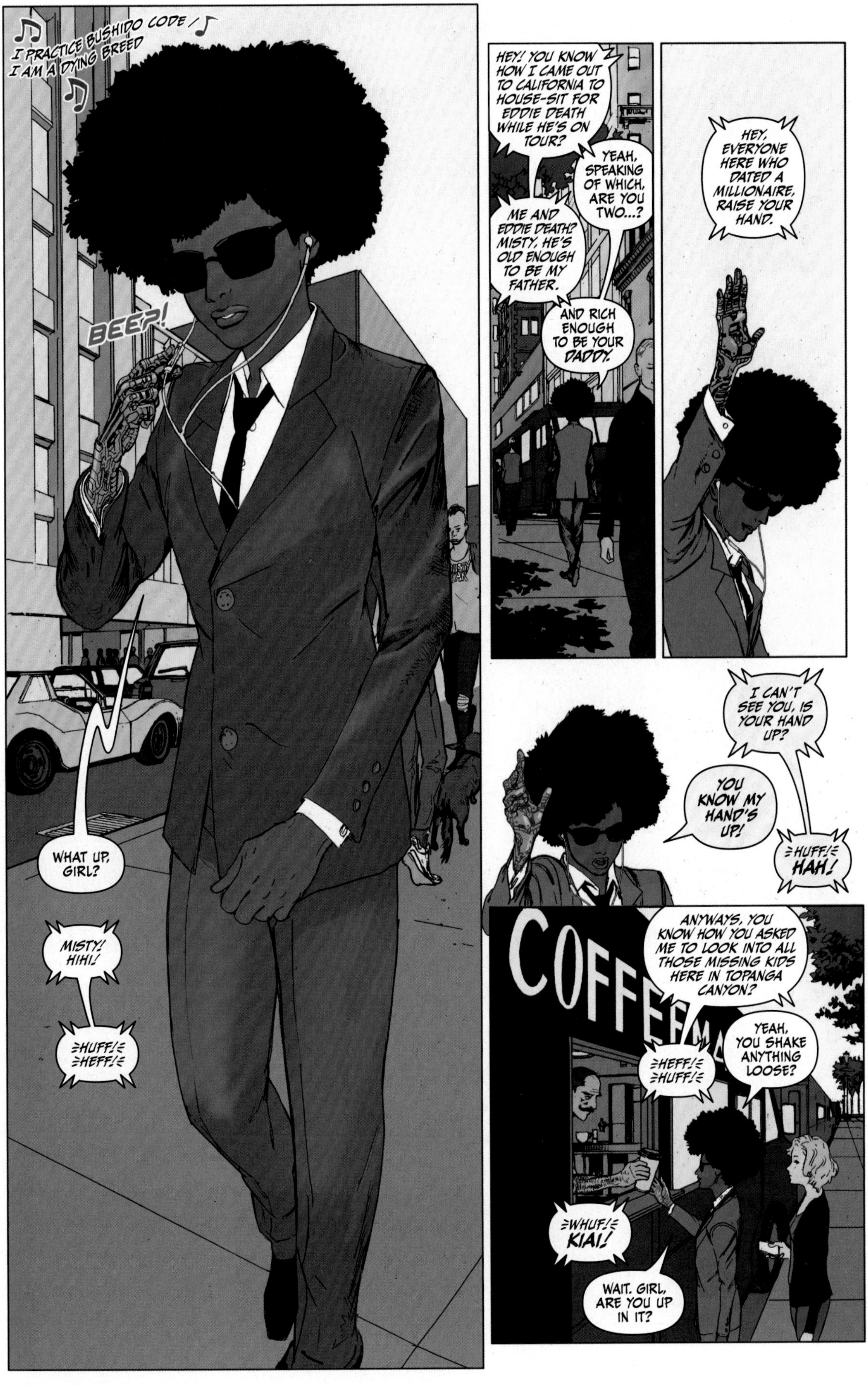
I PRACTICE BUSHIDO CODE / I AM A DYING BREED
BEEP!
WHAT UP, GIRL?
MISTY! HIHI!
HUFF! HEFF!
HEY! YOU KNOW HOW I CAME OUT TO CALIFORNIA TO HOUSE-SIT FOR EDDIE DEATH WHILE HE'S ON TOUR?
YEAH, SPEAKING OF WHICH, ARE YOU TWO...?
ME AND EDDIE DEATH? MISTY. HE'S OLD ENOUGH TO BE MY FATHER.
AND RICH ENOUGH TO BE YOUR DADDY.
HEY, EVERYONE HERE WHO DATED A MILLIONAIRE, RAISE YOUR HAND.
I CAN'T SEE YOU. IS YOUR HAND UP?
YOU KNOW MY HAND'S UP!
HUFF! HAH!
COFFEEMA
ANYWAYS, YOU KNOW HOW YOU ASKED ME TO LOOK INTO ALL THOSE MISSING KIDS HERE IN TOPANGA CANYON?
HEFF! HUFF!
YEAH, YOU SHAKE ANYTHING LOOSE?
WHUF! KIAI!
WAIT. GIRL, ARE YOU UP IN IT?

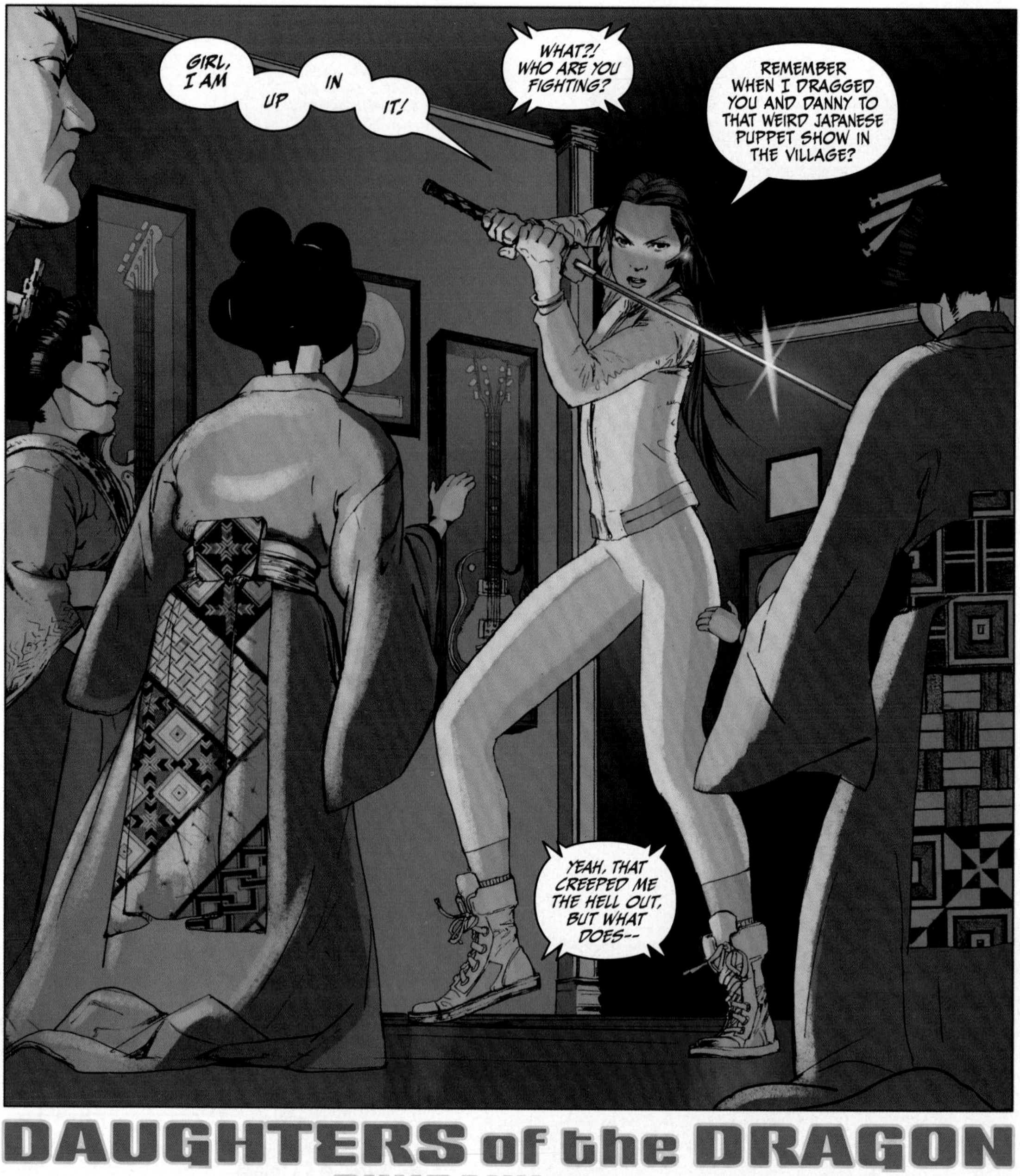
GIRL, I AM UP IN IT!
WHAT?! WHO ARE YOU FIGHTING?
REMEMBER WHEN I DRAGGED YOU AND DANNY TO THAT WEIRD JAPANESE PUPPET SHOW IN THE VILLAGE?
YEAH, THAT CREEPED ME THE HELL OUT, BUT WHAT DOES--

DAUGHTERS of the DRAGON

BUNRAKU: Part 1

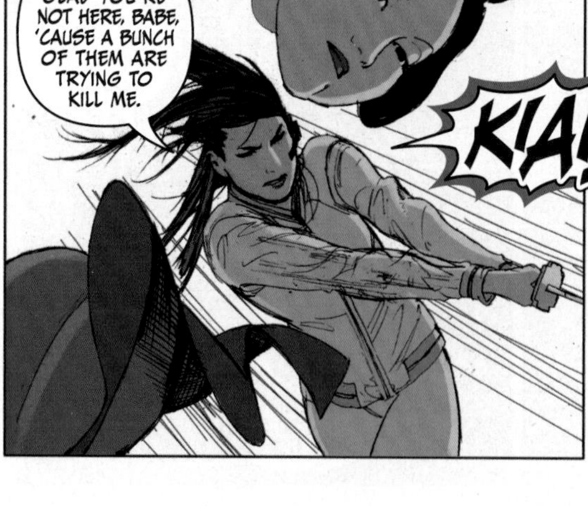
THEN BE GLAD YOU'RE NOT HERE, BABE, 'CAUSE A BUNCH OF THEM ARE TRYING TO KILL ME.
KIA!!

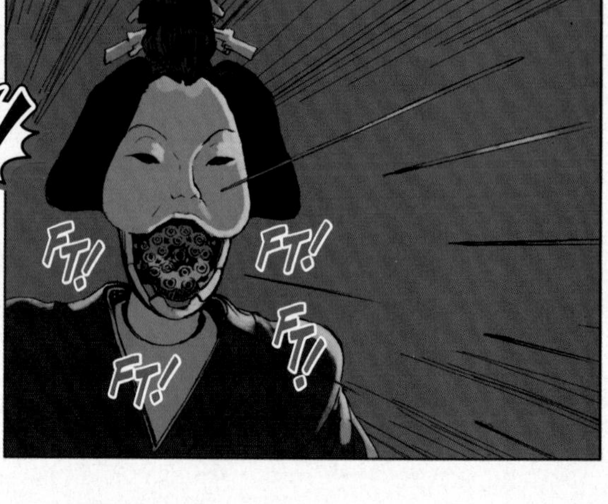
FT!
FT!
FT!
FT!

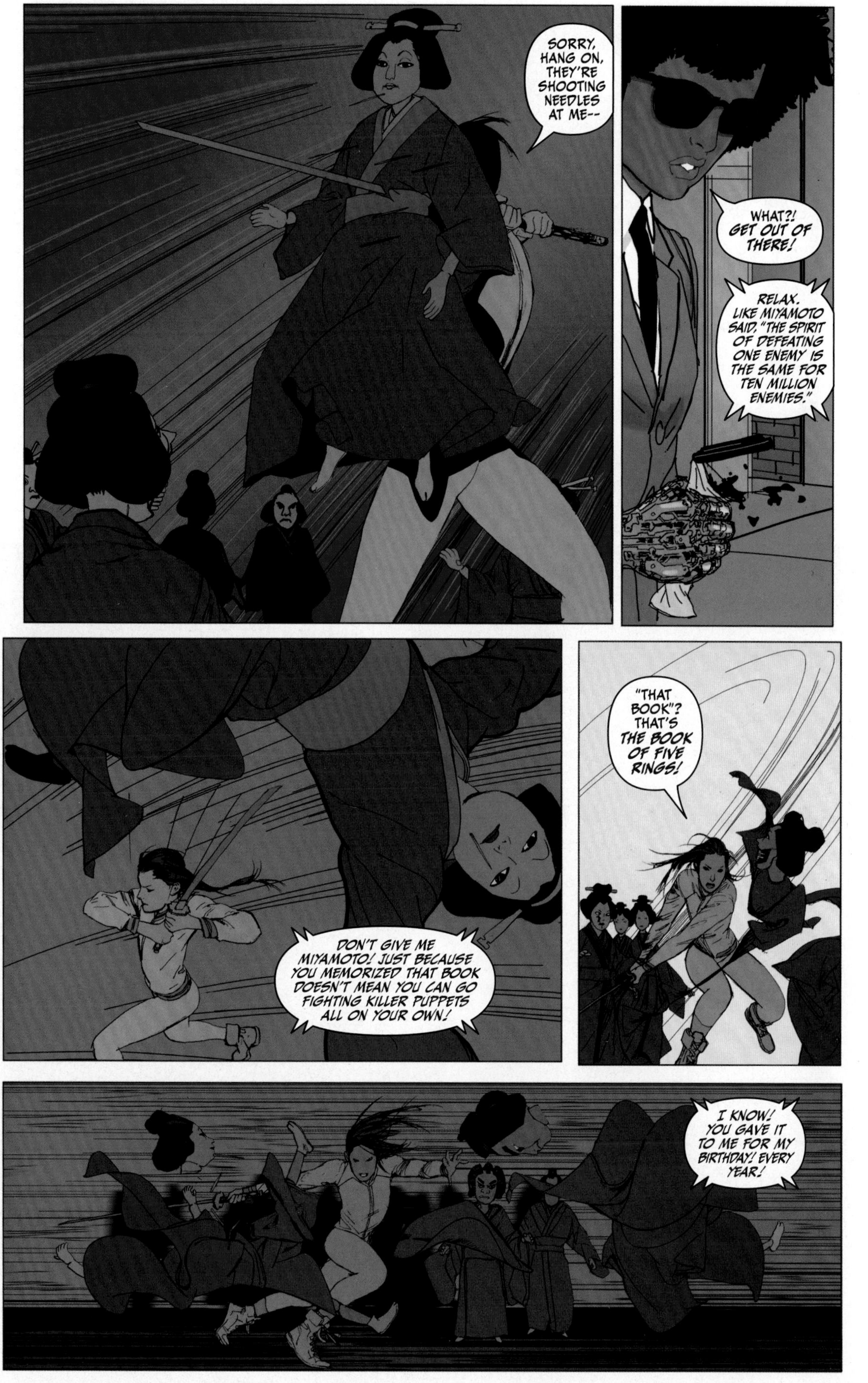
SORRY, HANG ON, THEY'RE SHOOTING NEEDLES AT ME--
WHAT?! GET OUT OF THERE!
RELAX. LIKE MIYAMOTO SAID, "THE SPIRIT OF DEFEATING ONE ENEMY IS THE SAME FOR TEN MILLION ENEMIES."
DON'T GIVE ME MIYAMOTO! JUST BECAUSE YOU MEMORIZED THAT BOOK DOESN'T MEAN YOU CAN GO FIGHTING KILLER PUPPETS ALL ON YOUR OWN!
"THAT BOOK"? THAT'S THE BOOK OF FIVE RINGS!
I KNOW! YOU GAVE IT TO ME FOR MY BIRTHDAY! EVERY YEAR!

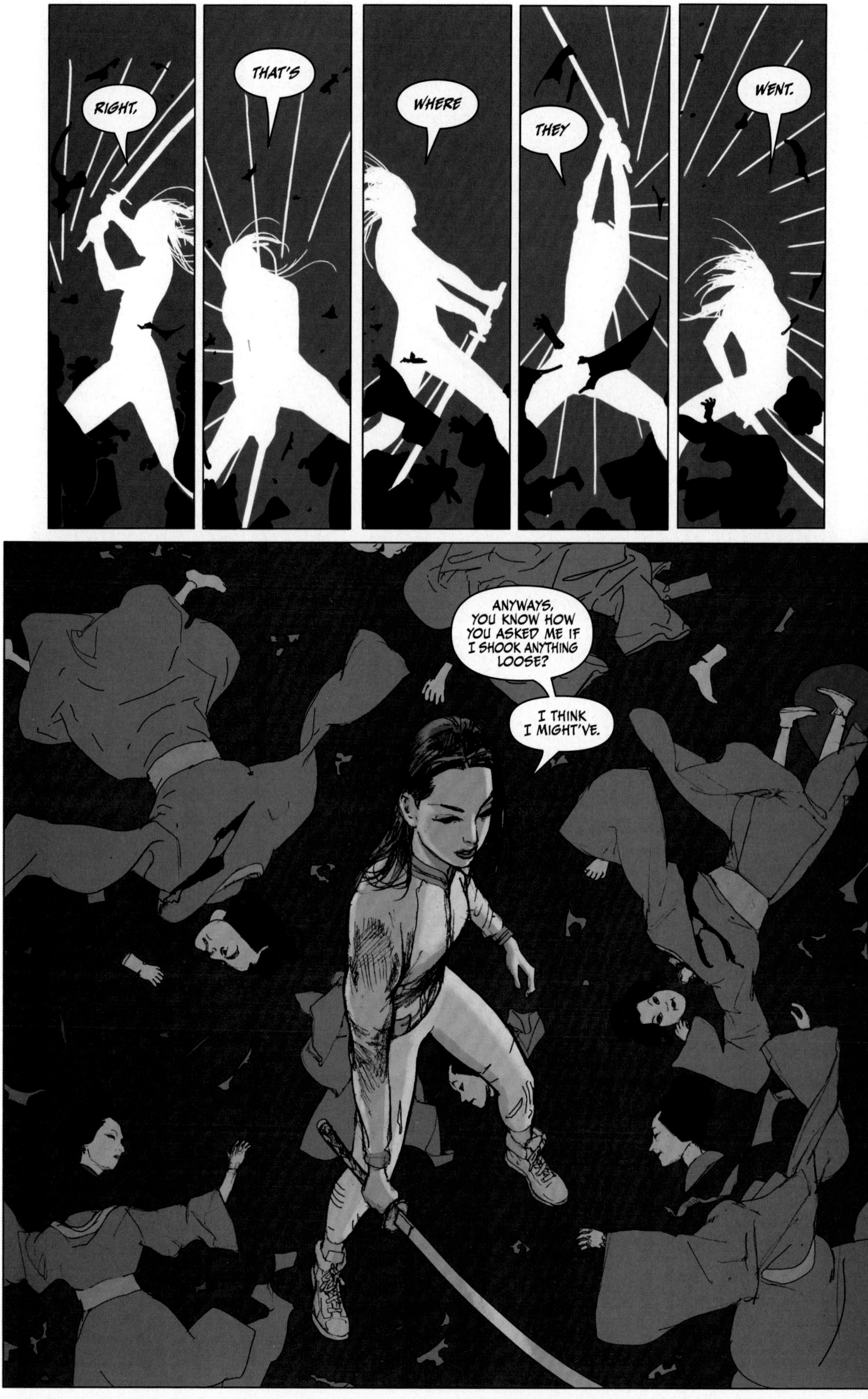
RIGHT,
THAT'S
WHERE
THEY
WENT.
ANYWAYS, YOU KNOW HOW YOU ASKED ME IF I SHOOK ANYTHING LOOSE?
I THINK I MIGHT'VE.

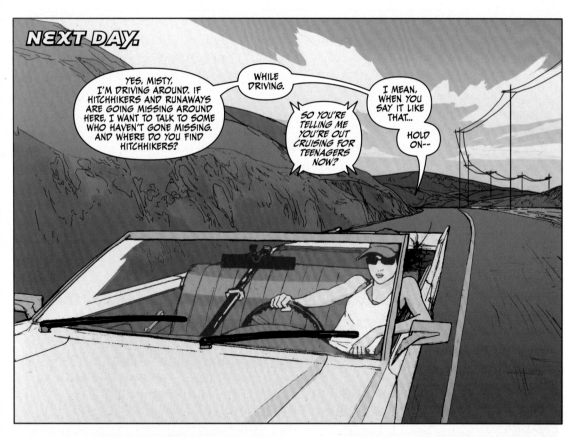

YES, MISTY, I'M DRIVING AROUND. IF HITCHHIKERS AND RUNAWAYS ARE GOING MISSING AROUND HERE, I WANT TO TALK TO SOME WHO HAVEN'T GONE MISSING. AND WHERE DO YOU FIND HITCHHIKERS?

WHILE DRIVING.

SO YOU'RE TELLING ME YOU'RE OUT CRUISING FOR TEENAGERS NOW?

I MEAN, WHEN YOU SAY IT LIKE THAT...

HOLD ON--

KRRRNNCH!

YO! JUMP IN, KIDS, I'M NOT A WEIRDO!

I MEAN, I'M PROBABLY A WEIRDO, BUT NOT A *WEIRDO* WEIRDO, YOU DIG?

WE DIG!

I'M WREN, AND THIS IS CARLOS.

COLLEEN WING.

WHERE YOU KARMIC YOUTH HEADED?

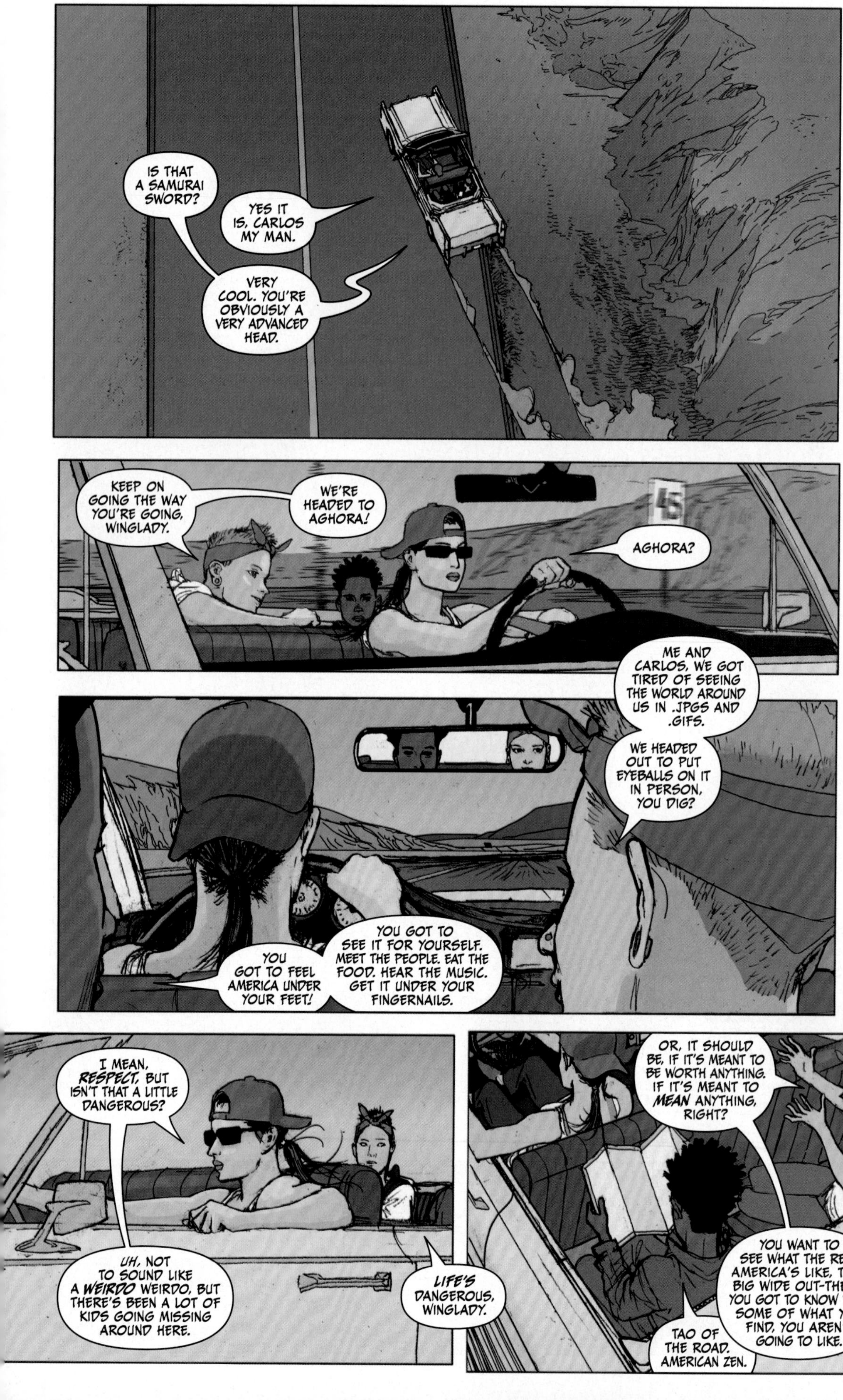
IS THAT A SAMURAI SWORD?
YES IT IS, CARLOS MY MAN.
VERY COOL. YOU'RE OBVIOUSLY A VERY ADVANCED HEAD.
KEEP ON GOING THE WAY YOU'RE GOING, WINGLADY.
WE'RE HEADED TO AGHORA!
AGHORA?
ME AND CARLOS, WE GOT TIRED OF SEEING THE WORLD AROUND US IN .JPGS AND .GIFS.
WE HEADED OUT TO PUT EYEBALLS ON IT IN PERSON, YOU DIG?
YOU GOT TO FEEL AMERICA UNDER YOUR FEET!
YOU GOT TO SEE IT FOR YOURSELF. MEET THE PEOPLE. EAT THE FOOD. HEAR THE MUSIC. GET IT UNDER YOUR FINGERNAILS.
I MEAN, RESPECT, BUT ISN'T THAT A LITTLE DANGEROUS?
UH, NOT TO SOUND LIKE A WEIRDO WEIRDO, BUT THERE'S BEEN A LOT OF KIDS GOING MISSING AROUND HERE.
LIFE'S DANGEROUS, WINGLADY.
OR, IT SHOULD BE, IF IT'S MEANT TO BE WORTH ANYTHING. IF IT'S MEANT TO MEAN ANYTHING, RIGHT?
YOU WANT TO SEE WHAT THE REAL AMERICA'S LIKE, THAT BIG WIDE OUT-THERE, YOU GOT TO KNOW THAT SOME OF WHAT YOU FIND, YOU AREN'T GOING TO LIKE.
TAO OF THE ROAD. AMERICAN ZEN.

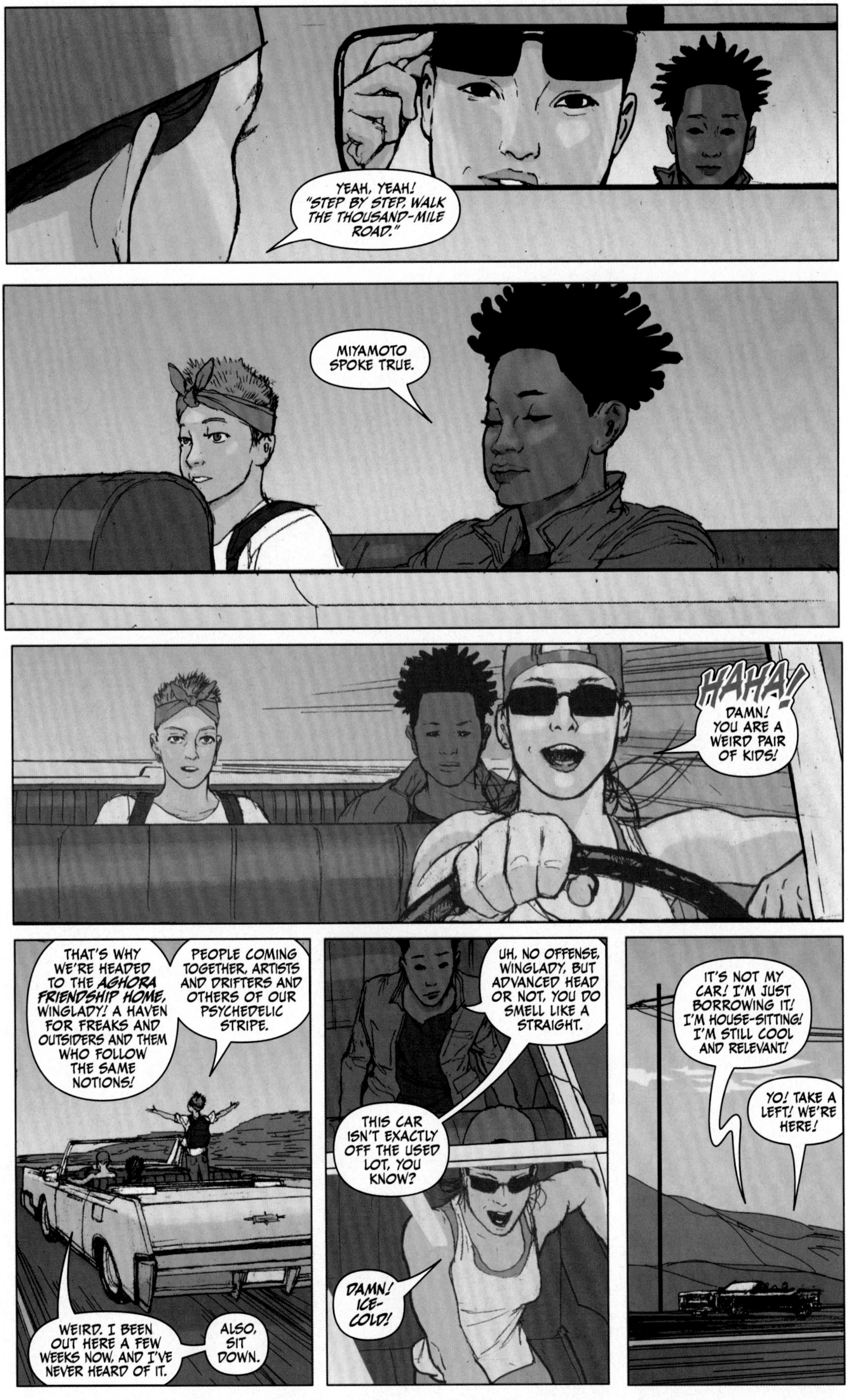
YEAH, YEAH! "STEP BY STEP, WALK THE THOUSAND-MILE ROAD."
MIYAMOTO SPOKE TRUE.
HAHA!
DAMN! YOU ARE A WEIRD PAIR OF KIDS!
THAT'S WHY WE'RE HEADED TO THE AGHORA FRIENDSHIP HOME, WINGLADY! A HAVEN FOR FREAKS AND OUTSIDERS AND THEM WHO FOLLOW THE SAME NOTIONS!
PEOPLE COMING TOGETHER, ARTISTS AND DRIFTERS AND OTHERS OF OUR PSYCHEDELIC STRIPE.
WEIRD. I BEEN OUT HERE A FEW WEEKS NOW, AND I'VE NEVER HEARD OF IT.
ALSO, SIT DOWN.
UH, NO OFFENSE, WINGLADY, BUT ADVANCED HEAD OR NOT, YOU DO SMELL LIKE A STRAIGHT.
THIS CAR ISN'T EXACTLY OFF THE USED LOT, YOU KNOW?
DAMN! ICE-COLD!
IT'S NOT MY CAR! I'M JUST BORROWING IT! I'M HOUSE-SITTING! I'M STILL COOL AND RELEVANT!
YO! TAKE A LEFT! WE'RE HERE!

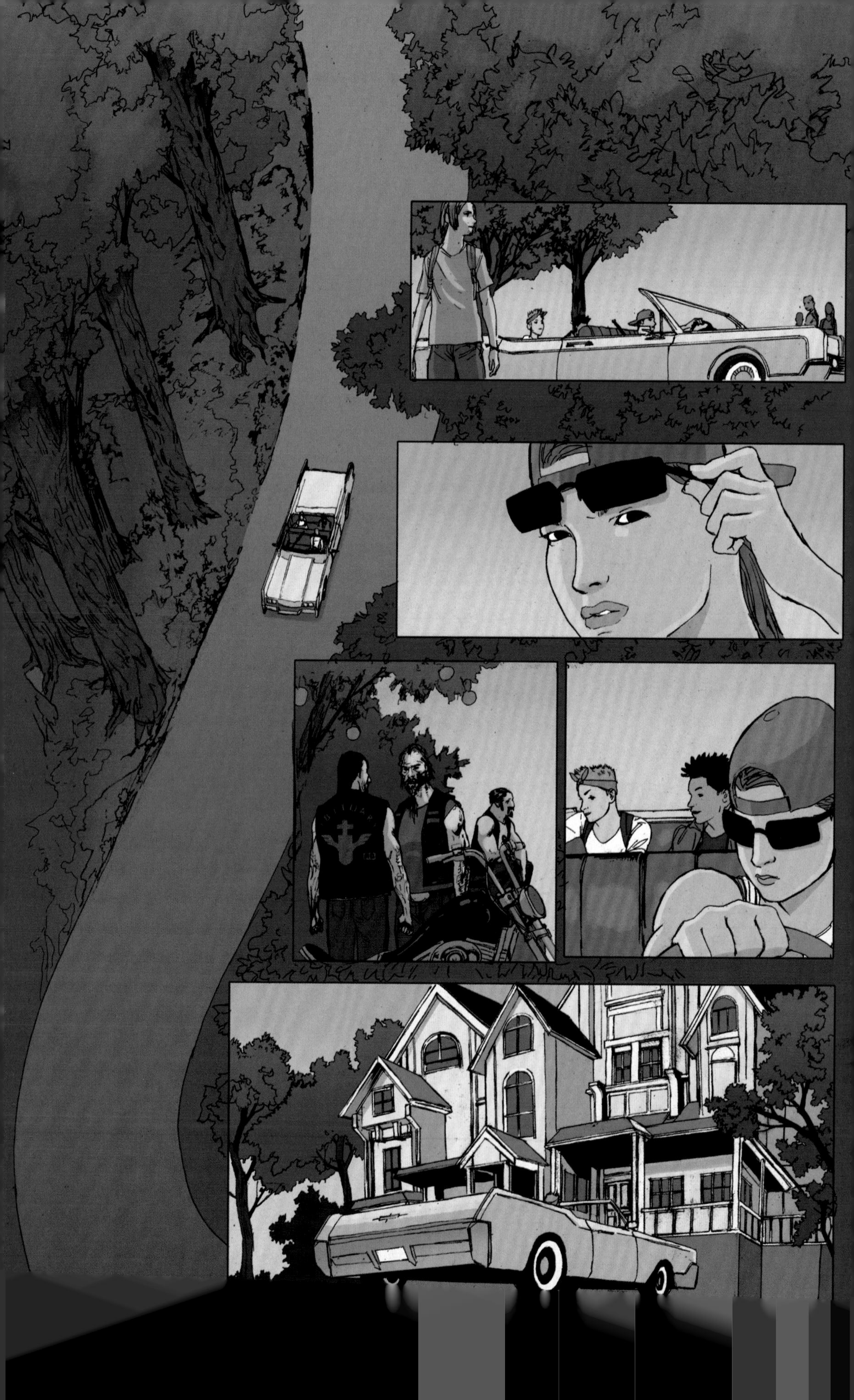

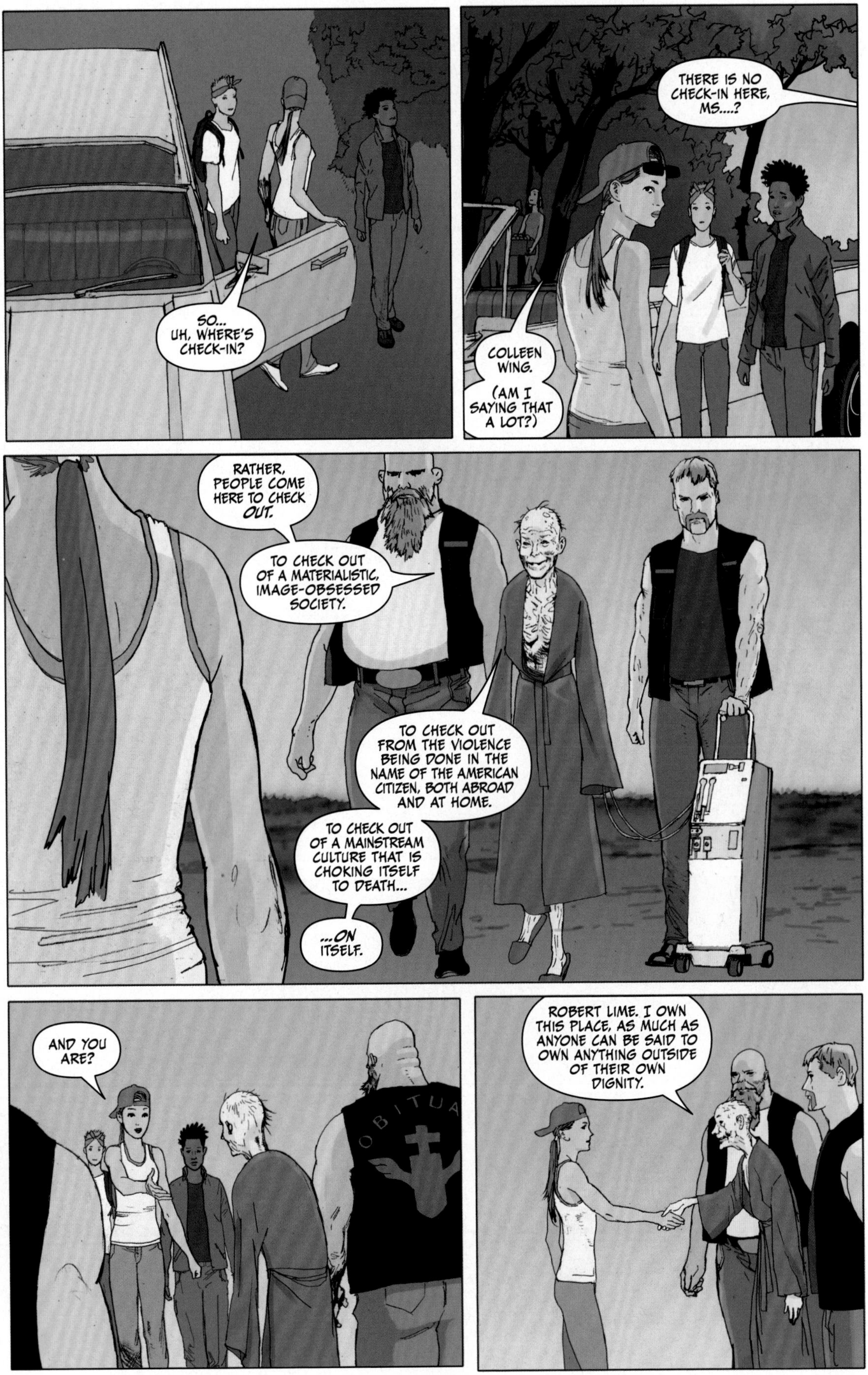
SO... UH, WHERE'S CHECK-IN?
THERE IS NO CHECK-IN HERE, MS....?
COLLEEN WING.
(AM I SAYING THAT A LOT?)
RATHER, PEOPLE COME HERE TO CHECK OUT.
TO CHECK OUT OF A MATERIALISTIC, IMAGE-OBSESSED SOCIETY.
TO CHECK OUT FROM THE VIOLENCE BEING DONE IN THE NAME OF THE AMERICAN CITIZEN, BOTH ABROAD AND AT HOME.
TO CHECK OUT OF A MAINSTREAM CULTURE THAT IS CHOKING ITSELF TO DEATH...
...ON ITSELF.
AND YOU ARE?
OBITUA
ROBERT LIME. I OWN THIS PLACE, AS MUCH AS ANYONE CAN BE SAID TO OWN ANYTHING OUTSIDE OF THEIR OWN DIGNITY.

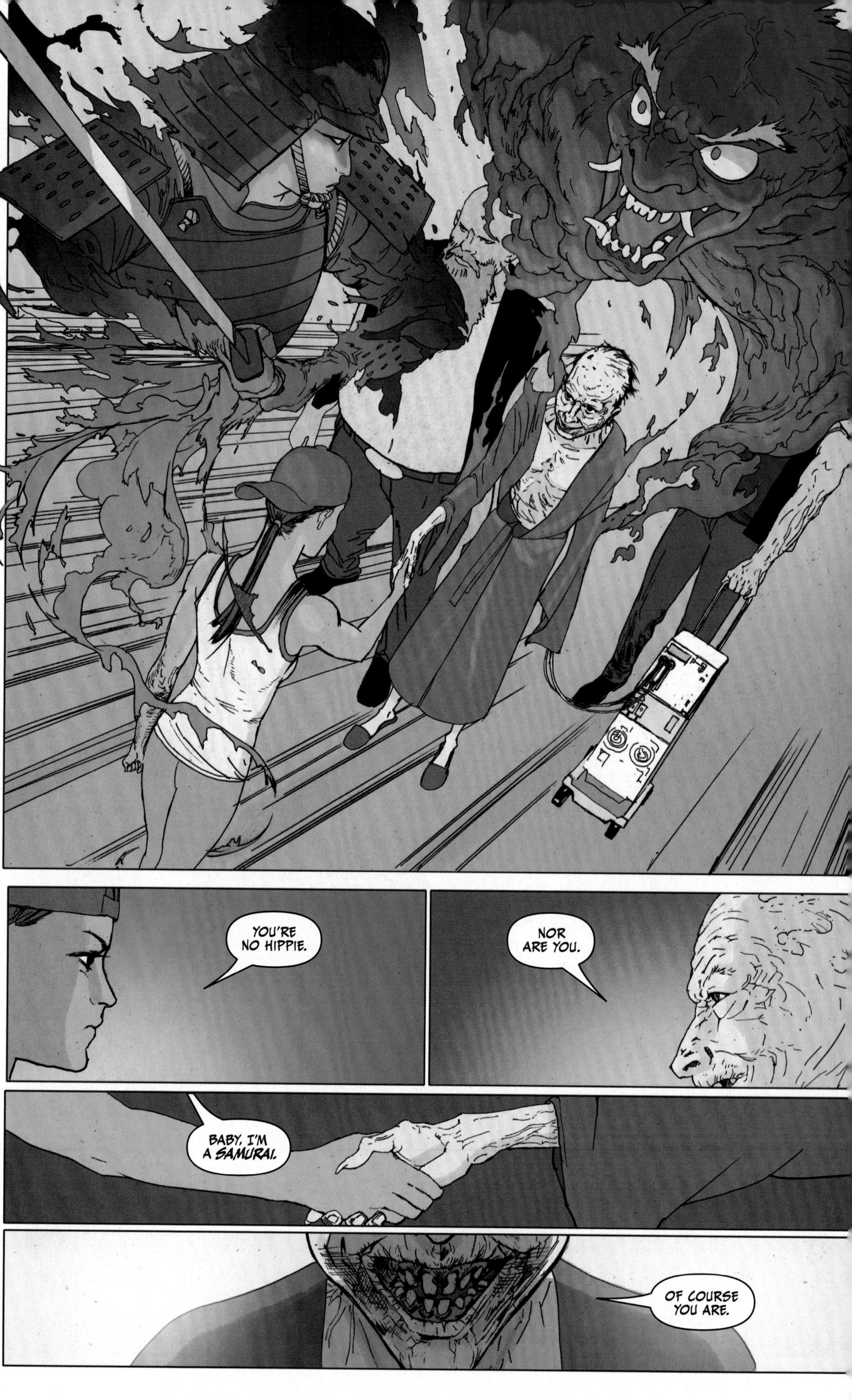
YOU'RE NO HIPPIE.
NOR ARE YOU.
BABY, I'M A SAMURAI.
OF COURSE YOU ARE.

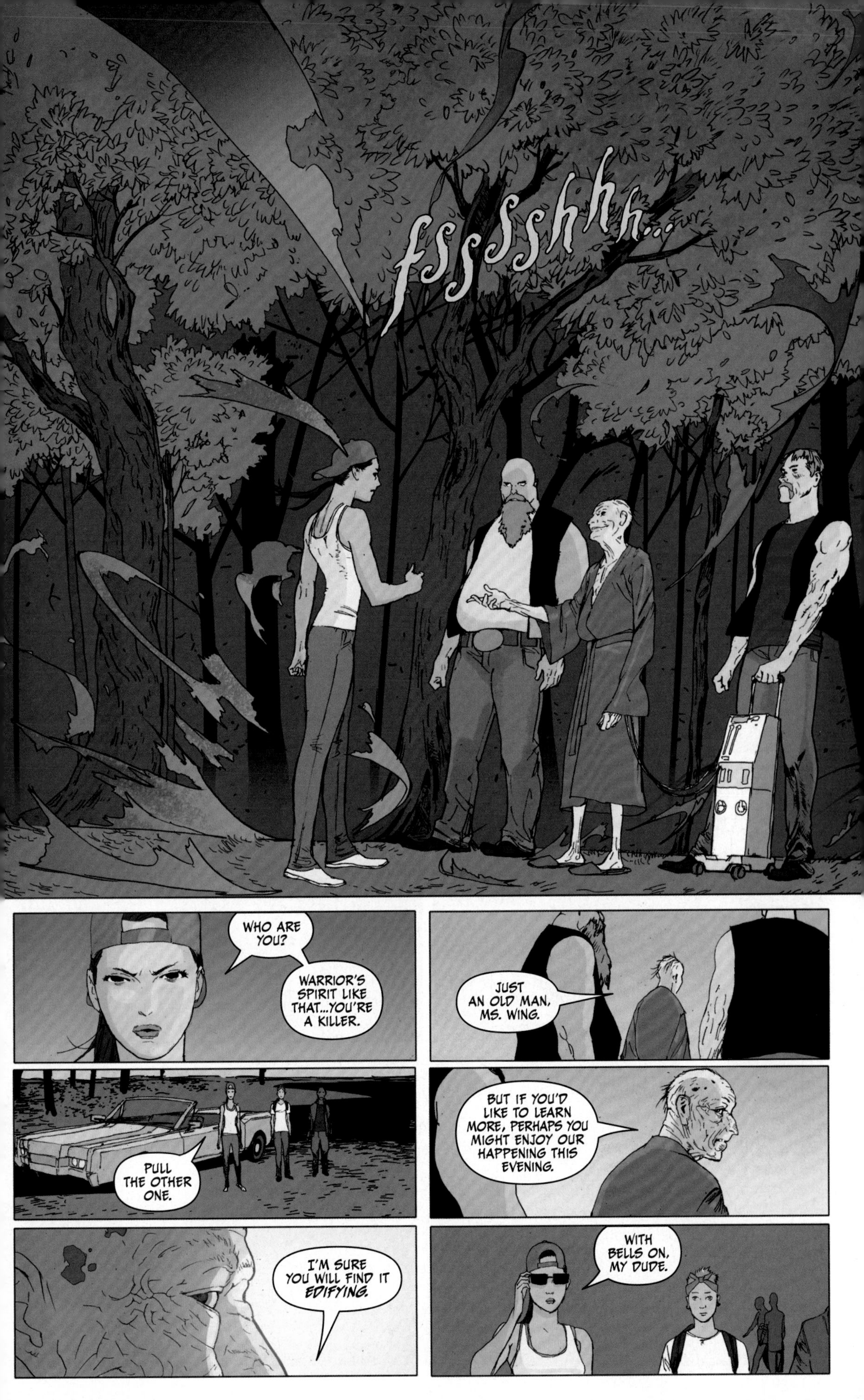
fssssshhh...
WHO ARE YOU?
WARRIOR'S SPIRIT LIKE THAT...YOU'RE A KILLER.
JUST AN OLD MAN, MS. WING.
PULL THE OTHER ONE.
BUT IF YOU'D LIKE TO LEARN MORE, PERHAPS YOU MIGHT ENJOY OUR HAPPENING THIS EVENING.
I'M SURE YOU WILL FIND IT *EDIFYING.*
WITH BELLS ON, MY DUDE.

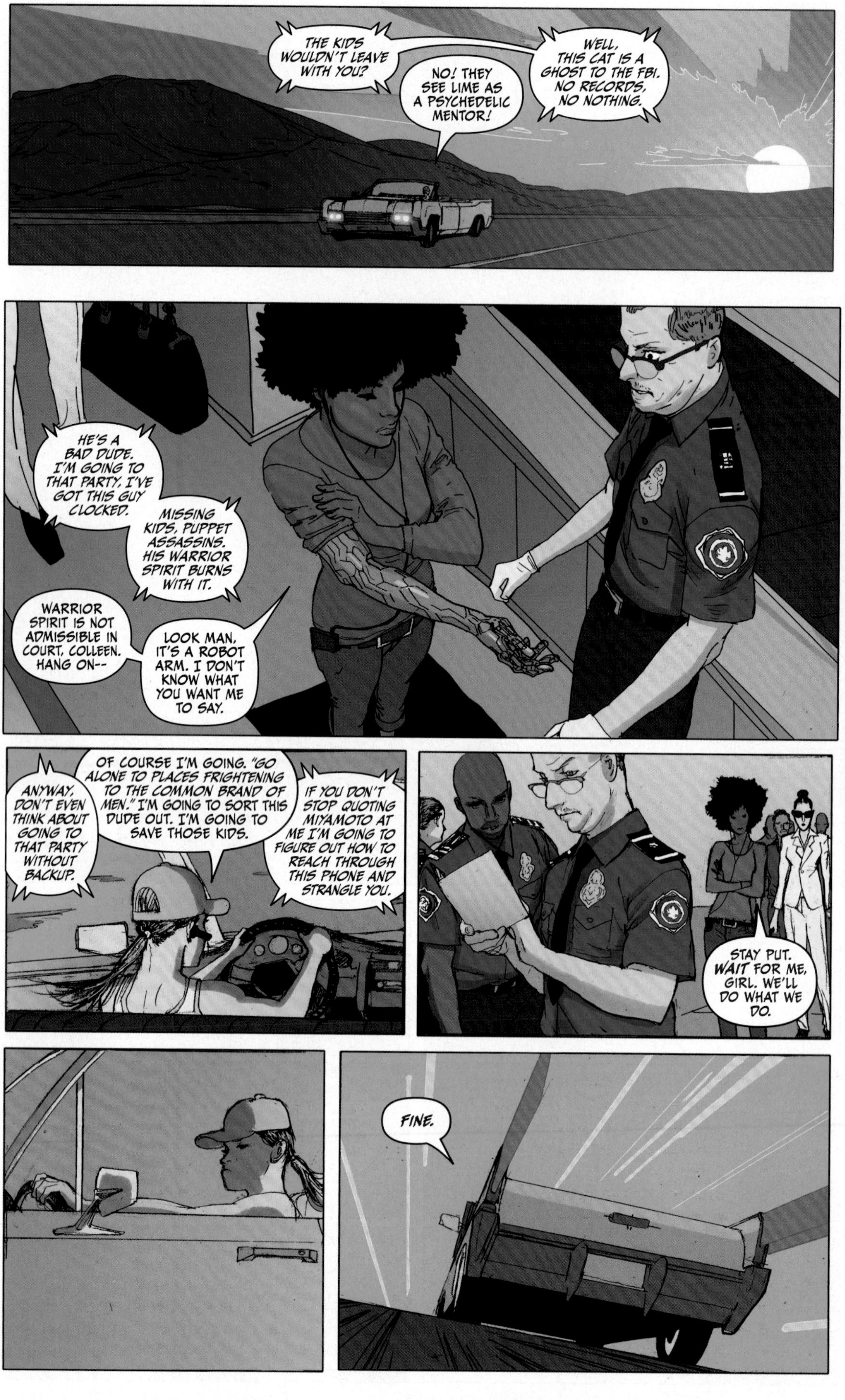
THE KIDS WOULDN'T LEAVE WITH YOU?
NO! THEY SEE LIME AS A PSYCHEDELIC MENTOR!
WELL, THIS CAT IS A GHOST TO THE FBI. NO RECORDS, NO NOTHING.
HE'S A BAD DUDE. I'M GOING TO THAT PARTY, I'VE GOT THIS GUY CLOCKED.
MISSING KIDS, PUPPET ASSASSINS. HIS WARRIOR SPIRIT BURNS WITH IT.
WARRIOR SPIRIT IS NOT ADMISSIBLE IN COURT, COLLEEN. HANG ON--
LOOK MAN, IT'S A ROBOT ARM. I DON'T KNOW WHAT YOU WANT ME TO SAY.
ANYWAY, DON'T EVEN THINK ABOUT GOING TO THAT PARTY WITHOUT BACKUP.
OF COURSE I'M GOING. "GO ALONE TO PLACES FRIGHTENING TO THE COMMON BRAND OF MEN." I'M GOING TO SORT THIS DUDE OUT. I'M GOING TO SAVE THOSE KIDS.
IF YOU DON'T STOP QUOTING MIYAMOTO AT ME I'M GOING TO FIGURE OUT HOW TO REACH THROUGH THIS PHONE AND STRANGLE YOU.
STAY PUT. WAIT FOR ME, GIRL. WE'LL DO WHAT WE DO.
FINE.

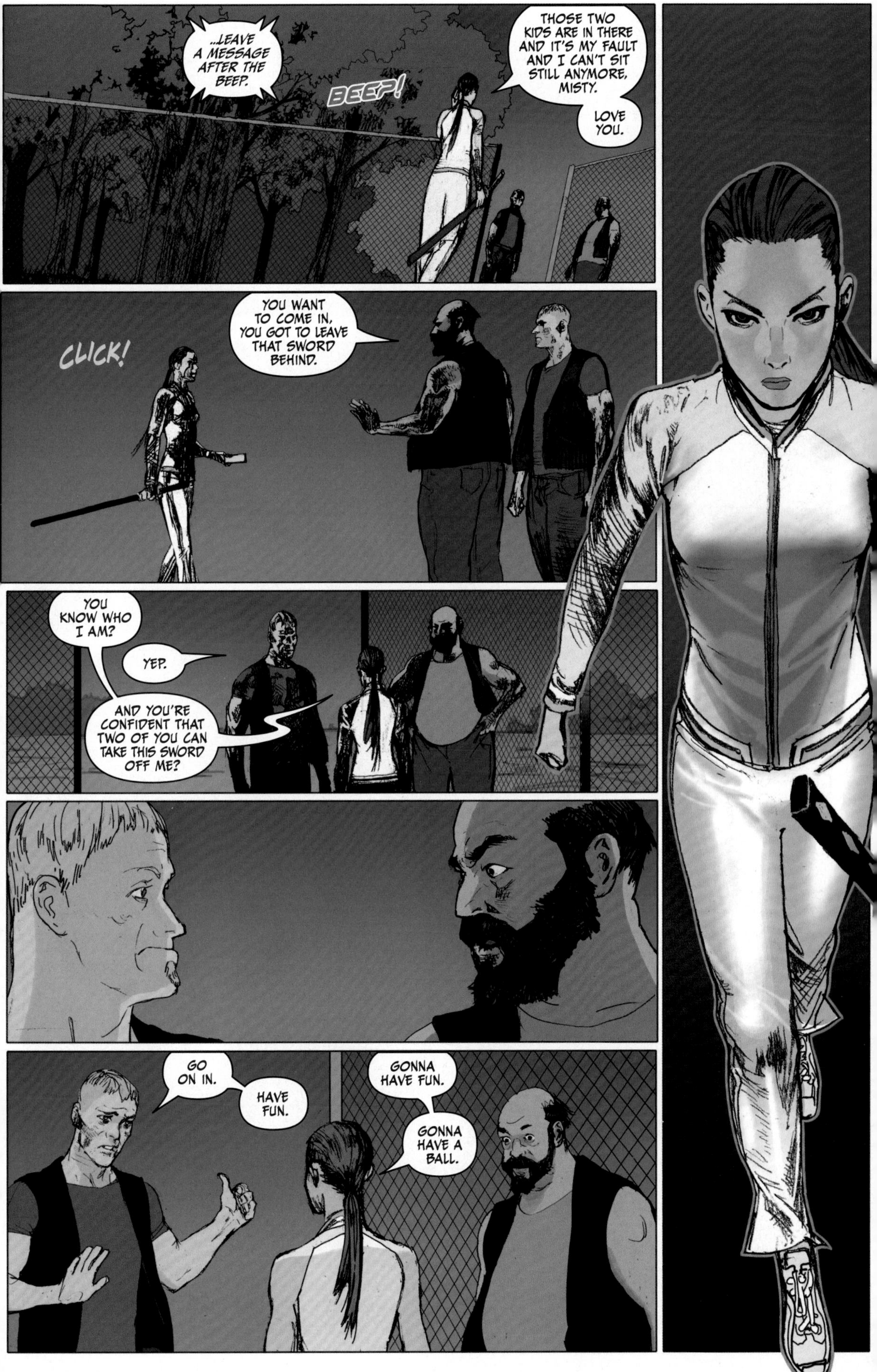
...LEAVE A MESSAGE AFTER THE BEEP.
BEEP!
THOSE TWO KIDS ARE IN THERE AND IT'S MY FAULT AND I CAN'T SIT STILL ANYMORE, MISTY.
LOVE YOU.
CLICK!
YOU WANT TO COME IN, YOU GOT TO LEAVE THAT SWORD BEHIND.
YOU KNOW WHO I AM?
YEP.
AND YOU'RE CONFIDENT THAT TWO OF YOU CAN TAKE THIS SWORD OFF ME?
GO ON IN.
HAVE FUN.
GONNA HAVE FUN.
GONNA HAVE A BALL.

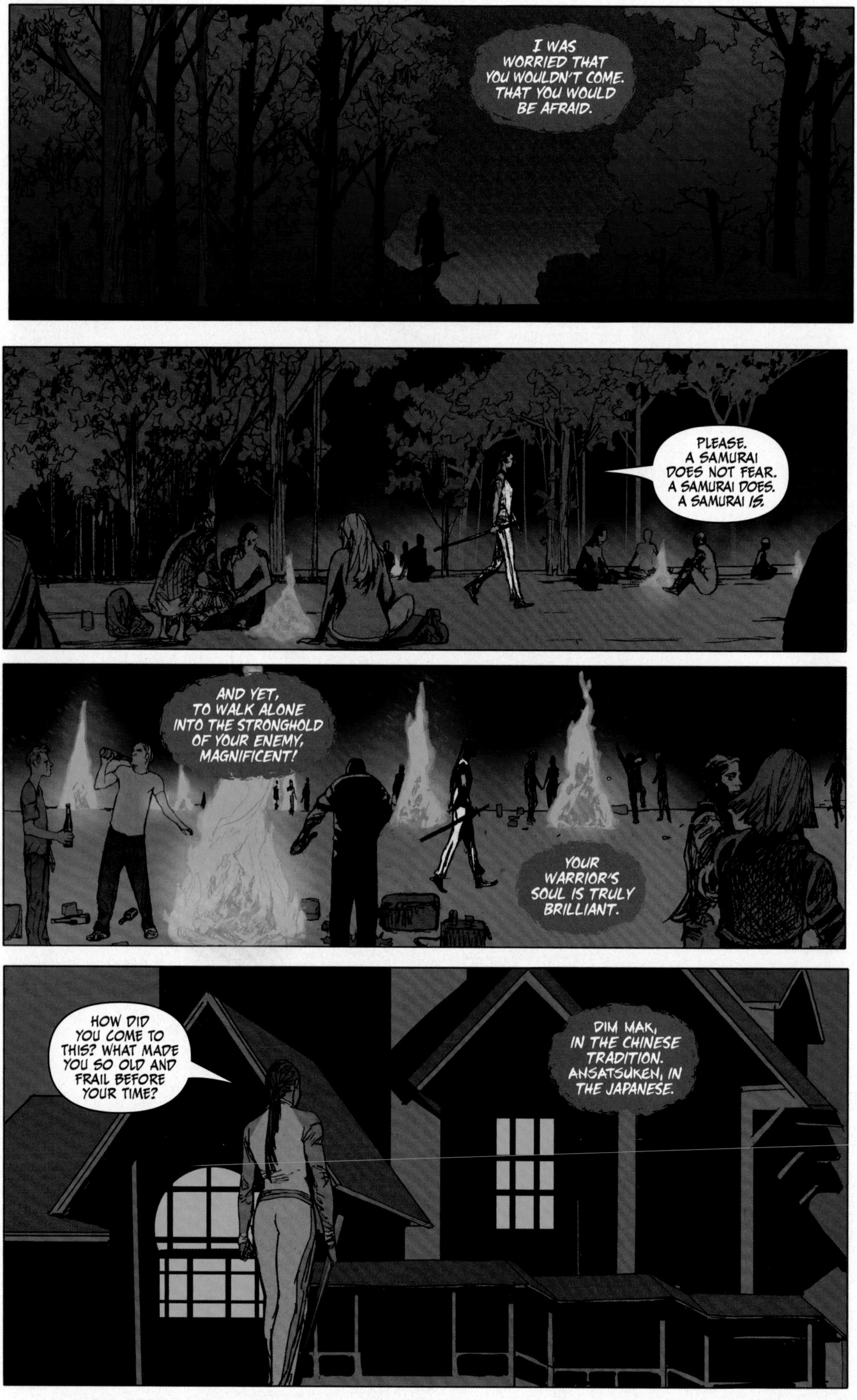
I WAS WORRIED THAT YOU WOULDN'T COME. THAT YOU WOULD BE AFRAID.
PLEASE. A SAMURAI DOES NOT FEAR. A SAMURAI DOES. A SAMURAI IS.
AND YET, TO WALK ALONE INTO THE STRONGHOLD OF YOUR ENEMY, MAGNIFICENT!
YOUR WARRIOR'S SOUL IS TRULY BRILLIANT.
HOW DID YOU COME TO THIS? WHAT MADE YOU SO OLD AND FRAIL BEFORE YOUR TIME?
DIM MAK, IN THE CHINESE TRADITION. ANSATSUKEN, IN THE JAPANESE.

THE DEATH TOUCH. ASSASSINATION FIST. YOU RAN INTO SOME DEADLY HANDS OF KUNG FU.

PRECISELY.

I WAS STRUCK BY A GREAT AND SUBLIME MASTER OF THE ART WHOM I ANGERED. I HAD DISAPPOINTED HER, AND THE DEATH TOUCH WAS MY PUNISHMENT.

I HAVE SINCE SOUGHT TO EVADE THAT DEATH THROUGH MEDICAL SCIENCE, THROUGH ORIENTAL MEDICINE, MARTIAL ARTS TECHNIQUES.

IT WAS ONLY WHEN YOU ENTERED MY STORY THAT MY PATH WAS CLEAR.

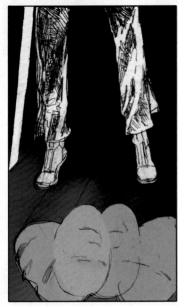

FTT!

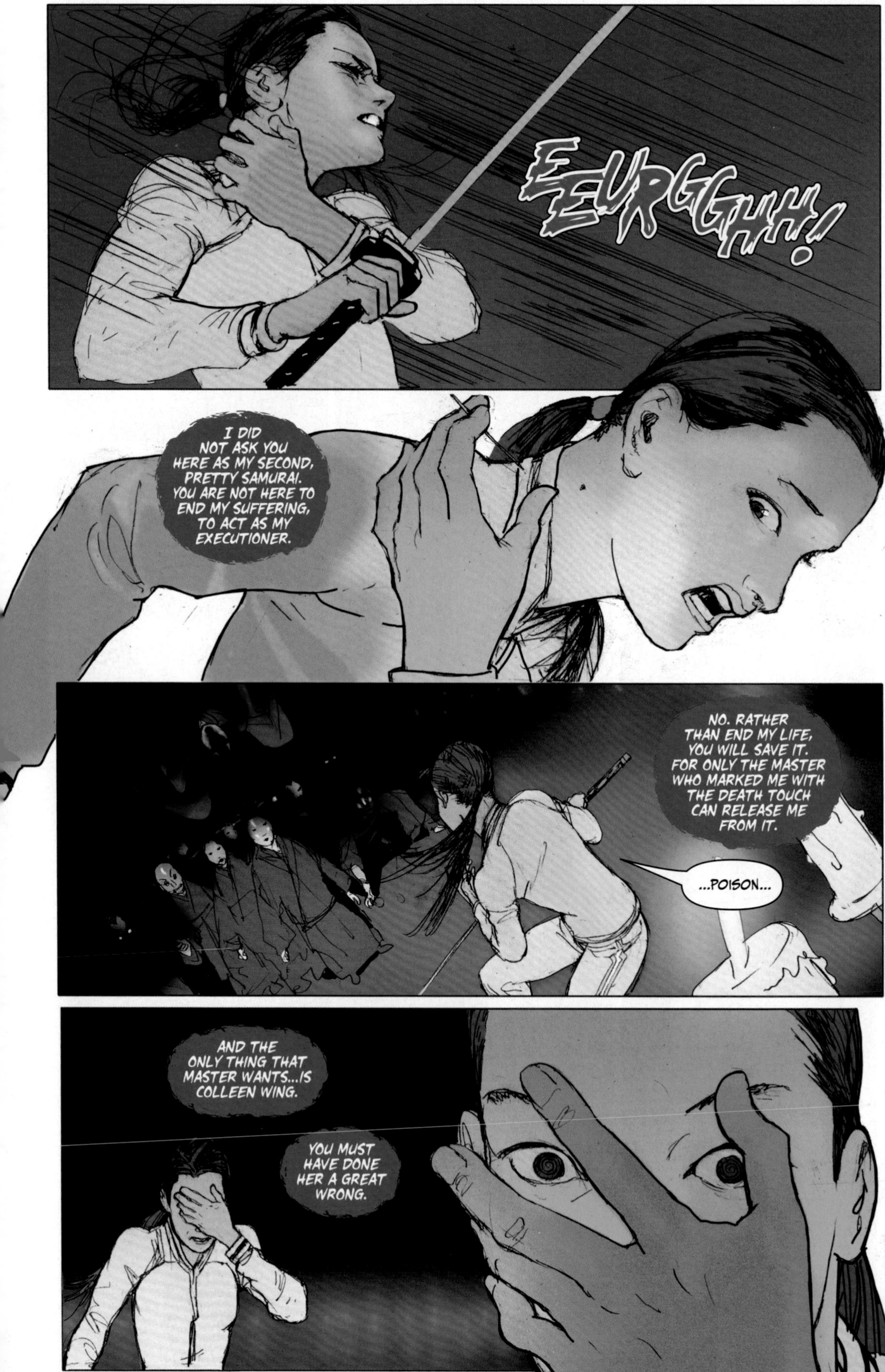
EEURGGHH!
I DID NOT ASK YOU HERE AS MY SECOND, PRETTY SAMURAI. YOU ARE NOT HERE TO END MY SUFFERING, TO ACT AS MY EXECUTIONER.
NO. RATHER THAN END MY LIFE, YOU WILL SAVE IT. FOR ONLY THE MASTER WHO MARKED ME WITH THE DEATH TOUCH CAN RELEASE ME FROM IT.
...POISON...
AND THE ONLY THING THAT MASTER WANTS...IS COLLEEN WING.
YOU MUST HAVE DONE HER A GREAT WRONG.

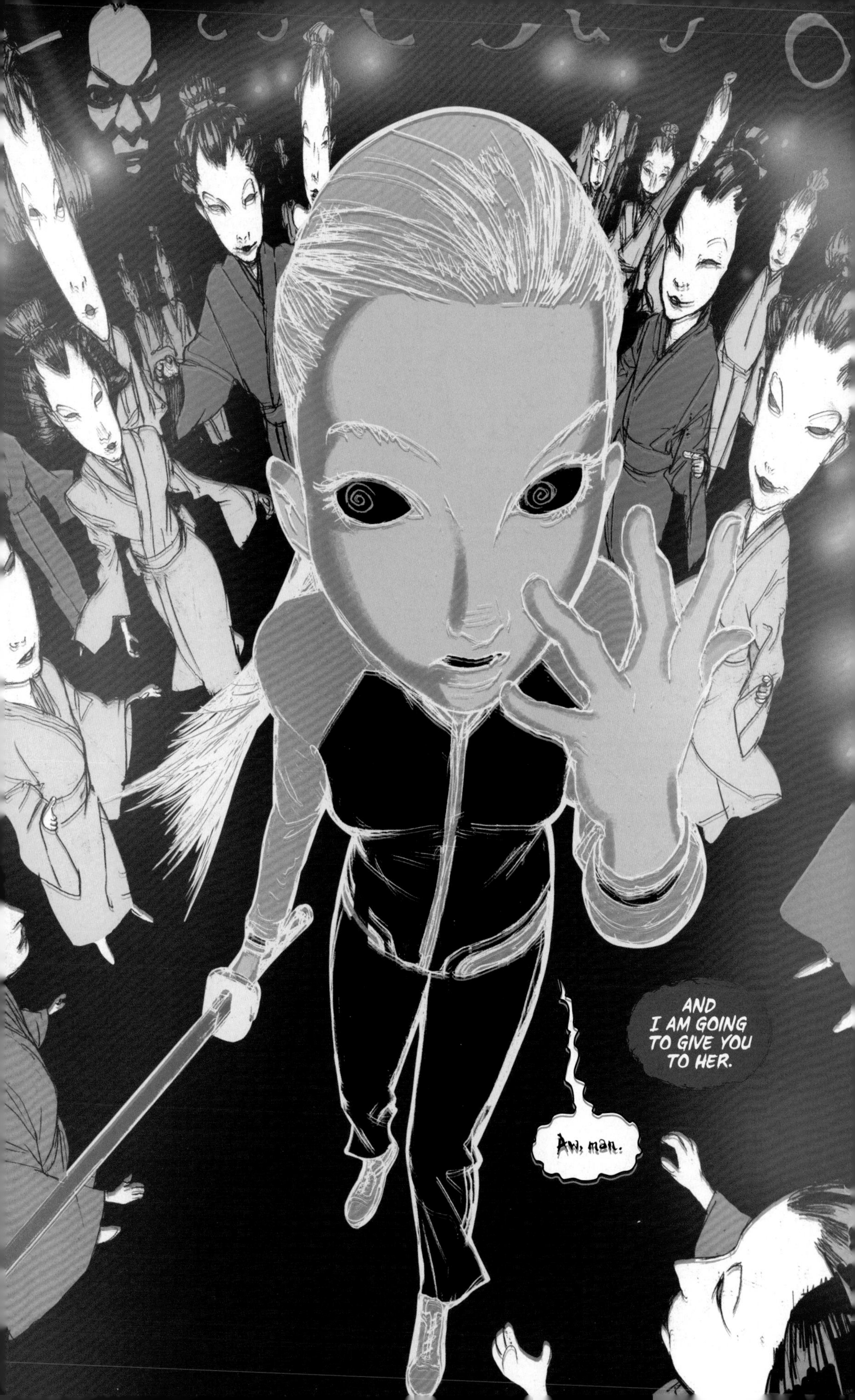
AND I AM GOING TO GIVE YOU TO HER.
Aw, man.

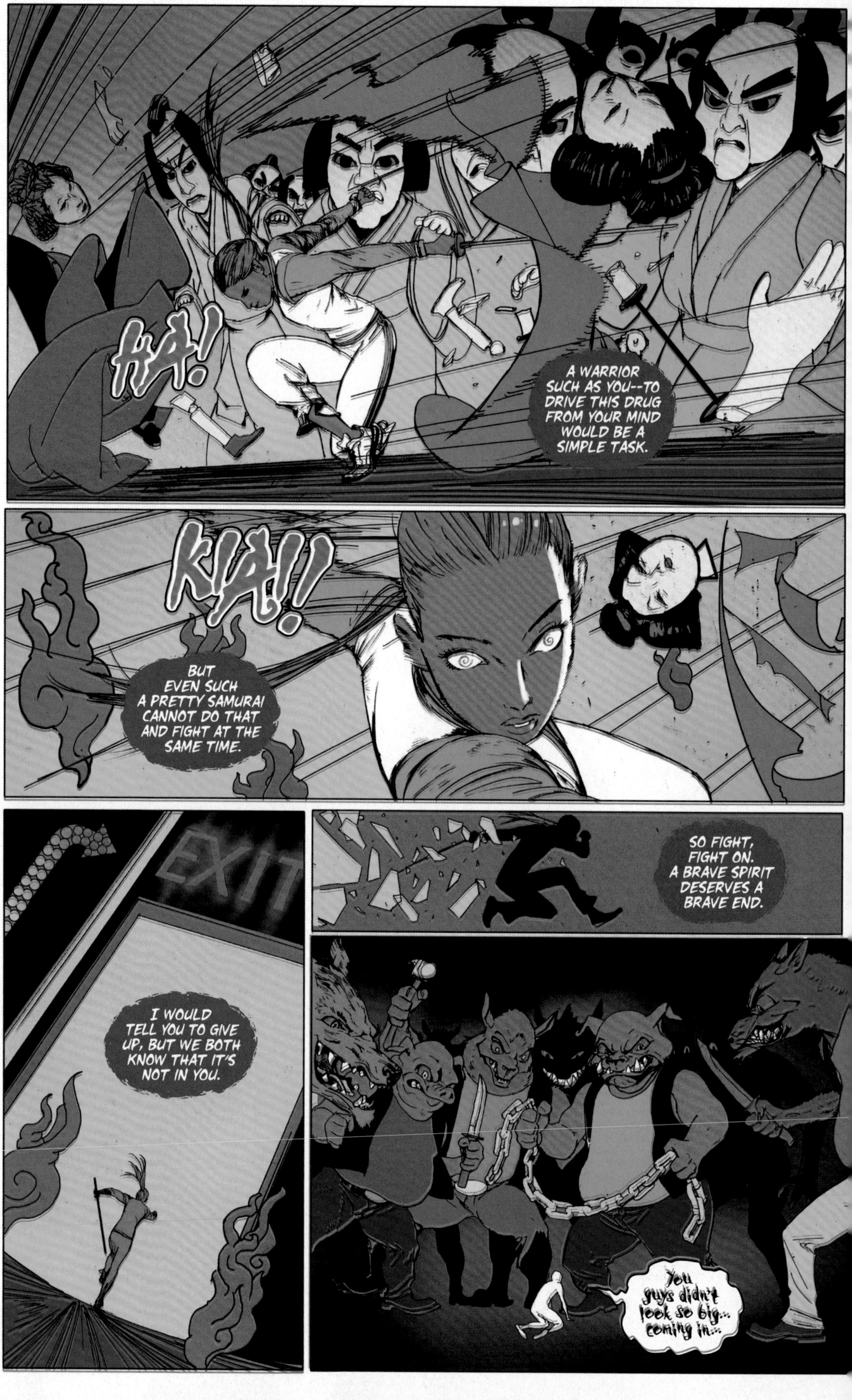
HA!
A WARRIOR SUCH AS YOU--TO DRIVE THIS DRUG FROM YOUR MIND WOULD BE A SIMPLE TASK.
KIA!!
BUT EVEN SUCH A PRETTY SAMURAI CANNOT DO THAT AND FIGHT AT THE SAME TIME.
EXIT
SO FIGHT, FIGHT ON. A BRAVE SPIRIT DESERVES A BRAVE END.
I WOULD TELL YOU TO GIVE UP, BUT WE BOTH KNOW THAT IT'S NOT IN YOU.
You guys didn't look so big... coming in...

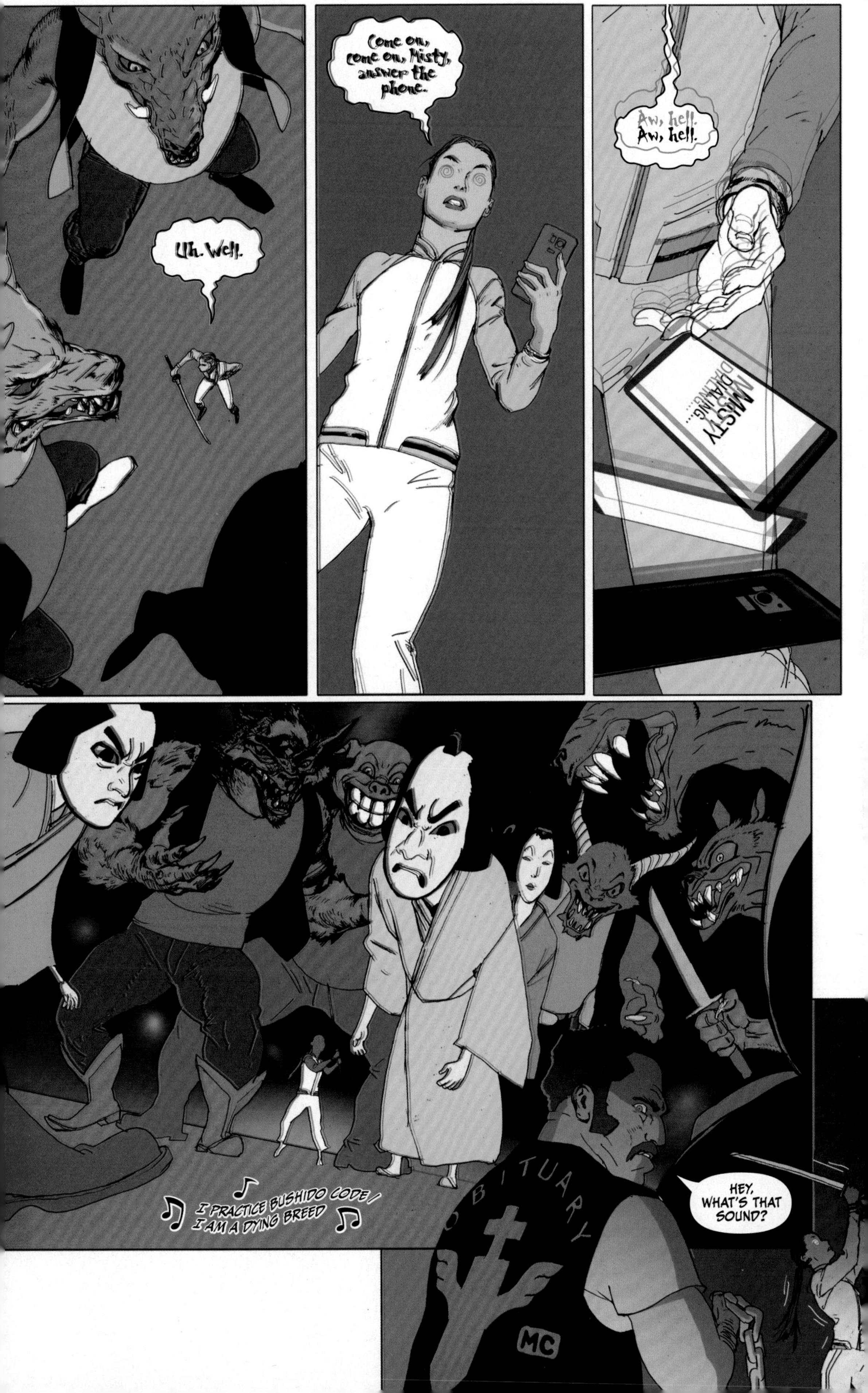
Uh. Well.
Come on, come on, Misty, answer the phone.
Aw, hell. Aw, hell.
MISTY
DIALING......
I PRACTICE BUSHIDO CODE / I AM A DYING BREED
HEY, WHAT'S THAT SOUND?
OBITUARY
MC

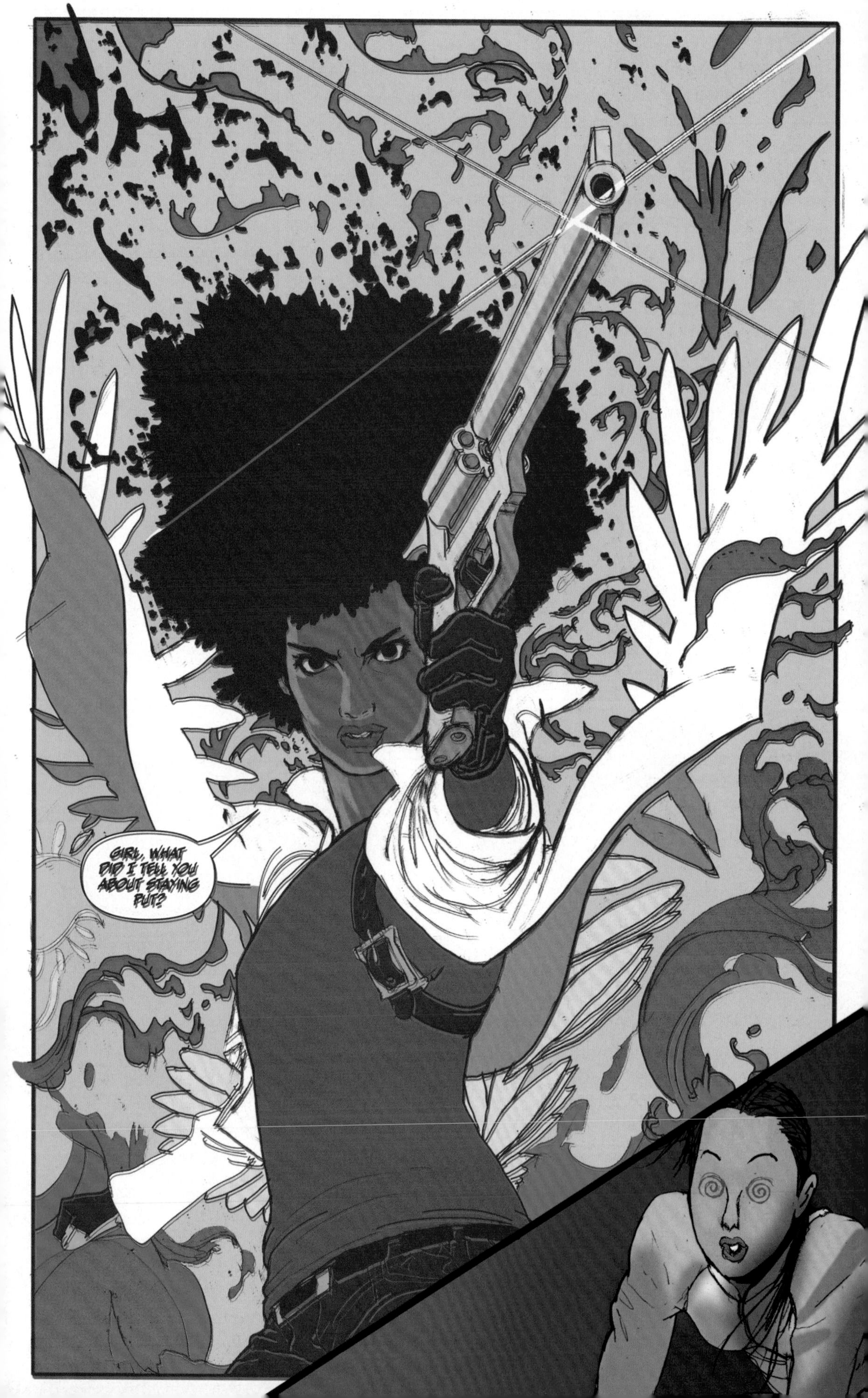
GIRL, WHAT DID I TELL YOU ABOUT STAYING PUT?

CHAPTER 2

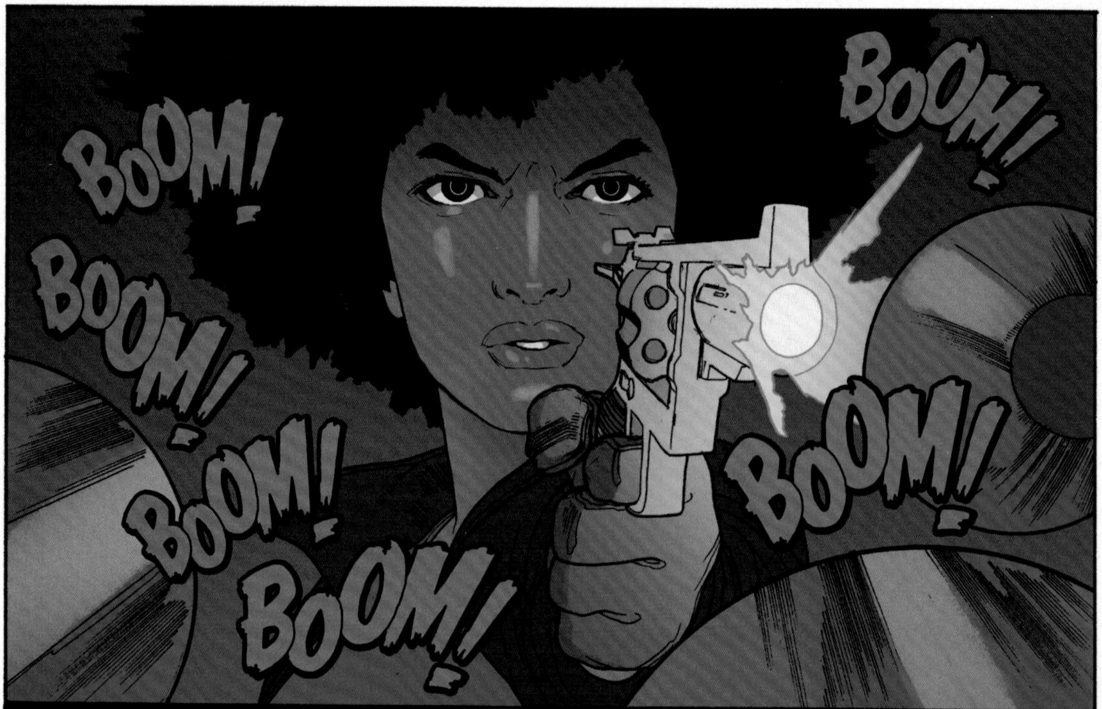
BOOM!
BOOM!
BOOM!
BOOM!
BOOM!
BOOM!

DAUGHTERS of the DRAGON

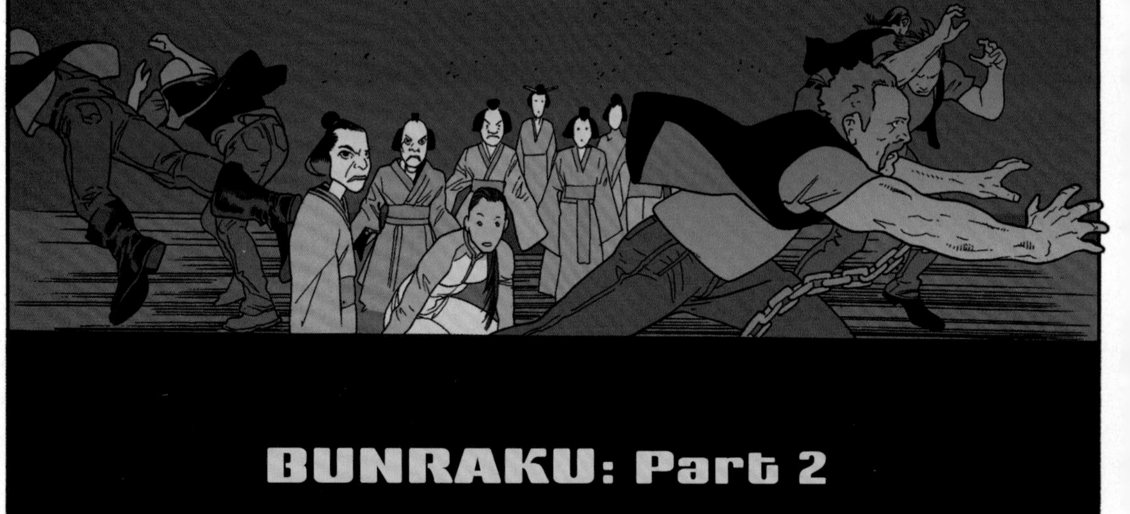

BUNRAKU: Part 2

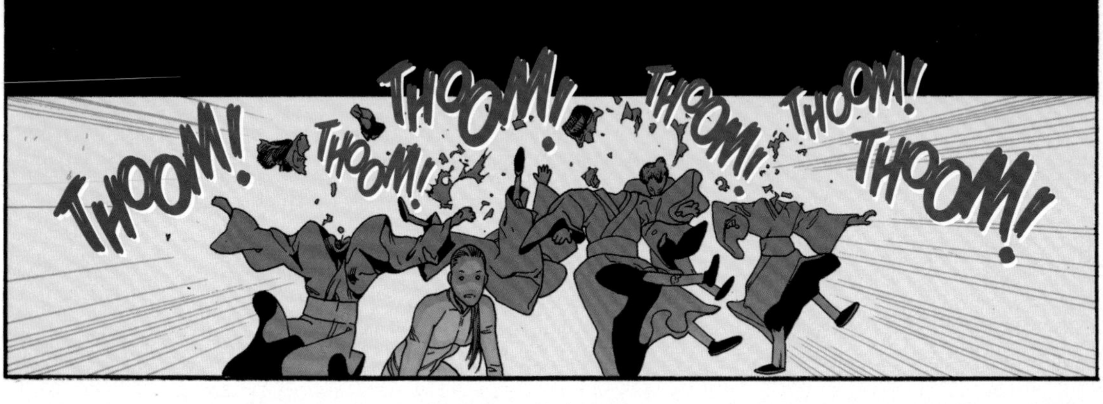
THOOM!
THOOM!
THOOM!
THOOM!
THOOM!
THOOM!

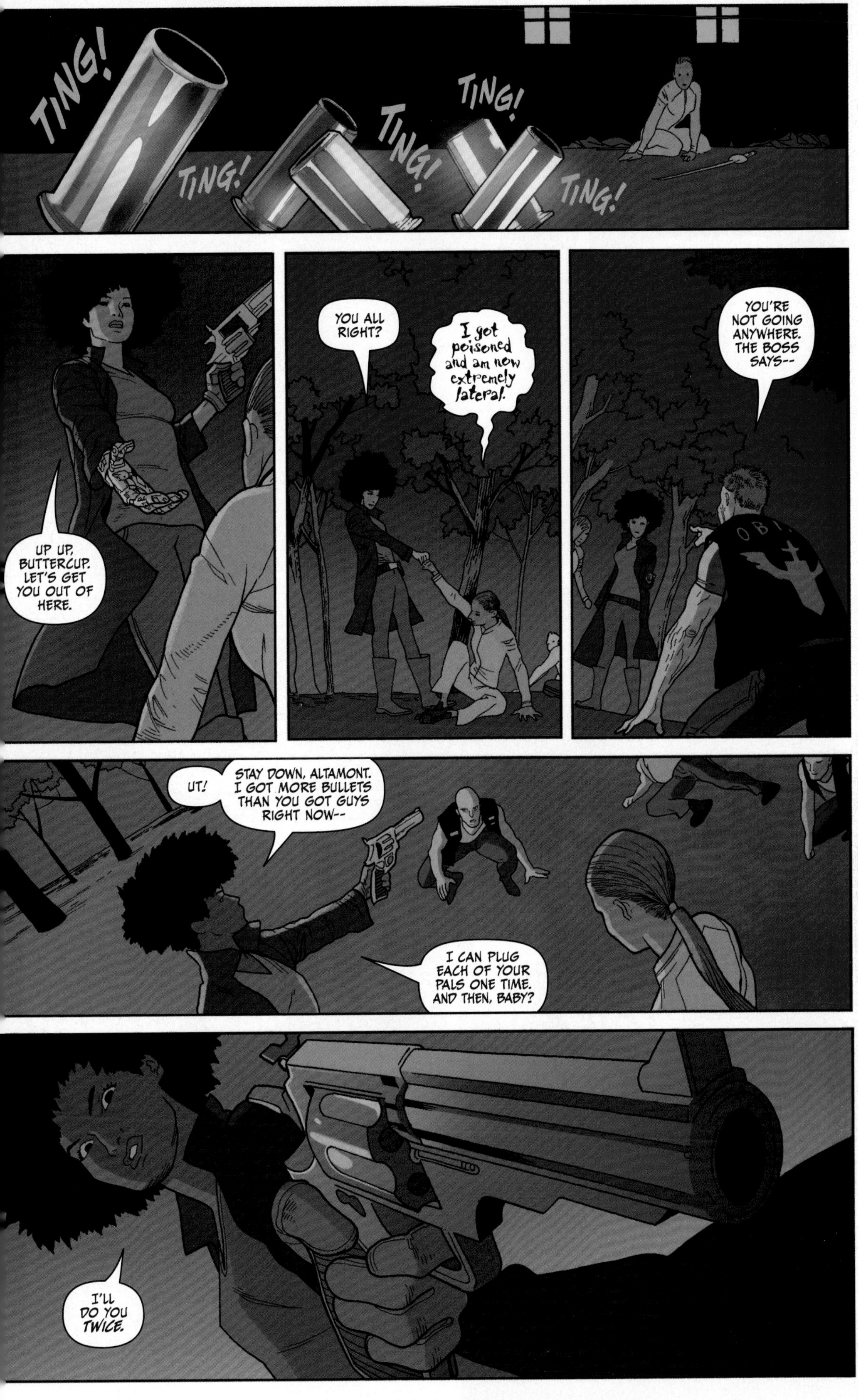
TING!
TING!
TING!
TING!
TING!
UP UP, BUTTERCUP. LET'S GET YOU OUT OF HERE.
YOU ALL RIGHT?
I got poisoned and am now extremely lateral.
YOU'RE NOT GOING ANYWHERE. THE BOSS SAYS--
UT!
STAY DOWN, ALTAMONT. I GOT MORE BULLETS THAN YOU GOT GUYS RIGHT NOW--
I CAN PLUG EACH OF YOUR PALS ONE TIME. AND THEN, BABY?
I'LL DO YOU TWICE.

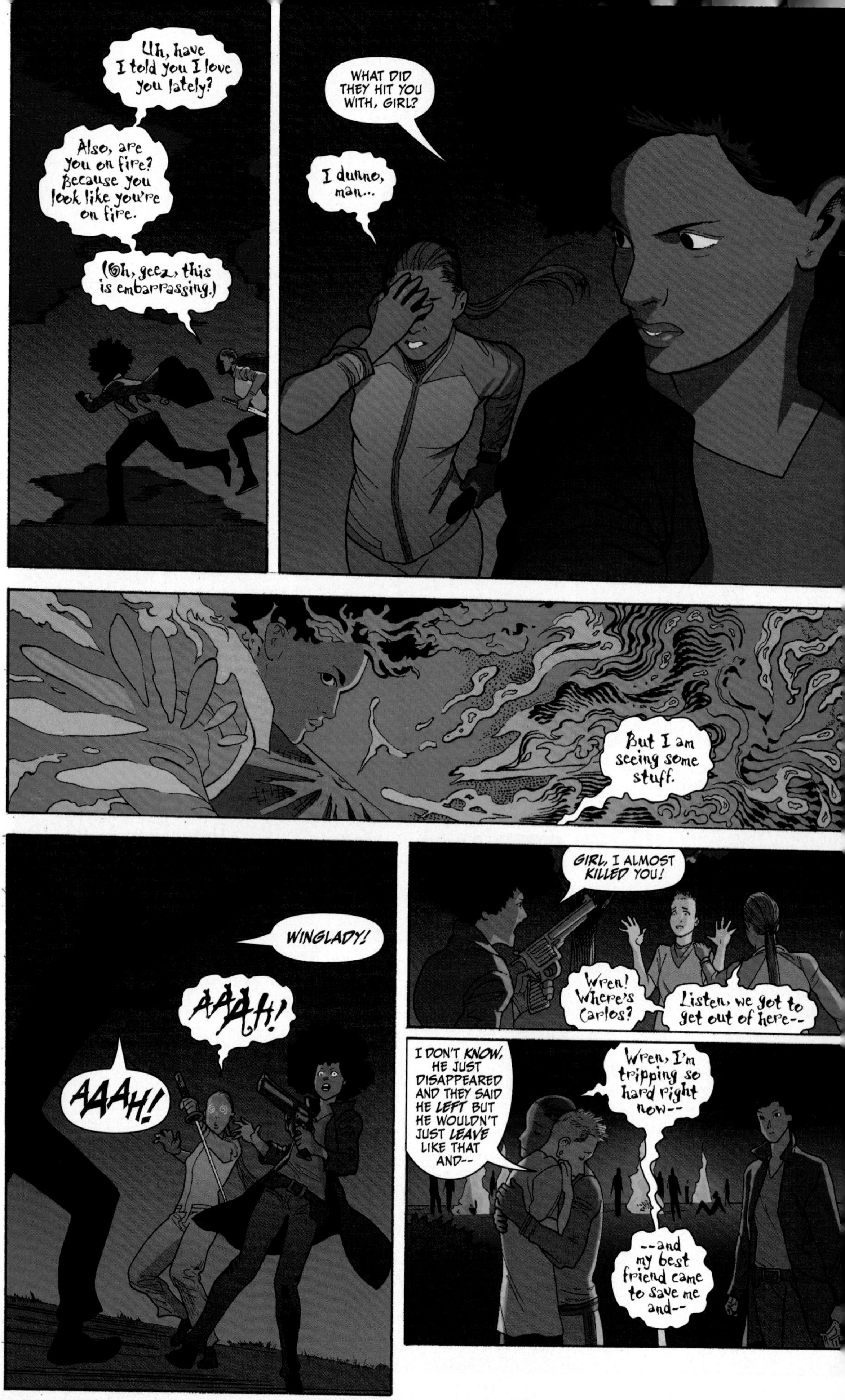

Uh, have I told you I love you lately?
Also, are you on fire? Because you look like you're on fire.
(Oh, geez, this is embarrassing.)
WHAT DID THEY HIT YOU WITH, GIRL?
I dunno, man...
But I am seeing some stuff.
WINGLADY!
AAAH!
AAAH!
GIRL, I ALMOST KILLED YOU!
Wren! Where's Carlos?
Listen, we got to get out of here--
I DON'T KNOW, HE JUST DISAPPEARED AND THEY SAID HE LEFT BUT HE WOULDN'T JUST LEAVE LIKE THAT AND--
Wren, I'm tripping so hard right now--
--and my best friend came to save me and--

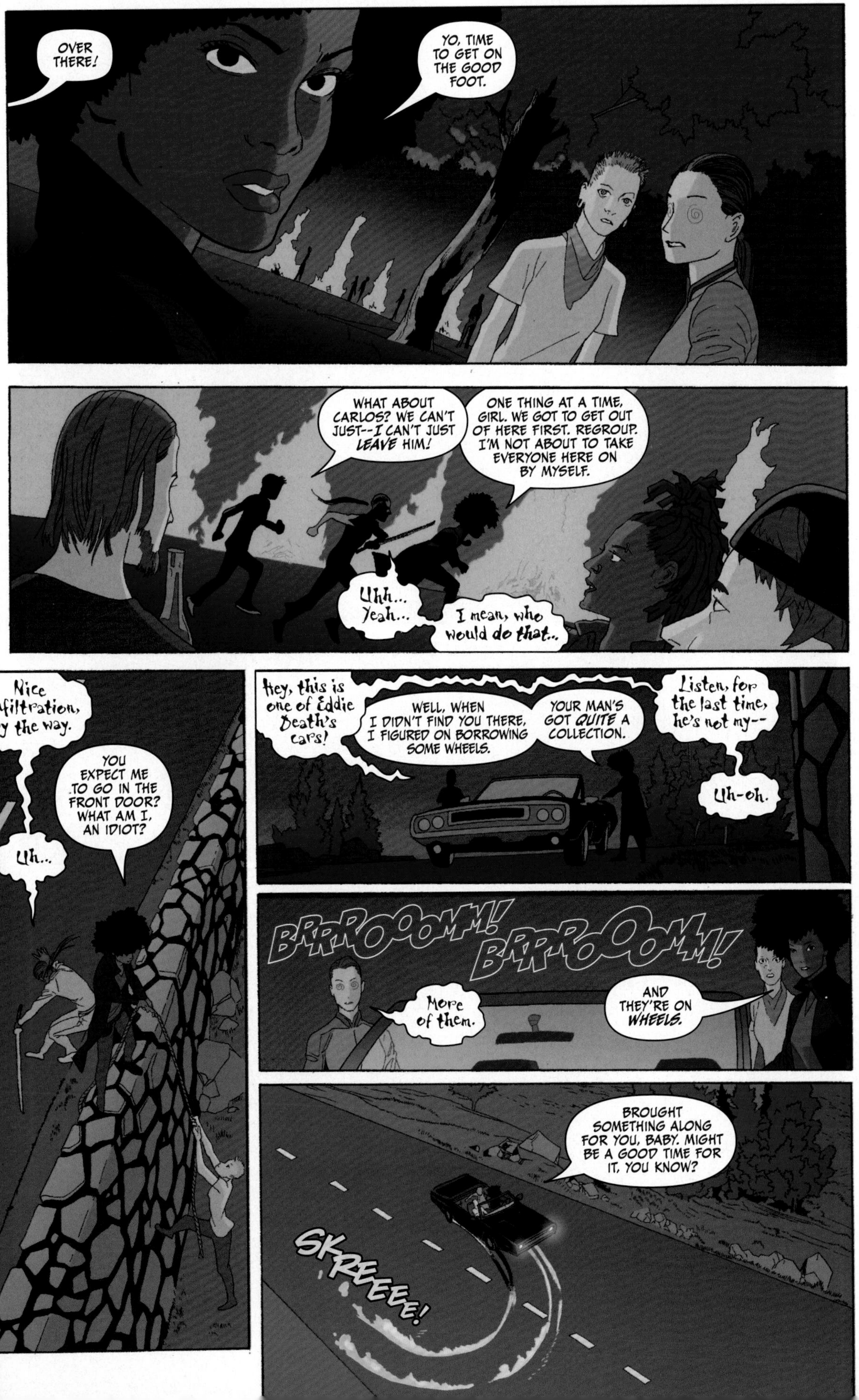
OVER THERE!
YO, TIME TO GET ON THE GOOD FOOT.
WHAT ABOUT CARLOS? WE CAN'T JUST--I CAN'T JUST LEAVE HIM!
ONE THING AT A TIME, GIRL. WE GOT TO GET OUT OF HERE FIRST. REGROUP. I'M NOT ABOUT TO TAKE EVERYONE HERE ON BY MYSELF.
Uhh... Yeah...
I mean, who would do that...
Nice infiltration, by the way.
YOU EXPECT ME TO GO IN THE FRONT DOOR? WHAT AM I, AN IDIOT?
Uh...
Hey, this is one of Eddie Death's cars!
WELL, WHEN I DIDN'T FIND YOU THERE, I FIGURED ON BORROWING SOME WHEELS.
YOUR MAN'S GOT QUITE A COLLECTION.
Listen, for the last time, he's not my--
Uh-oh.
BRRROOOMM! BRRROOOMM!
More of them.
AND THEY'RE ON WHEELS.
BROUGHT SOMETHING ALONG FOR YOU, BABY. MIGHT BE A GOOD TIME FOR IT, YOU KNOW?
SKREEEEE!

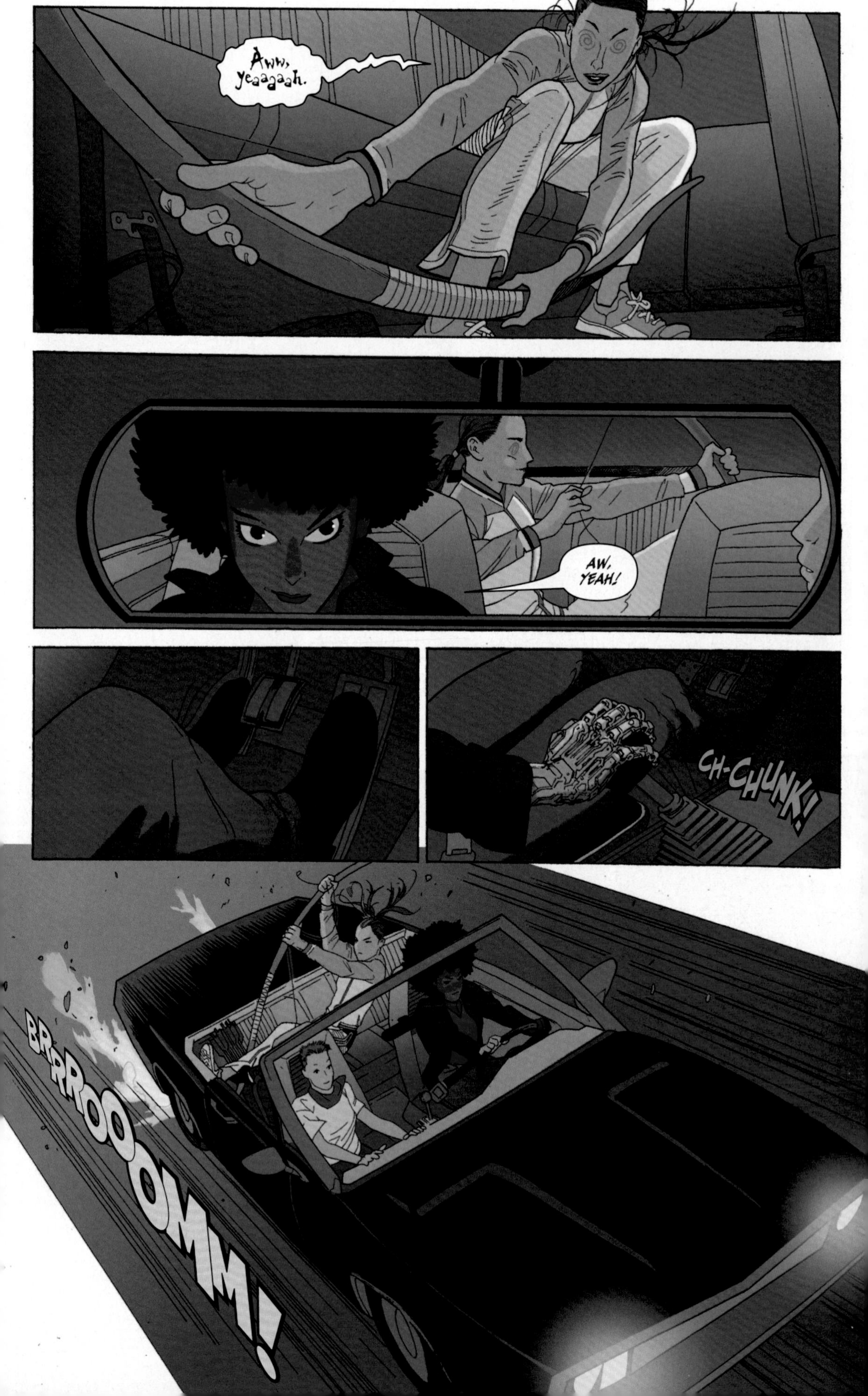
Aww, yeaaaaah.
AW, YEAH!
CH-CHUNK!
BRRROOOMM!

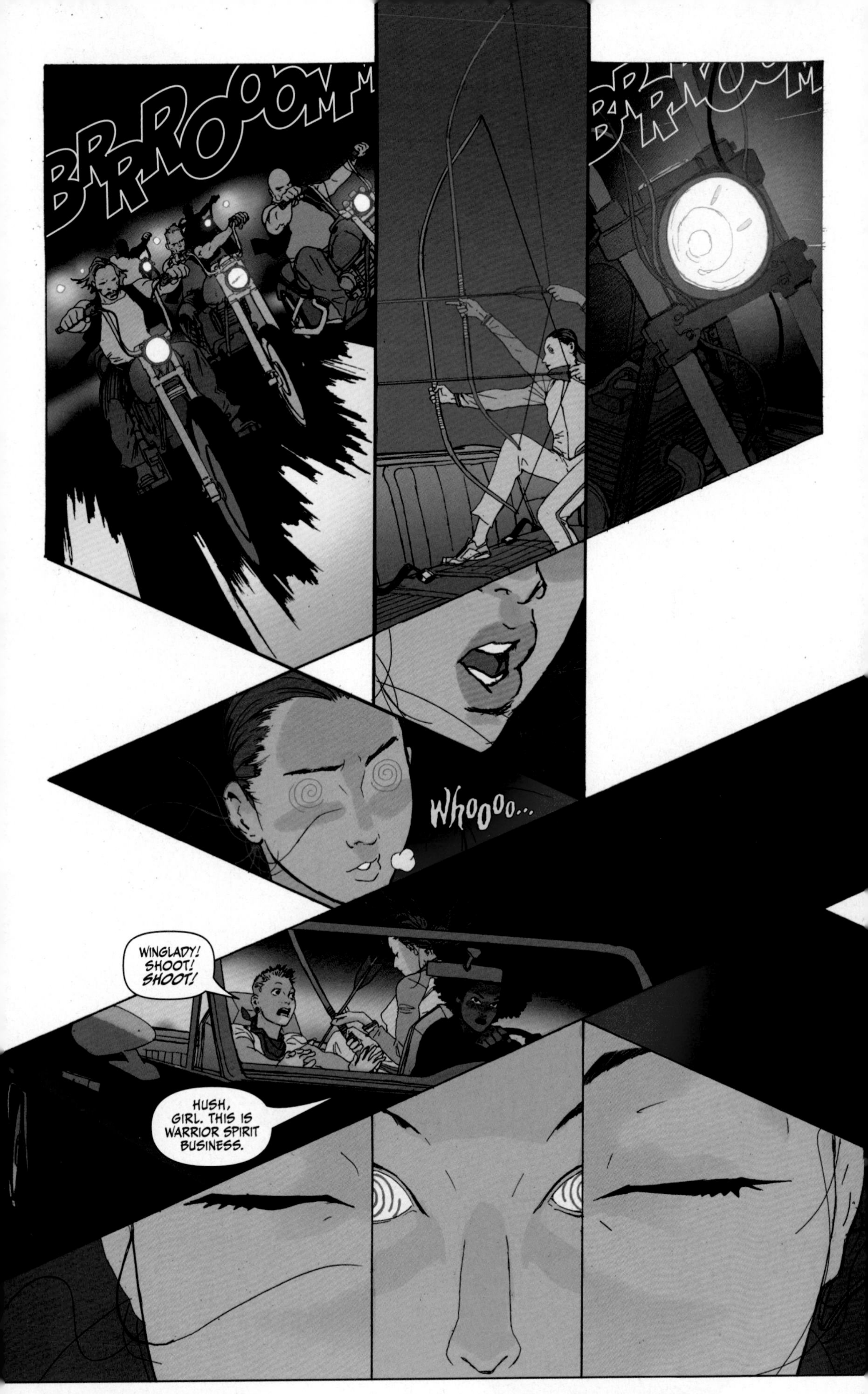
BRRROOOMM
BRRROOOM
Whoooo...
WINGLADY! SHOOT! SHOOT!
HUSH, GIRL. THIS IS WARRIOR SPIRIT BUSINESS.

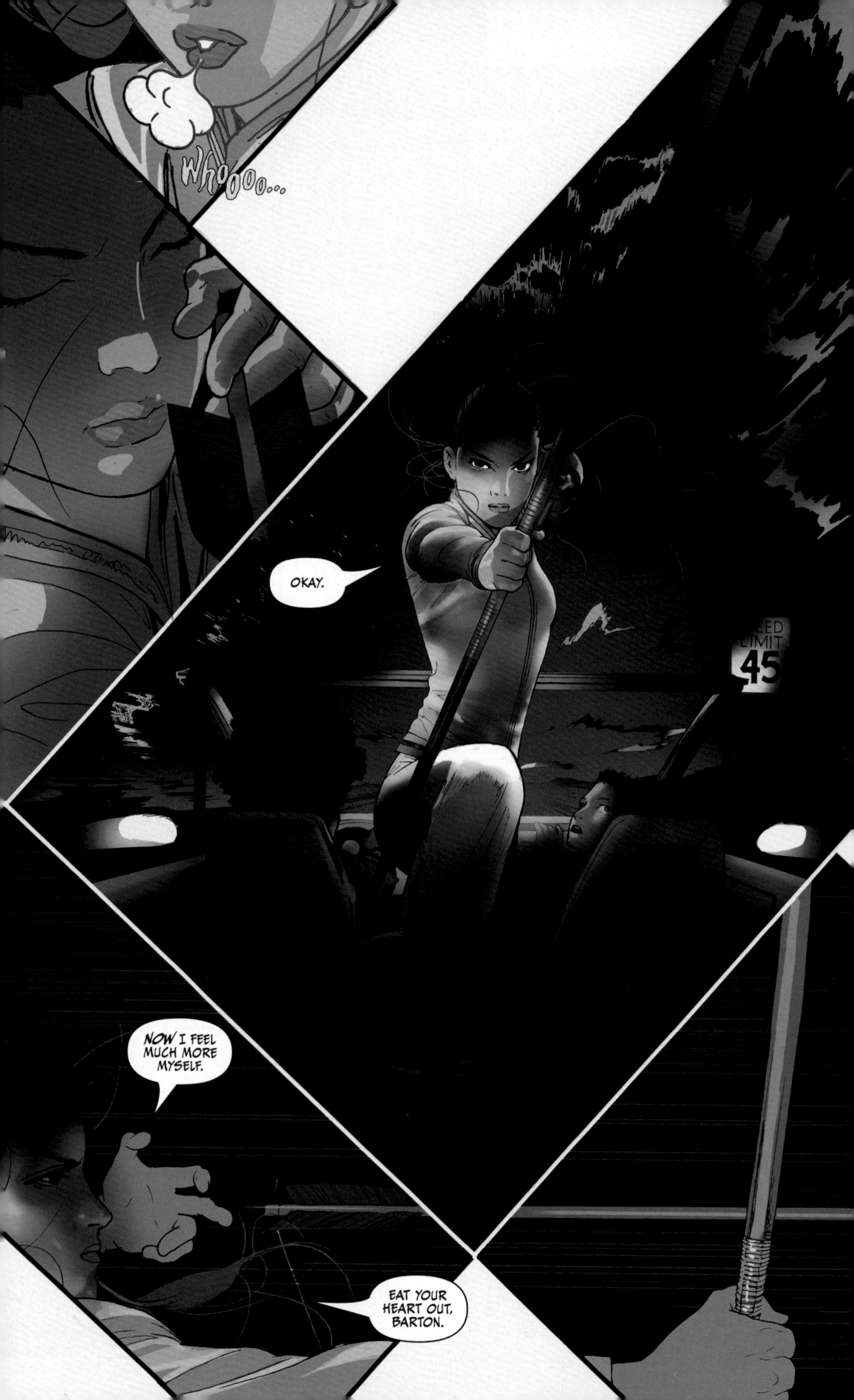
WHOOOO...
OKAY.
SPEED LIMIT 45
NOW I FEEL MUCH MORE MYSELF.
EAT YOUR HEART OUT, BARTON.

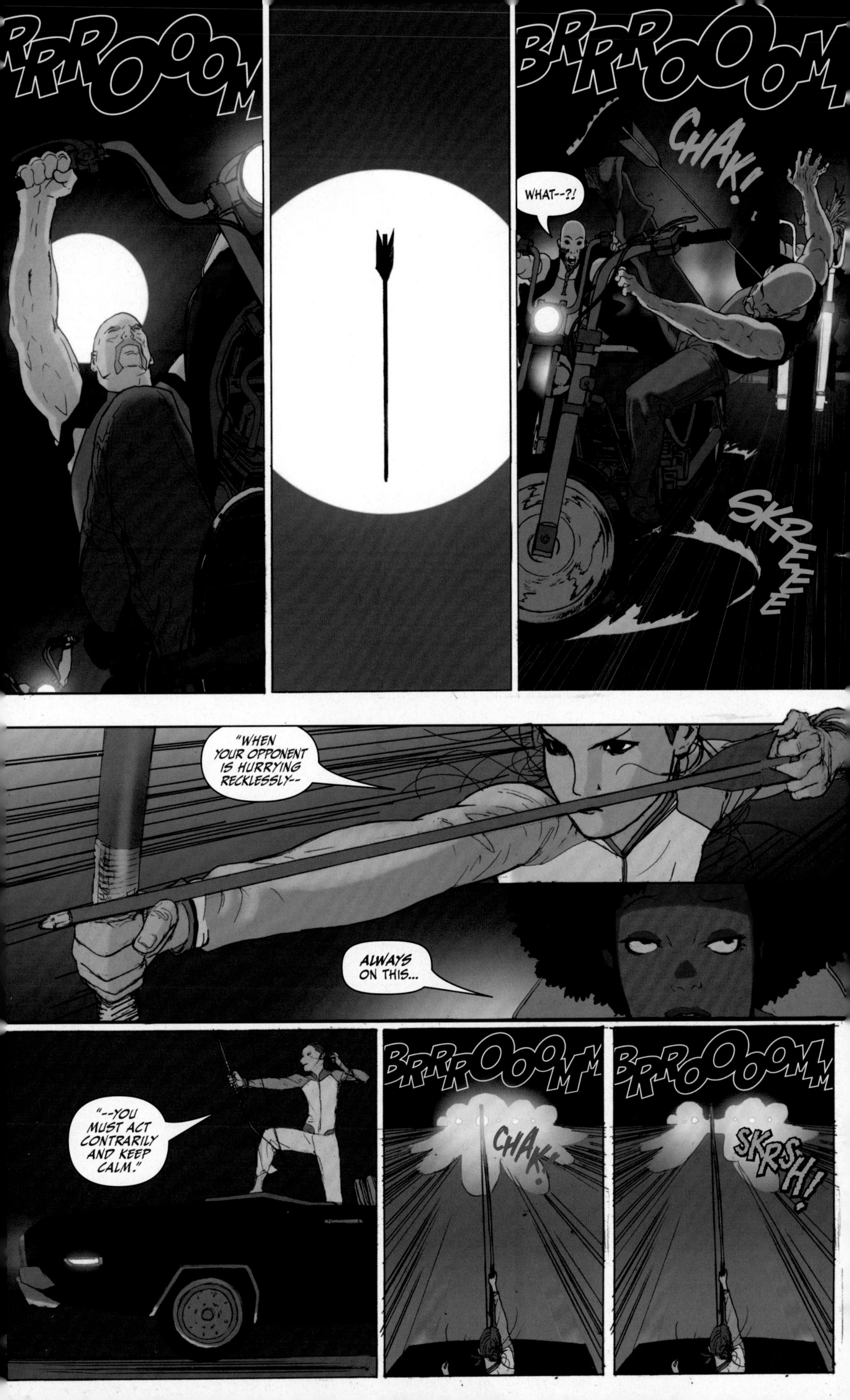
BRRROOOOMM
BRRROOOOOMM
CHAK!
WHAT--?!
SKREEEEE
"WHEN YOUR OPPONENT IS HURRYING RECKLESSLY--
ALWAYS ON THIS...
"--YOU MUST ACT CONTRARILY AND KEEP CALM."
BRRROOOOMM
CHAK!
BRRROOOOMM
SKRSH!

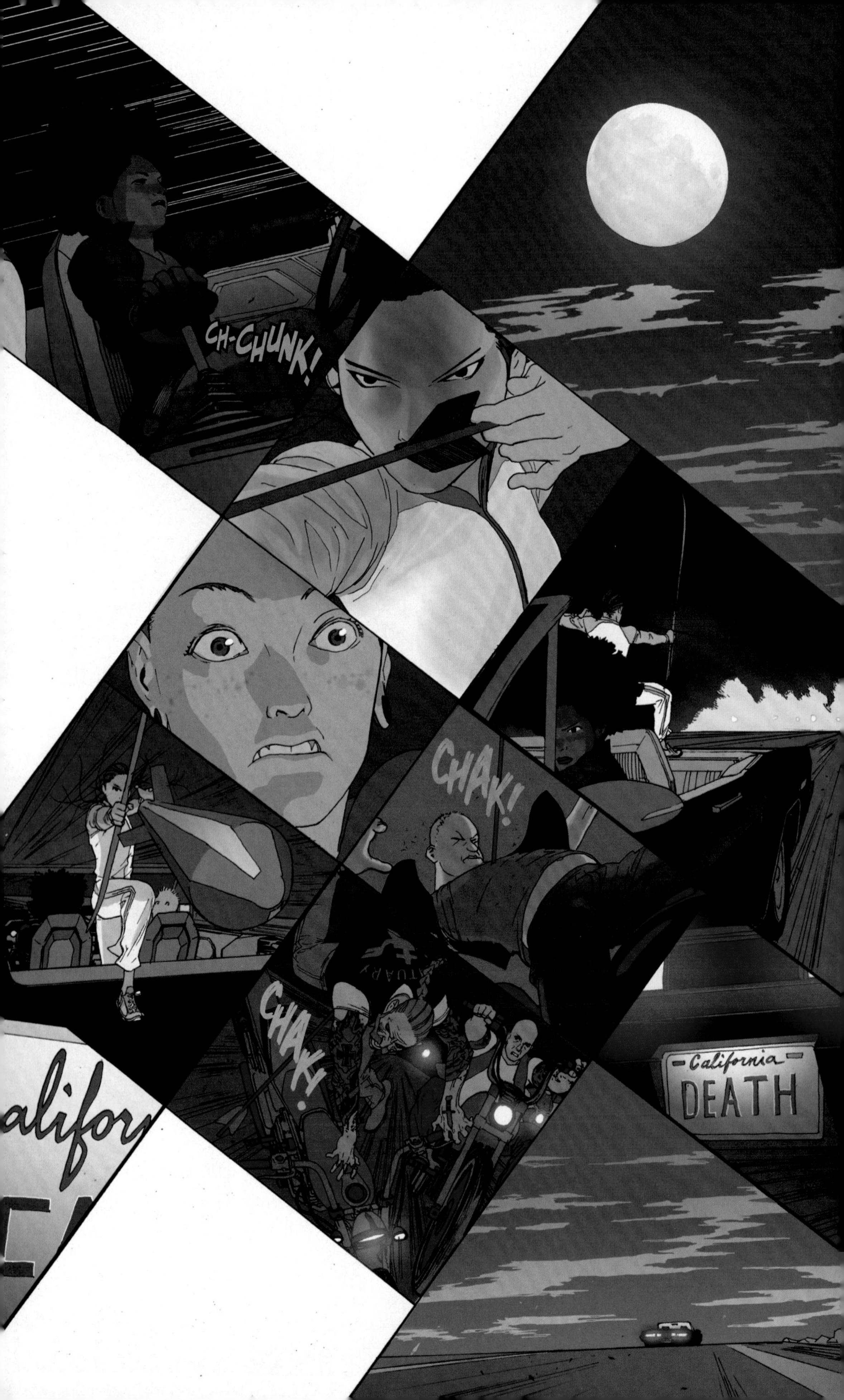
CH-CHUNK!
CHAK!
CHAK!
California
DEATH

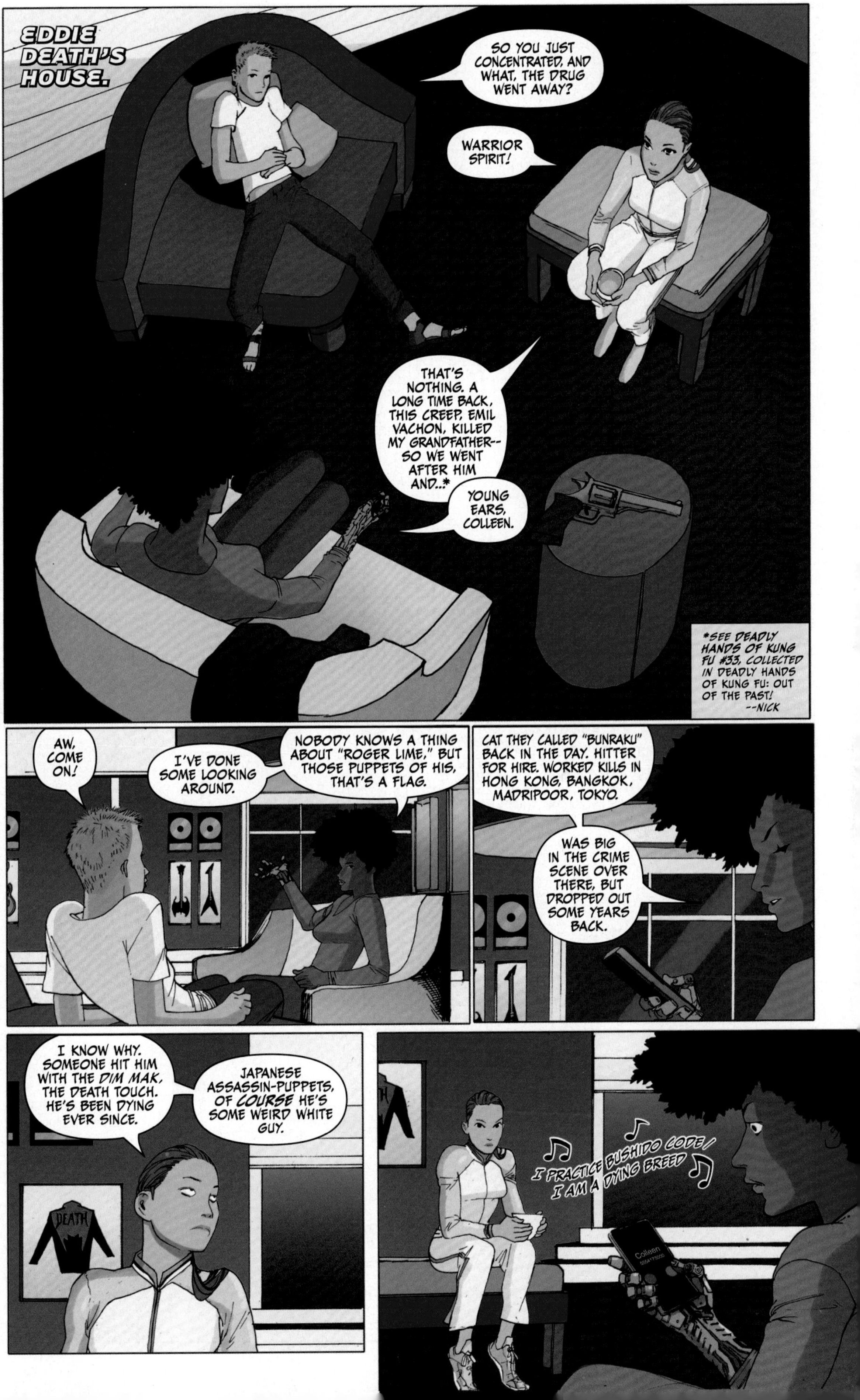
EDDIE DEATH'S HOUSE.
SO YOU JUST CONCENTRATED, AND WHAT, THE DRUG WENT AWAY?
WARRIOR SPIRIT!
THAT'S NOTHING. A LONG TIME BACK, THIS CREEP, EMIL VACHON, KILLED MY GRANDFATHER-- SO WE WENT AFTER HIM AND...*
YOUNG EARS, COLLEEN.
*SEE DEADLY HANDS OF KUNG FU #33, COLLECTED IN DEADLY HANDS OF KUNG FU: OUT OF THE PAST! --NICK
AW, COME ON!
I'VE DONE SOME LOOKING AROUND.
NOBODY KNOWS A THING ABOUT "ROGER LIME," BUT THOSE PUPPETS OF HIS, THAT'S A FLAG.
CAT THEY CALLED "BUNRAKU" BACK IN THE DAY. HITTER FOR HIRE. WORKED KILLS IN HONG KONG, BANGKOK, MADRIPOOR, TOKYO.
WAS BIG IN THE CRIME SCENE OVER THERE, BUT DROPPED OUT SOME YEARS BACK.
I KNOW WHY. SOMEONE HIT HIM WITH THE DIM MAK, THE DEATH TOUCH. HE'S BEEN DYING EVER SINCE.
JAPANESE ASSASSIN-PUPPETS, OF COURSE HE'S SOME WEIRD WHITE GUY.
DEATH
I PRACTICE BUSHIDO CODE / I AM A DYING BREED
Colleen

I LEFT MY PHONE AT AGHORA!

♪ I PRACTICE BUSHIDO CODE! ♪
I AM A DYING BREED ♪

IT'S HIM.

Colleen
5554175000

00:35

HELLO, PRETTY SAMURAI. ONCE AGAIN, I MUST APPLAUD YOUR WARRIOR SPIRIT.

JUST SO I CAN HEAR YOU SAY IT: YOU GOT THOSE KIDS, DON'T YOU? THE MISSING ONES?

OF COURSE I DO.

AND I'LL WAGER YOU'RE DYING TO KNOW WHY.

ESPECIALLY SINCE YOU DELIVERED ONE OF THEM TO ME, PRETTY SAMURAI.

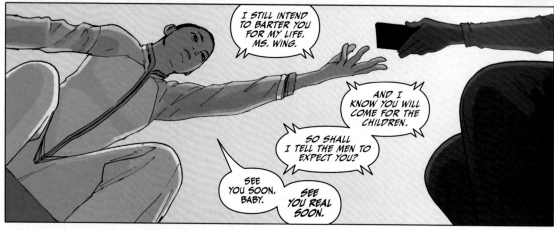

I STILL INTEND TO BARTER YOU FOR MY LIFE, MS. WING.

AND I KNOW YOU WILL COME FOR THE CHILDREN.

SO SHALL I TELL THE MEN TO EXPECT YOU?

SEE YOU SOON, BABY.

SEE YOU REAL SOON.

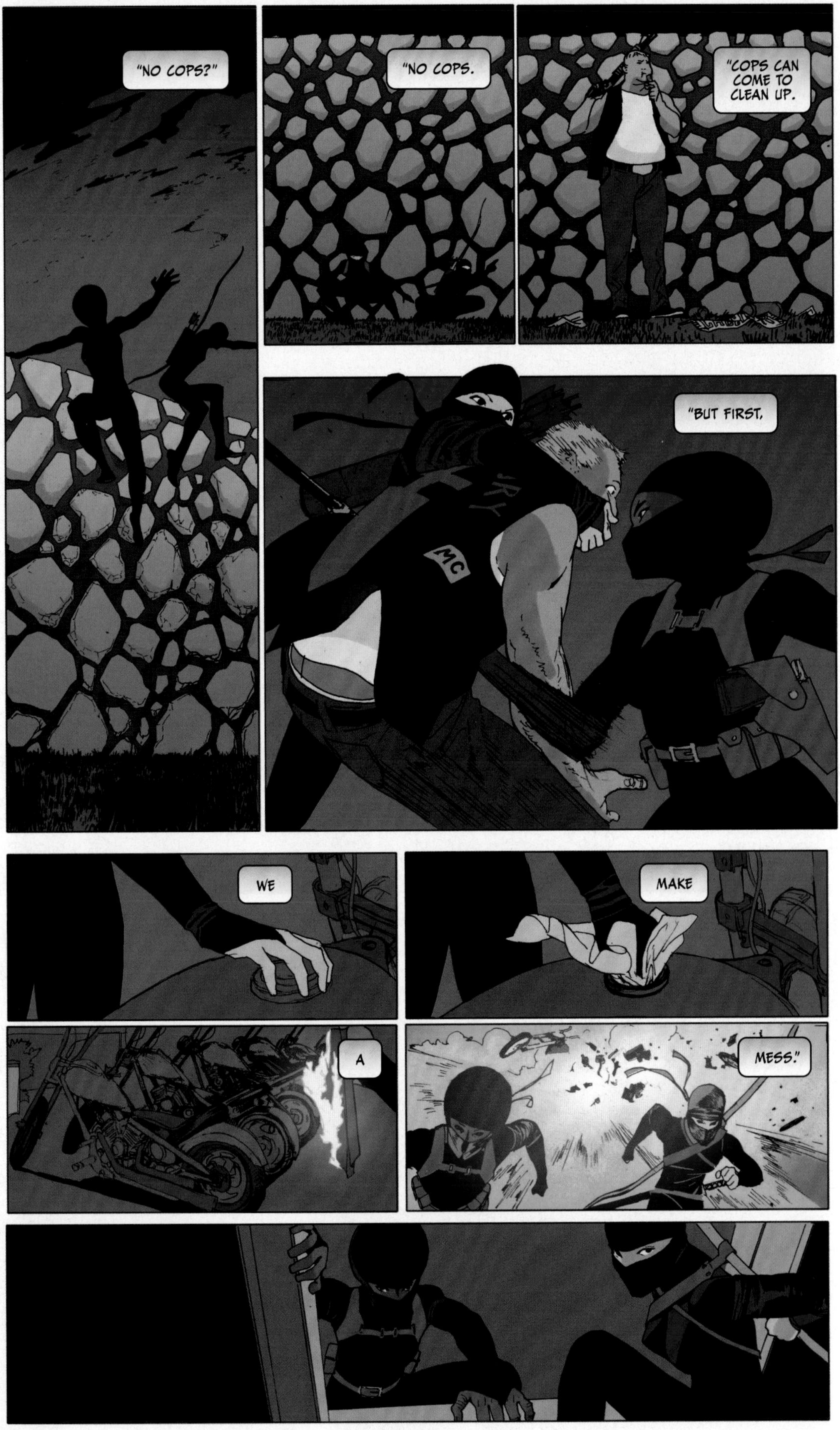
"NO COPS?"
"NO COPS.
"COPS CAN COME TO CLEAN UP.
"BUT FIRST,
MC
WE
MAKE
A
MESS."

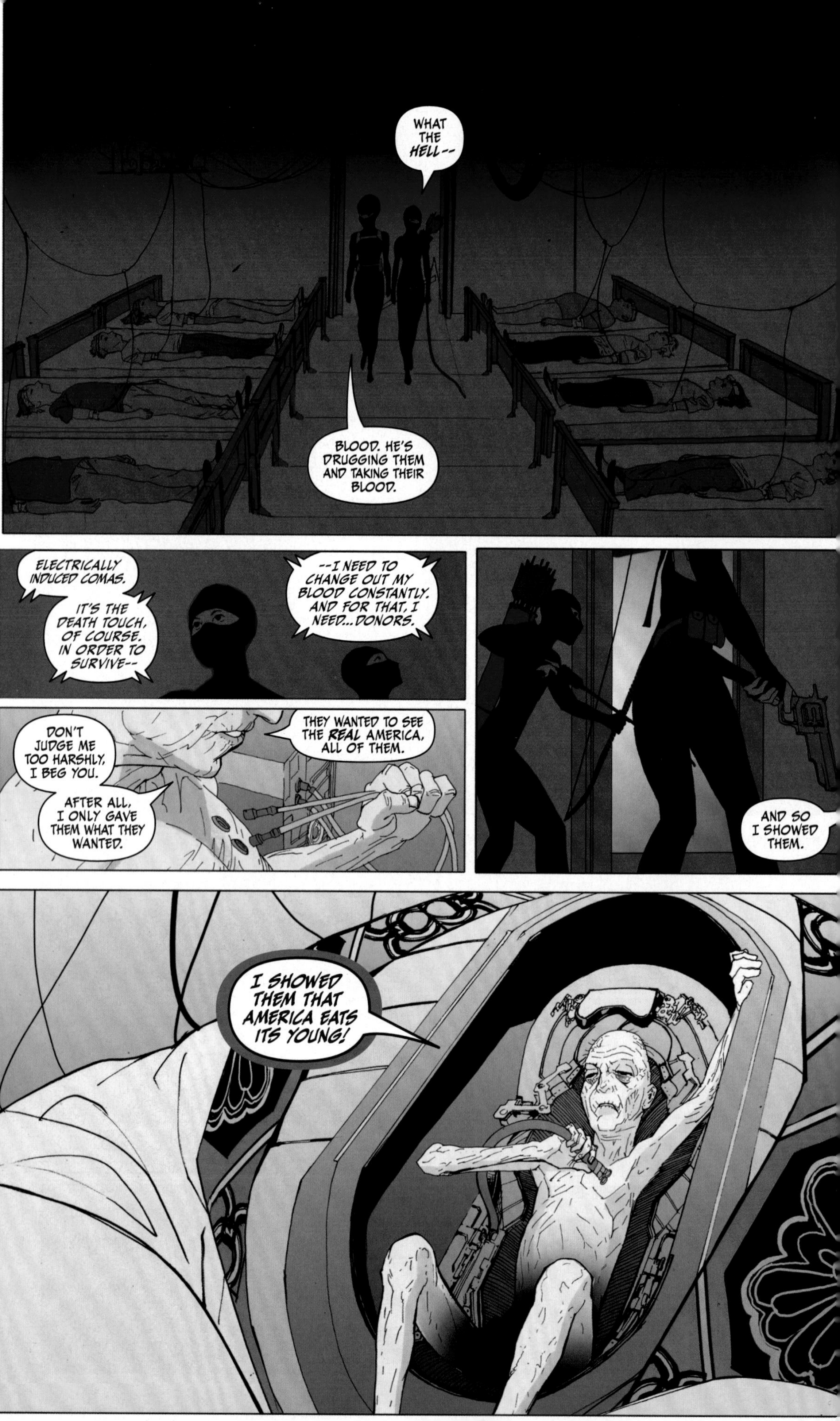
WHAT THE HELL--
BLOOD. HE'S DRUGGING THEM AND TAKING THEIR BLOOD.
ELECTRICALLY INDUCED COMAS.
IT'S THE DEATH TOUCH, OF COURSE. IN ORDER TO SURVIVE--
--I NEED TO CHANGE OUT MY BLOOD CONSTANTLY. AND FOR THAT, I NEED...DONORS.
DON'T JUDGE ME TOO HARSHLY, I BEG YOU.
AFTER ALL, I ONLY GAVE THEM WHAT THEY WANTED.
THEY WANTED TO SEE THE REAL AMERICA, ALL OF THEM.
AND SO I SHOWED THEM.
I SHOWED THEM THAT AMERICA EATS ITS YOUNG!

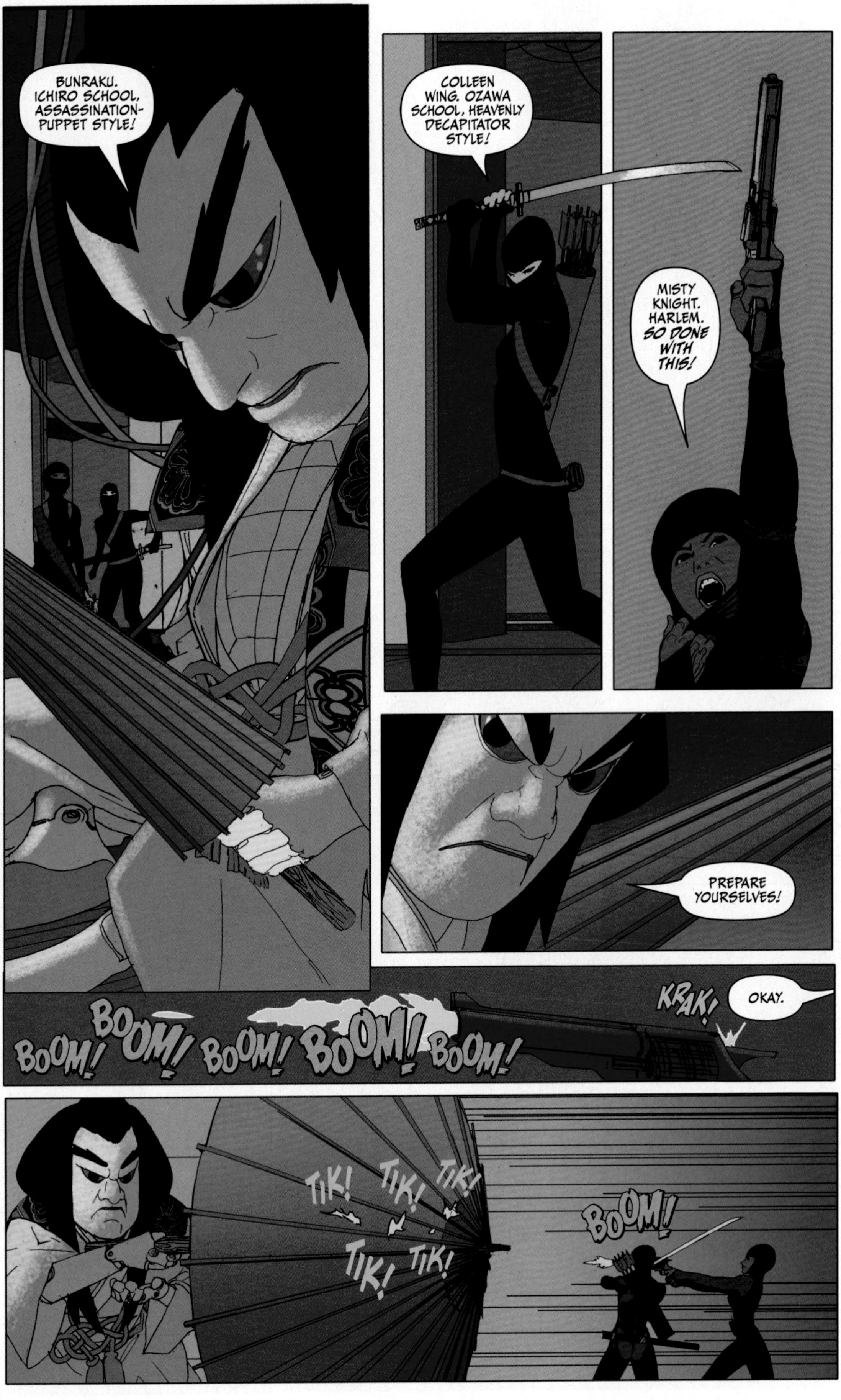
BUNRAKU. ICHIRO SCHOOL, ASSASSINATION-PUPPET STYLE!
COLLEEN WING. OZAWA SCHOOL, HEAVENLY DECAPITATOR STYLE!
MISTY KNIGHT. HARLEM. SO DONE WITH THIS!
PREPARE YOURSELVES!
BOOM! BOOM! BOOM! BOOM! BOOM!
KRAK!
OKAY.
TIK! TIK! TIK! TIK! TIK!
BOOM!

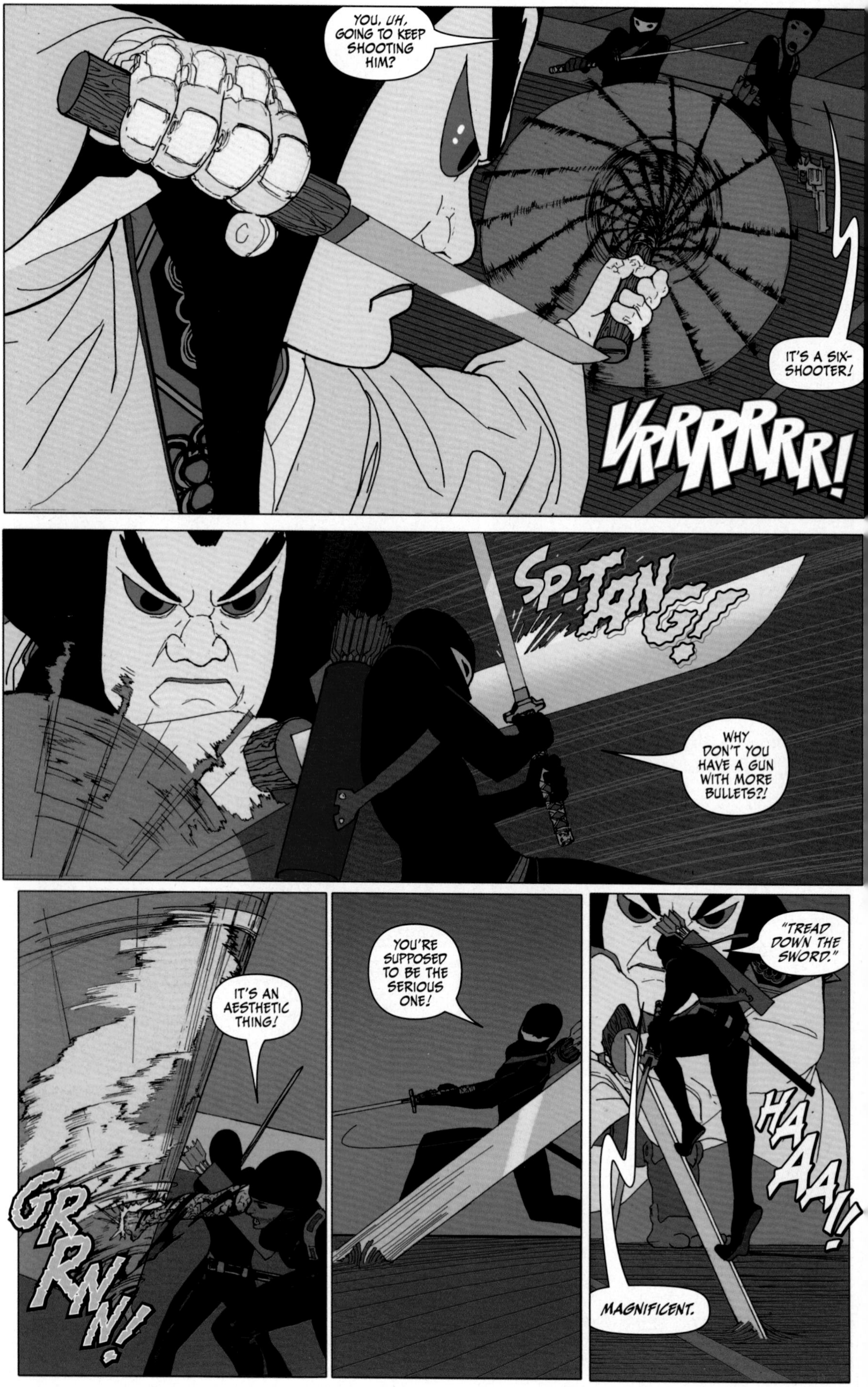
YOU, UH, GOING TO KEEP SHOOTING HIM?
IT'S A SIX-SHOOTER!
VRRRRRR!
SP-TANG!!
WHY DON'T YOU HAVE A GUN WITH MORE BULLETS?!
IT'S AN AESTHETIC THING!
GRNN!
YOU'RE SUPPOSED TO BE THE SERIOUS ONE!
"TREAD DOWN THE SWORD."
HAAAA!!
MAGNIFICENT.

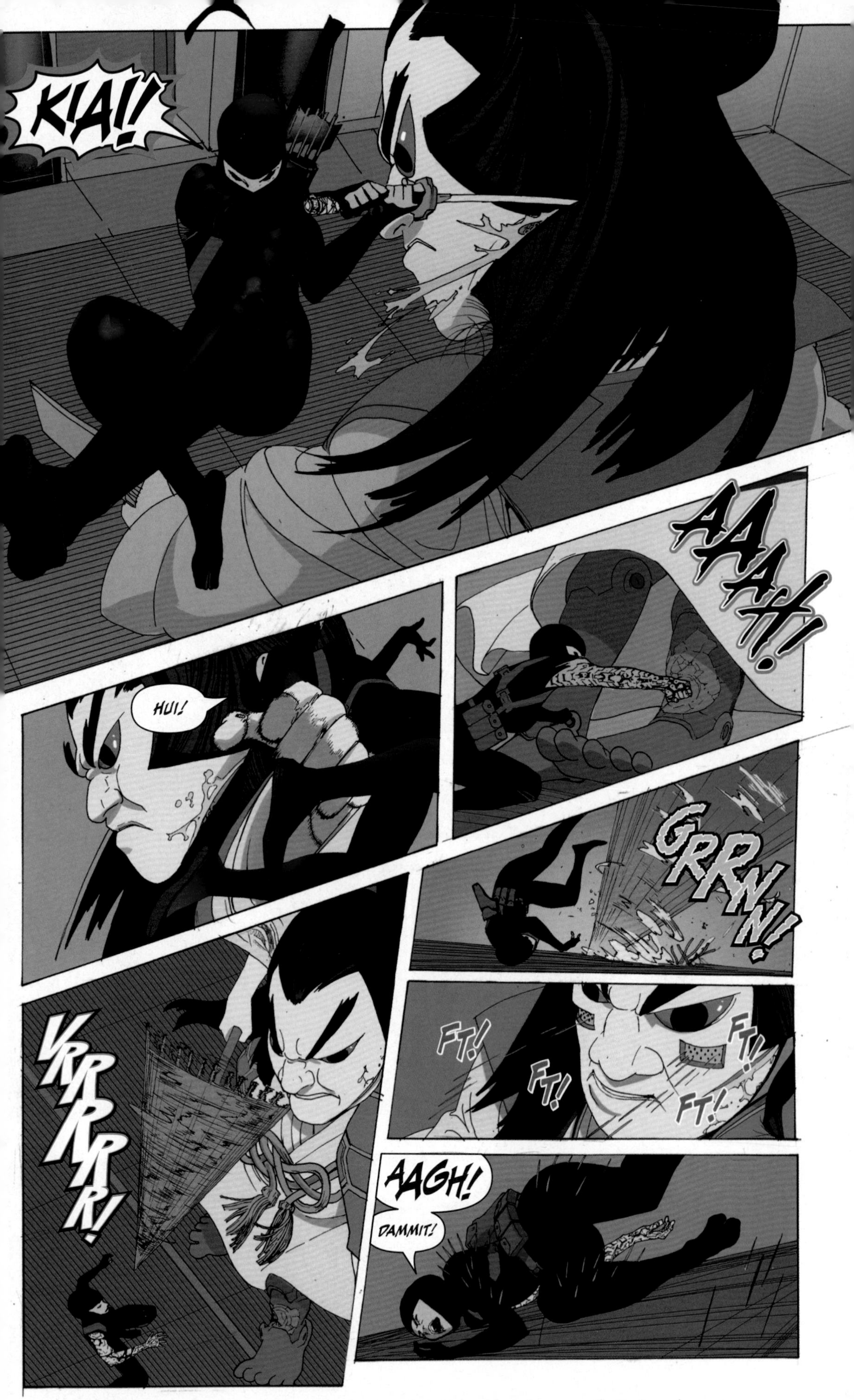

KIA!!
AAAH!
HUI!
GRRNN!
VRRRRRR!
FT!
FT!
FT!
FT!
AAGH!
DAMMIT!

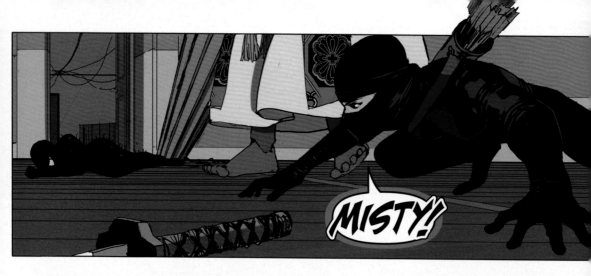

MISTY!

WORRY ABOUT YOURSELF, PRETTY SAMURAI.

Sp-TANG!

≡HUFF!≡

TANG! TANG! TANG!

AND SO IT ENDS.

SURE, BUNRAKU, YOU GOT ALL THESE BIKERS AND PUPPETS AND A GREAT PAD AND AN ADMITTEDLY DOPE ROBOT SUIT.

BUT YOU KNOW WHAT I GOT?

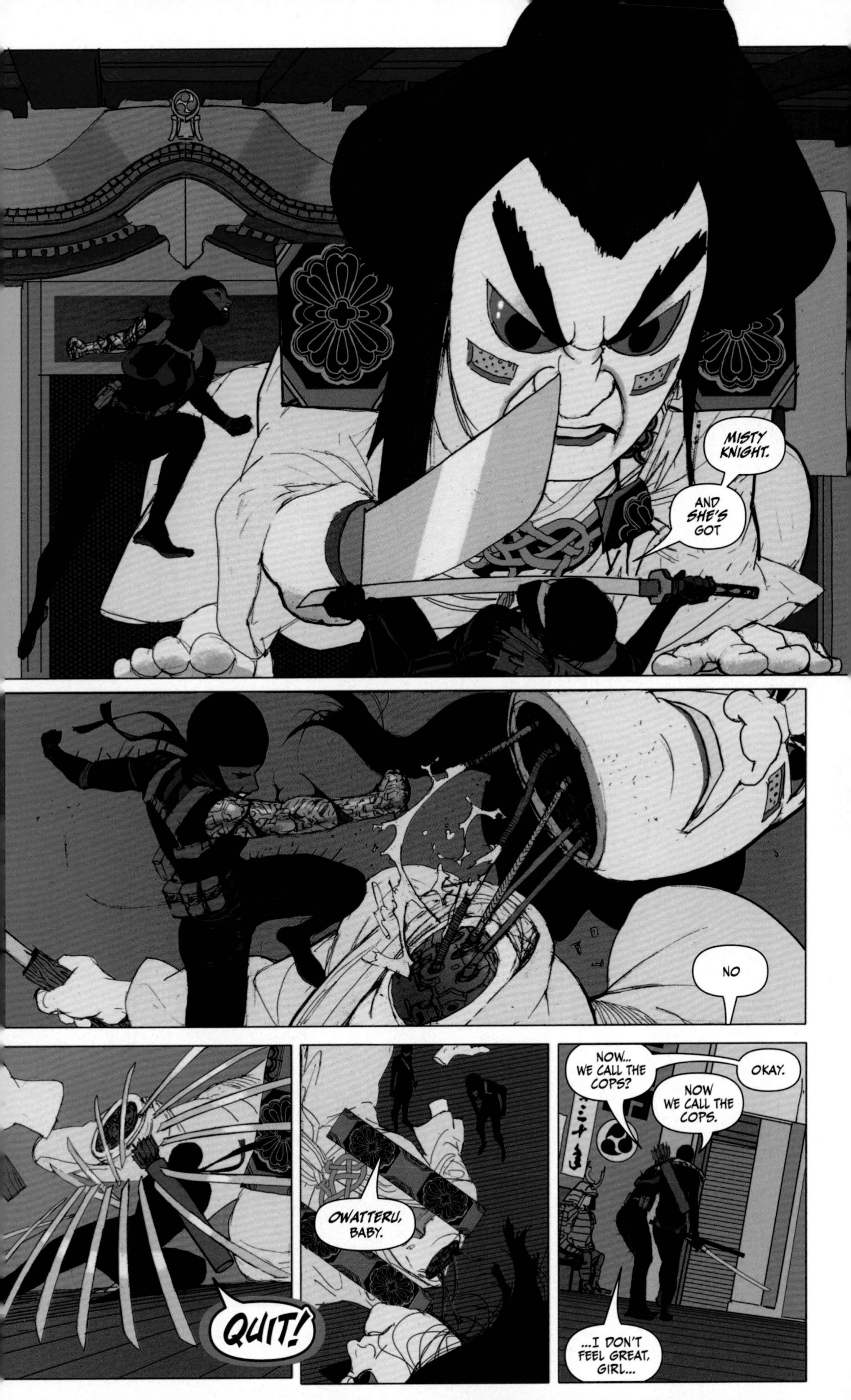
MISTY KNIGHT.
AND SHE'S GOT
NO
QUIT!
OWATTERU, BABY.
NOW... WE CALL THE COPS?
OKAY.
NOW WE CALL THE COPS.
...I DON'T FEEL GREAT, GIRL...

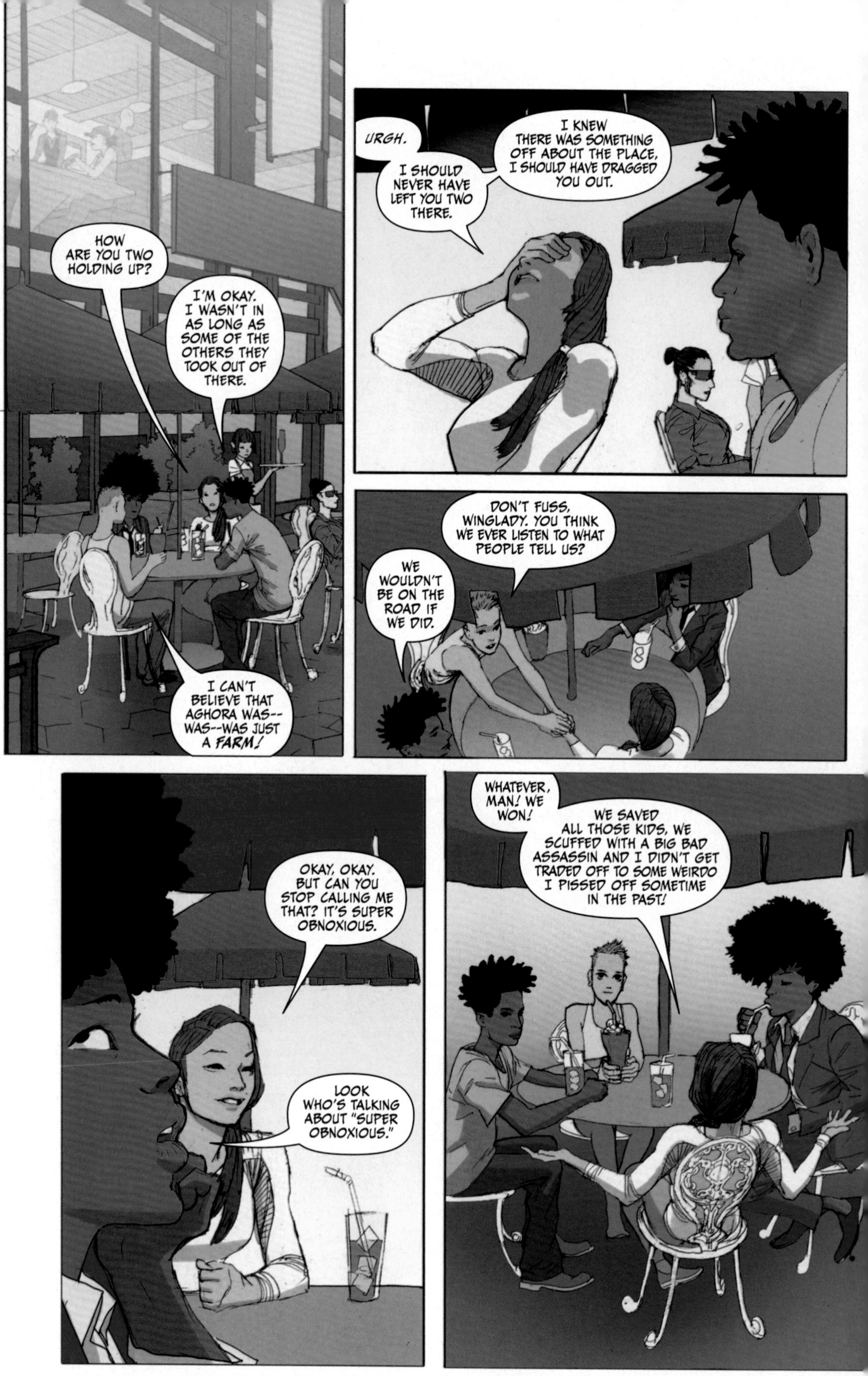
HOW ARE YOU TWO HOLDING UP?
I'M OKAY. I WASN'T IN AS LONG AS SOME OF THE OTHERS THEY TOOK OUT OF THERE.
I CAN'T BELIEVE THAT AGHORA WAS--WAS--WAS JUST A FARM!
URGH.
I SHOULD NEVER HAVE LEFT YOU TWO THERE.
I KNEW THERE WAS SOMETHING OFF ABOUT THE PLACE, I SHOULD HAVE DRAGGED YOU OUT.
DON'T FUSS, WINGLADY. YOU THINK WE EVER LISTEN TO WHAT PEOPLE TELL US?
WE WOULDN'T BE ON THE ROAD IF WE DID.
OKAY, OKAY. BUT CAN YOU STOP CALLING ME THAT? IT'S SUPER OBNOXIOUS.
LOOK WHO'S TALKING ABOUT "SUPER OBNOXIOUS."
WHATEVER, MAN! WE WON!
WE SAVED ALL THOSE KIDS, WE SCUFFED WITH A BIG BAD ASSASSIN AND I DIDN'T GET TRADED OFF TO SOME WEIRDO I PISSED OFF SOMETIME IN THE PAST!

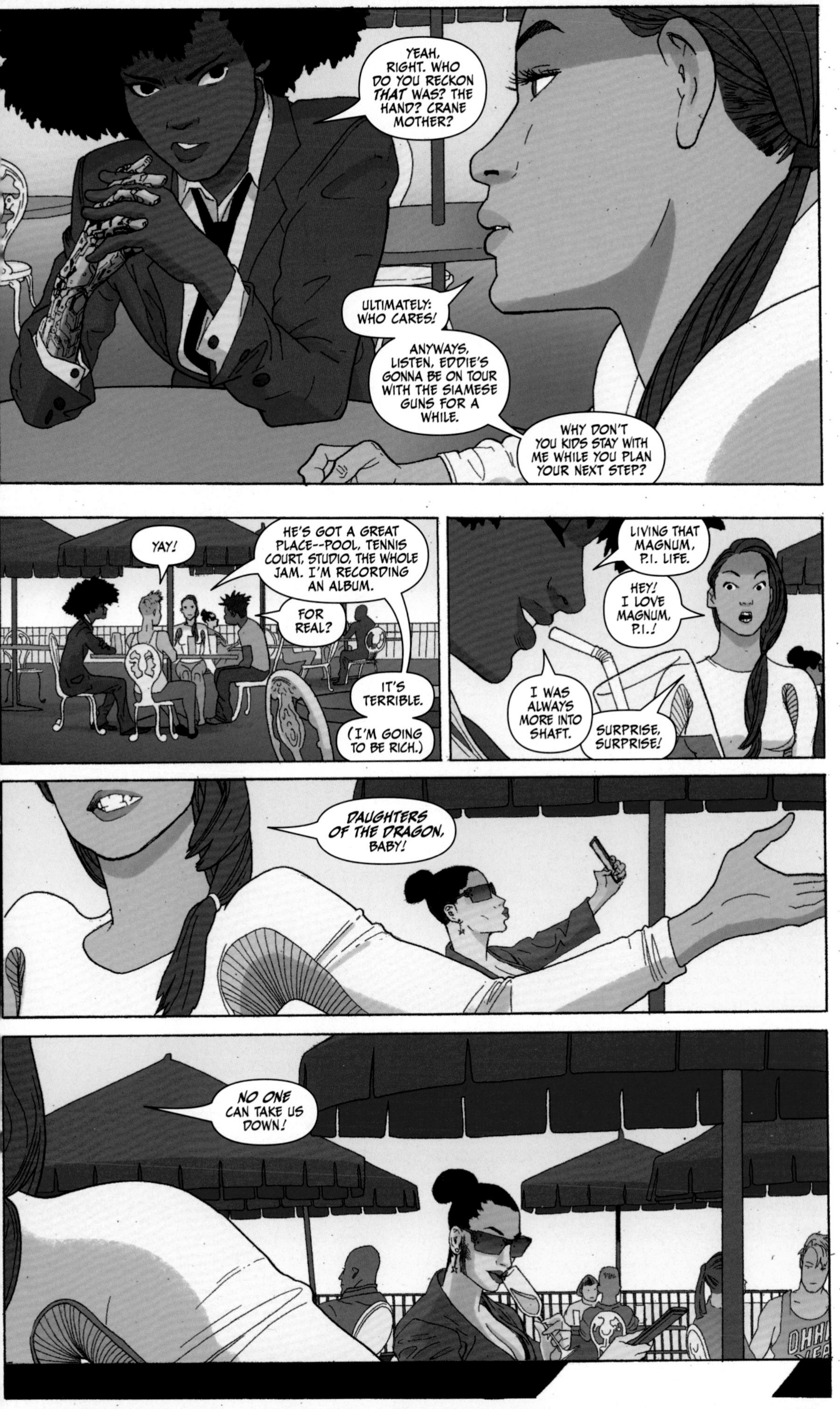
YEAH, RIGHT. WHO DO YOU RECKON THAT WAS? THE HAND? CRANE MOTHER?
ULTIMATELY: WHO CARES!
ANYWAYS, LISTEN, EDDIE'S GONNA BE ON TOUR WITH THE SIAMESE GUNS FOR A WHILE.
WHY DON'T YOU KIDS STAY WITH ME WHILE YOU PLAN YOUR NEXT STEP?
YAY!
HE'S GOT A GREAT PLACE--POOL, TENNIS COURT, STUDIO, THE WHOLE JAM. I'M RECORDING AN ALBUM.
FOR REAL?
IT'S TERRIBLE.
(I'M GOING TO BE RICH.)
LIVING THAT MAGNUM, P.I. LIFE.
HEY! I LOVE MAGNUM, P.I.!
I WAS ALWAYS MORE INTO SHAFT.
SURPRISE, SURPRISE!
DAUGHTERS OF THE DRAGON, BABY!
NO ONE CAN TAKE US DOWN!

CHAPTER 3

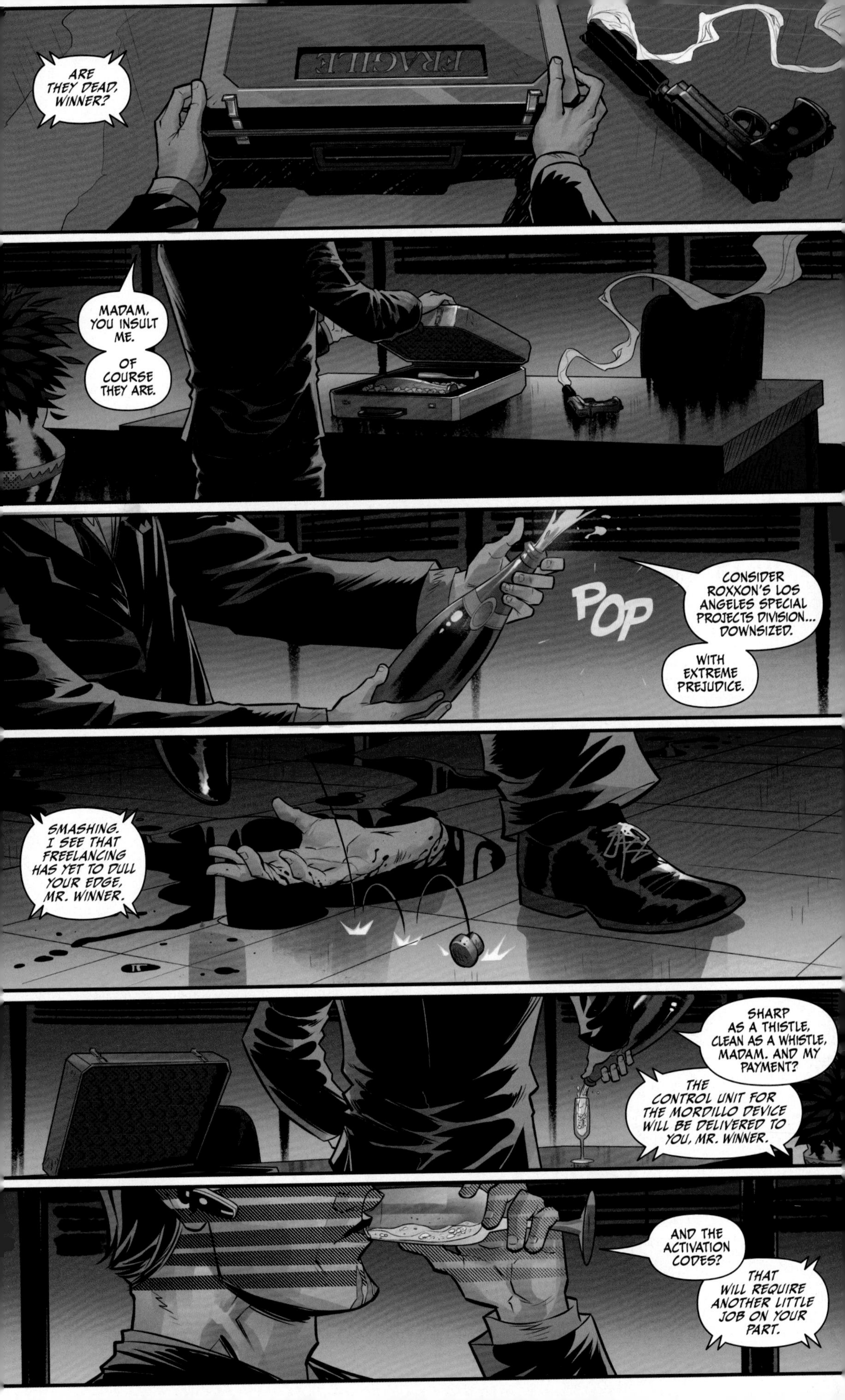
ARE THEY DEAD, WINNER?
MADAM, YOU INSULT ME.
OF COURSE THEY ARE.
POP
CONSIDER ROXXON'S LOS ANGELES SPECIAL PROJECTS DIVISION... DOWNSIZED.
WITH EXTREME PREJUDICE.
SMASHING. I SEE THAT FREELANCING HAS YET TO DULL YOUR EDGE, MR. WINNER.
SHARP AS A THISTLE, CLEAN AS A WHISTLE, MADAM. AND MY PAYMENT?
THE CONTROL UNIT FOR THE MORDILLO DEVICE WILL BE DELIVERED TO YOU, MR. WINNER.
AND THE ACTIVATION CODES?
THAT WILL REQUIRE ANOTHER LITTLE JOB ON YOUR PART.

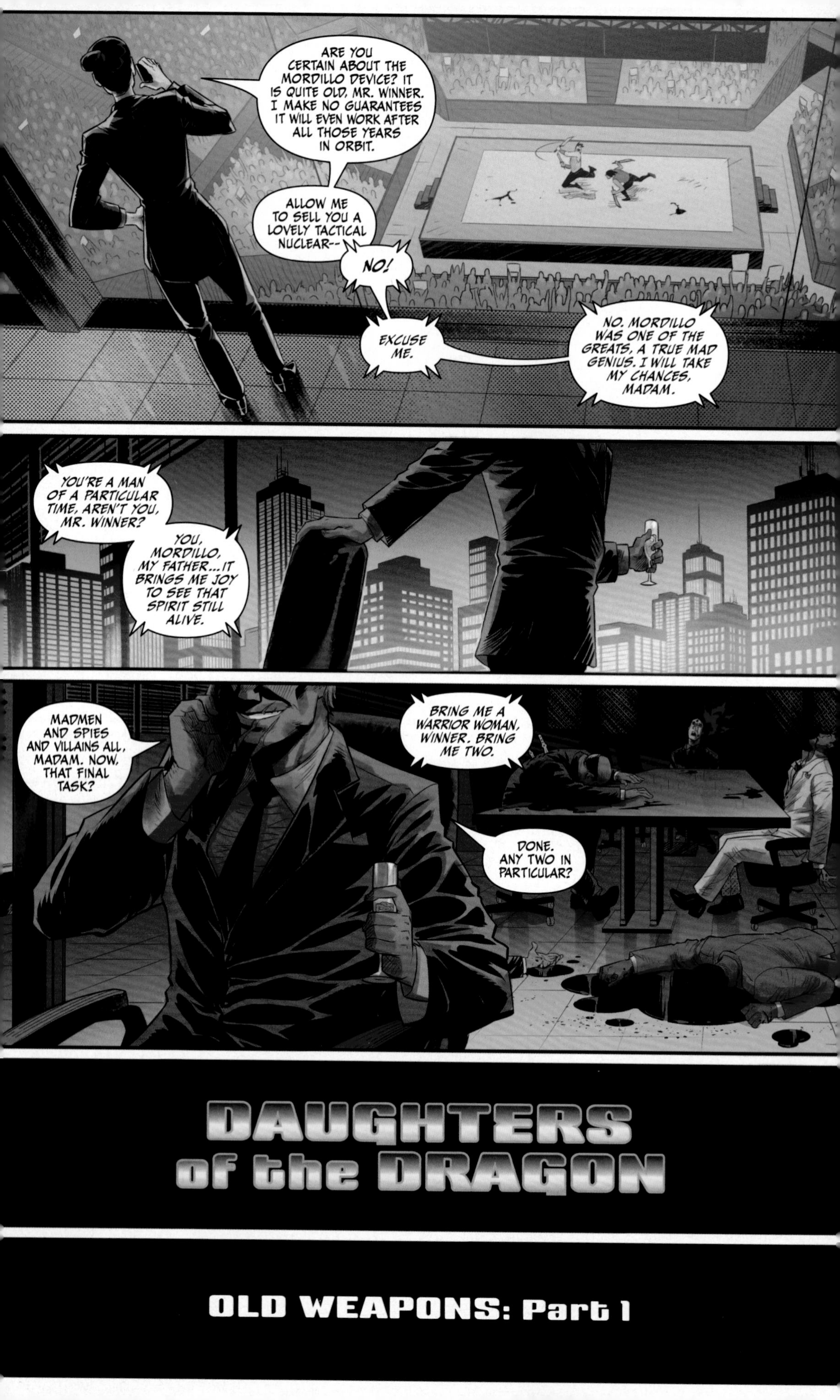
ARE YOU CERTAIN ABOUT THE MORDILLO DEVICE? IT IS QUITE OLD, MR. WINNER. I MAKE NO GUARANTEES IT WILL EVEN WORK AFTER ALL THOSE YEARS IN ORBIT.
ALLOW ME TO SELL YOU A LOVELY TACTICAL NUCLEAR--
NO!
EXCUSE ME.
NO. MORDILLO WAS ONE OF THE GREATS, A TRUE MAD GENIUS. I WILL TAKE MY CHANCES, MADAM.
YOU'RE A MAN OF A PARTICULAR TIME, AREN'T YOU, MR. WINNER?
YOU, MORDILLO, MY FATHER...IT BRINGS ME JOY TO SEE THAT SPIRIT STILL ALIVE.
MADMEN AND SPIES AND VILLAINS ALL, MADAM. NOW, THAT FINAL TASK?
BRING ME A WARRIOR WOMAN, WINNER. BRING ME TWO.
DONE. ANY TWO IN PARTICULAR?

DAUGHTERS of the DRAGON

OLD WEAPONS: Part 1

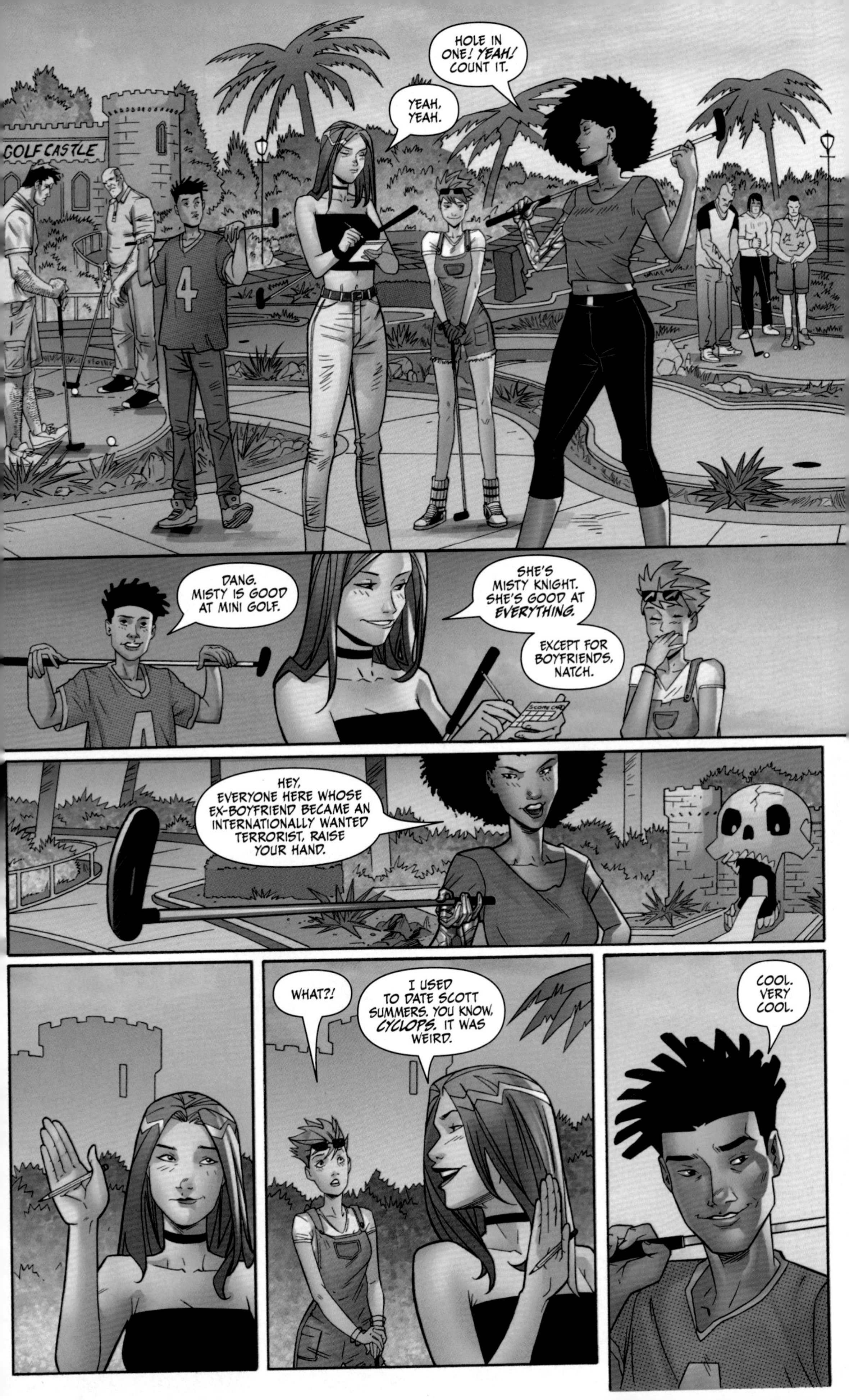
GOLF CASTLE
HOLE IN ONE! YEAH! COUNT IT.
YEAH, YEAH.
4
DANG. MISTY IS GOOD AT MINI GOLF.
SHE'S MISTY KNIGHT. SHE'S GOOD AT EVERYTHING.
EXCEPT FOR BOYFRIENDS, NATCH.
HEY, EVERYONE HERE WHOSE EX-BOYFRIEND BECAME AN INTERNATIONALLY WANTED TERRORIST, RAISE YOUR HAND.
WHAT?!
I USED TO DATE SCOTT SUMMERS. YOU KNOW, CYCLOPS. IT WAS WEIRD.
COOL. VERY COOL.

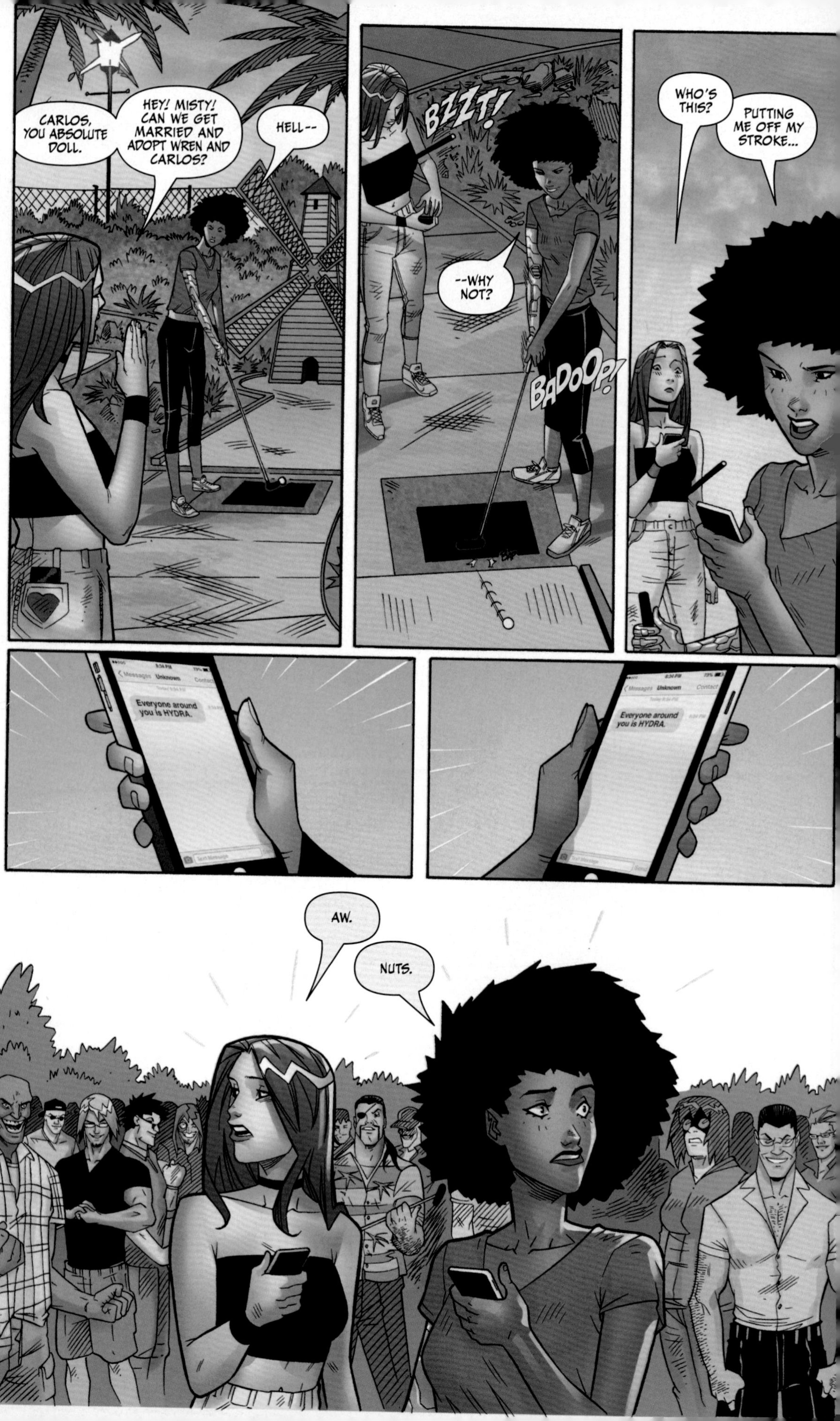
CARLOS, YOU ABSOLUTE DOLL.
HEY! MISTY! CAN WE GET MARRIED AND ADOPT WREN AND CARLOS?
HELL--
BZZT!
--WHY NOT?
BADOOP!
WHO'S THIS?
PUTTING ME OFF MY STROKE...
Everyone around you is HYDRA.
Everyone around you is HYDRA.
AW.
NUTS.

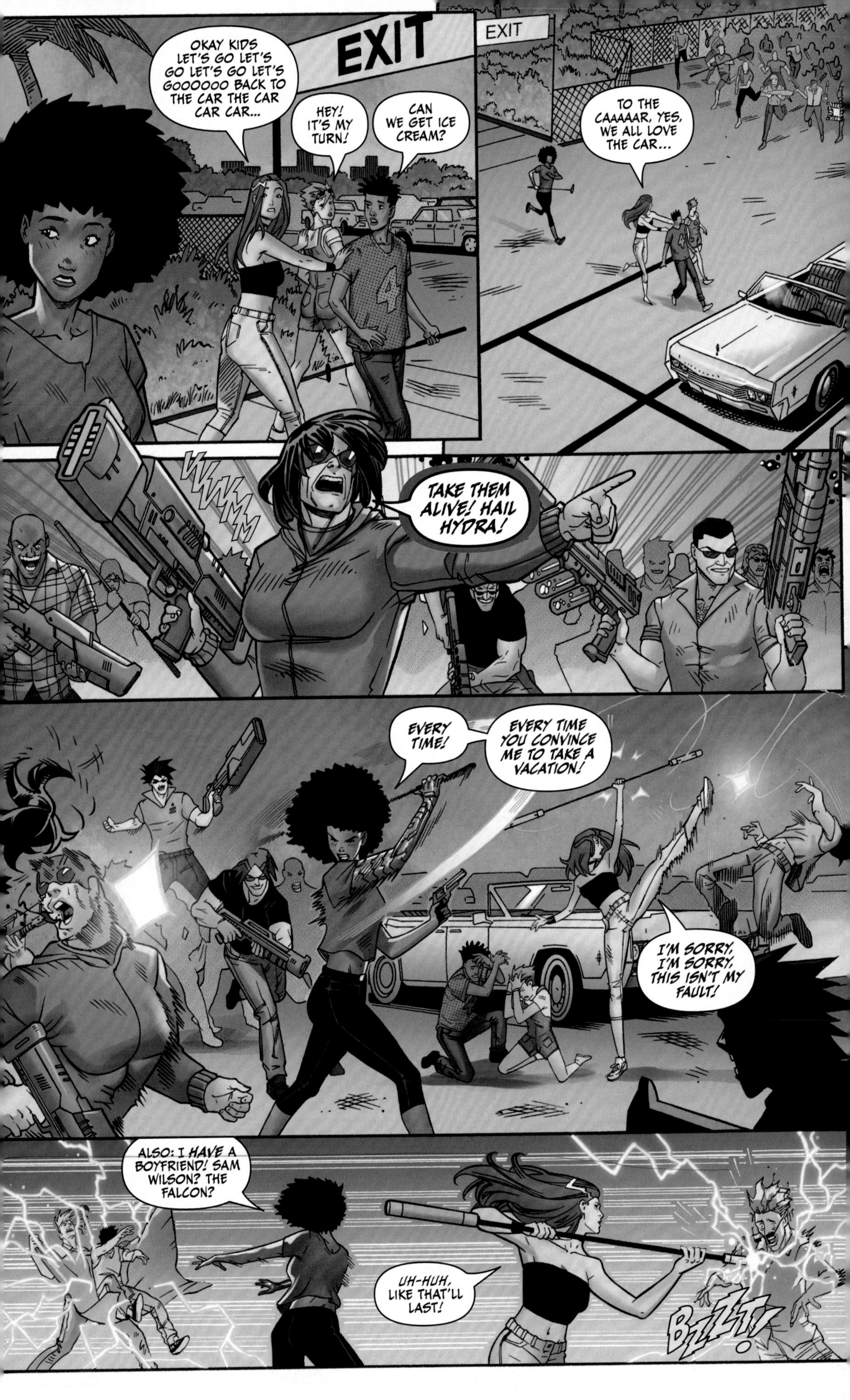
EXIT
OKAY KIDS LET'S GO LET'S GO LET'S GO LET'S GOOOOOO BACK TO THE CAR THE CAR CAR CAR...
HEY! IT'S MY TURN!
CAN WE GET ICE CREAM?
EXIT
TO THE CAAAAAR, YES, WE ALL LOVE THE CAR...
TAKE THEM ALIVE! HAIL HYDRA!
EVERY TIME!
EVERY TIME YOU CONVINCE ME TO TAKE A VACATION!
I'M SORRY, I'M SORRY, THIS ISN'T MY FAULT!
ALSO: I HAVE A BOYFRIEND! SAM WILSON? THE FALCON?
UH-HUH, LIKE THAT'LL LAST!
BZZT!

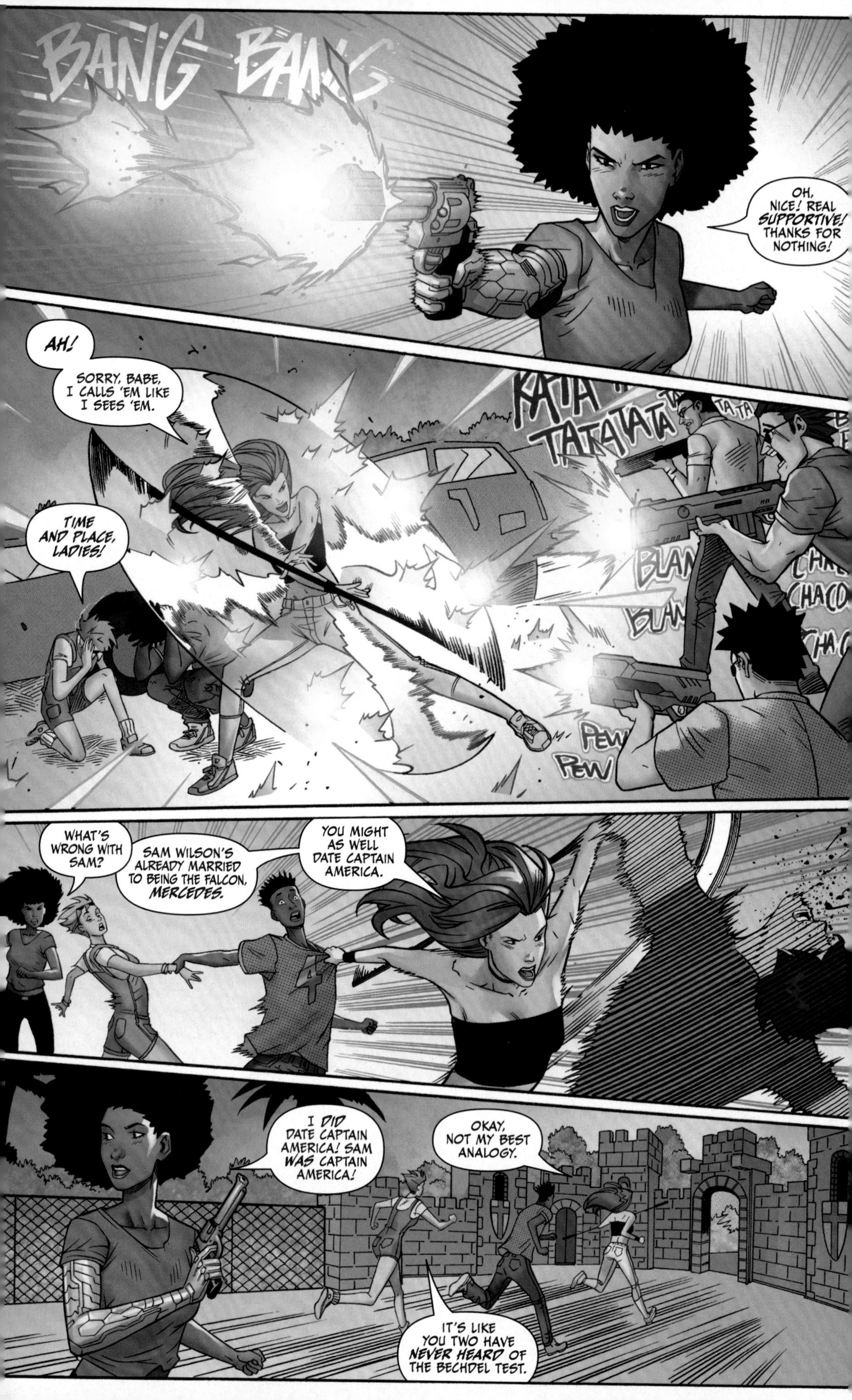

BANG BANG
OH, NICE! REAL *SUPPORTIVE!* THANKS FOR NOTHING!
AH!
SORRY, BABE, I CALLS 'EM LIKE I SEES 'EM.
KATA
TATATATA
TIME AND PLACE, LADIES!
PEW
PEW
WHAT'S WRONG WITH SAM?
SAM WILSON'S ALREADY MARRIED TO BEING THE FALCON, ***MERCEDES.***
YOU MIGHT AS WELL DATE CAPTAIN AMERICA.
I *DID* DATE CAPTAIN AMERICA! SAM ***WAS*** CAPTAIN AMERICA!
OKAY, NOT MY BEST ANALOGY.
IT'S LIKE YOU TWO HAVE ***NEVER HEARD*** OF THE BECHDEL TEST.

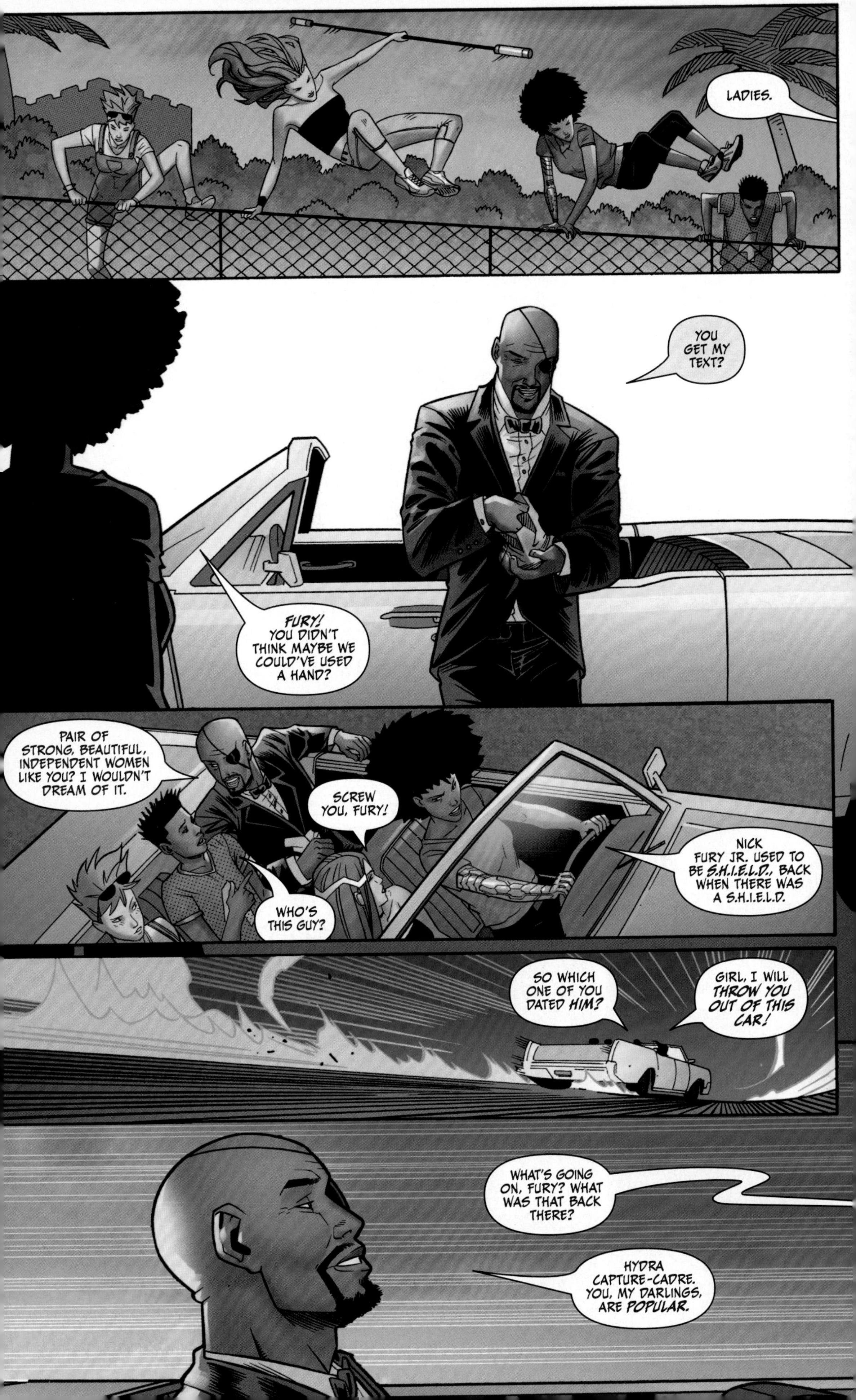
LADIES.
YOU GET MY TEXT?
FURY! YOU DIDN'T THINK MAYBE WE COULD'VE USED A HAND?
PAIR OF STRONG, BEAUTIFUL, INDEPENDENT WOMEN LIKE YOU? I WOULDN'T DREAM OF IT.
SCREW YOU, FURY!
WHO'S THIS GUY?
NICK FURY JR. USED TO BE S.H.I.E.L.D., BACK WHEN THERE WAS A S.H.I.E.L.D.
SO WHICH ONE OF YOU DATED HIM?
GIRL, I WILL THROW YOU OUT OF THIS CAR!
WHAT'S GOING ON, FURY? WHAT WAS THAT BACK THERE?
HYDRA CAPTURE-CADRE. YOU, MY DARLINGS, ARE POPULAR.

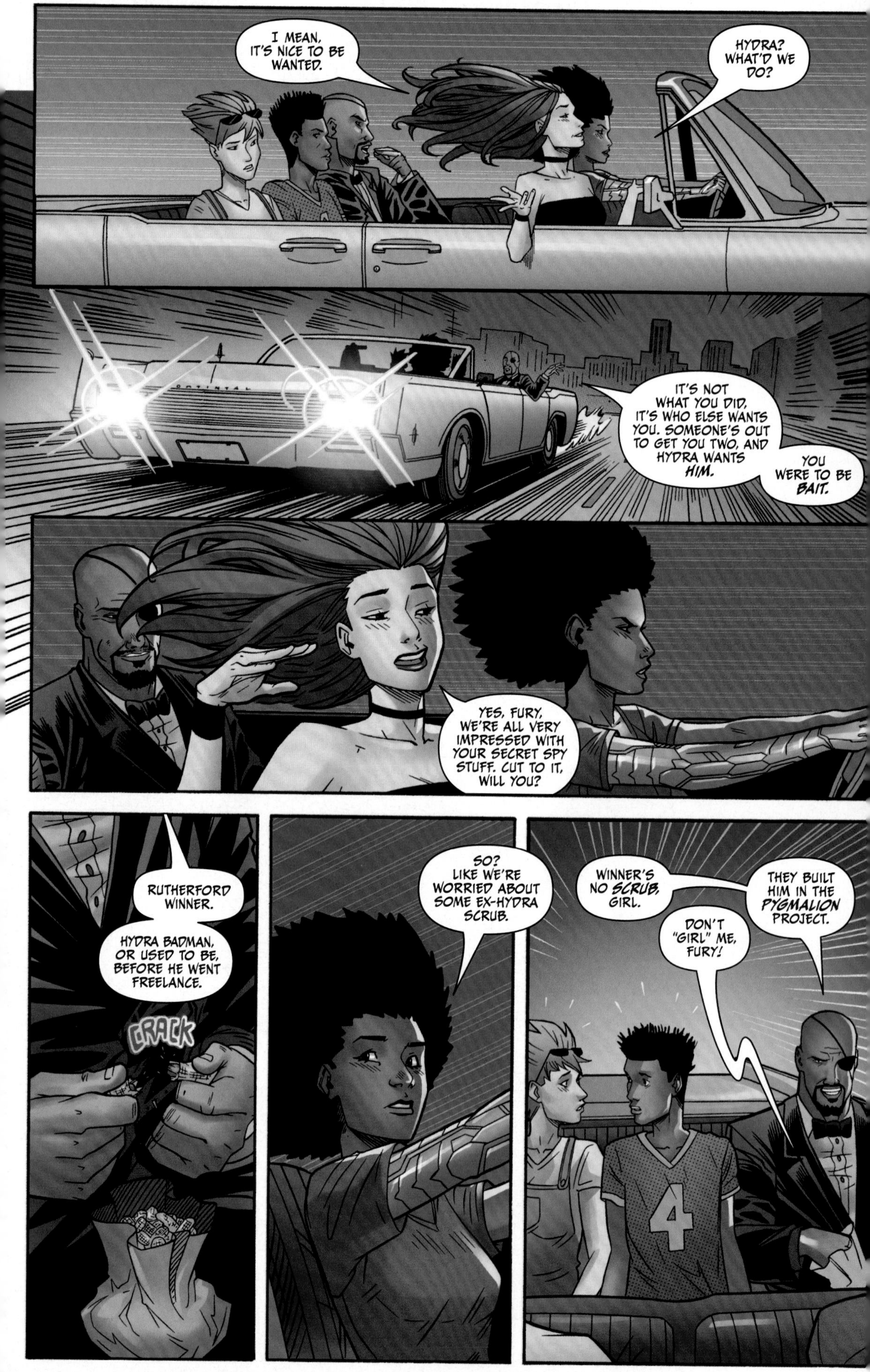
I MEAN, IT'S NICE TO BE WANTED.
HYDRA? WHAT'D WE DO?
IT'S NOT WHAT YOU DID, IT'S WHO ELSE WANTS YOU. SOMEONE'S OUT TO GET YOU TWO, AND HYDRA WANTS HIM.
YOU WERE TO BE BAIT.
YES, FURY, WE'RE ALL VERY IMPRESSED WITH YOUR SECRET SPY STUFF. CUT TO IT, WILL YOU?
RUTHERFORD WINNER.
HYDRA BADMAN, OR USED TO BE, BEFORE HE WENT FREELANCE.
CRACK
SO? LIKE WE'RE WORRIED ABOUT SOME EX-HYDRA SCRUB.
WINNER'S NO SCRUB, GIRL.
THEY BUILT HIM IN THE PYGMALION PROJECT.
DON'T "GIRL" ME, FURY!
4

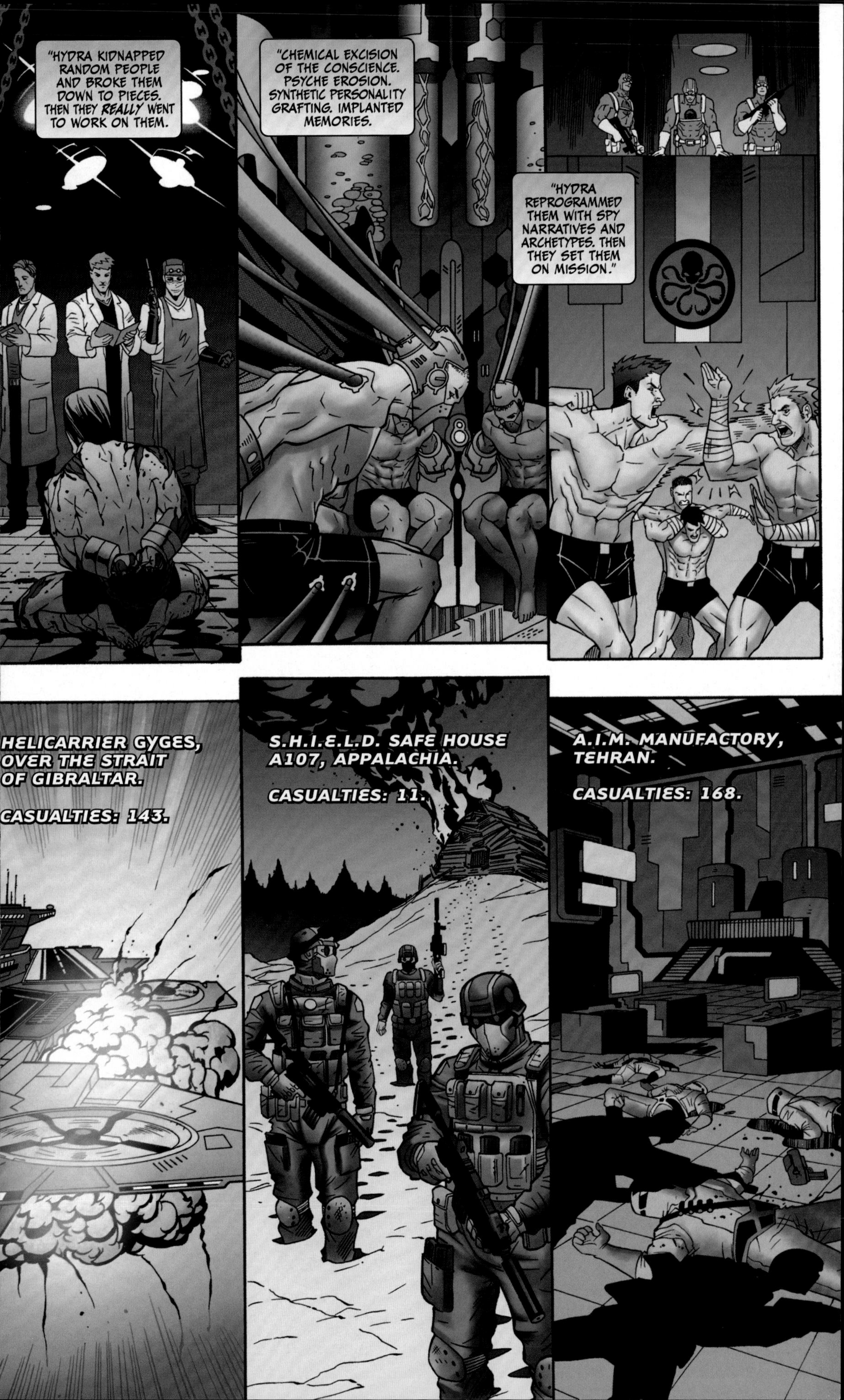
"HYDRA KIDNAPPED RANDOM PEOPLE AND BROKE THEM DOWN TO PIECES. THEN THEY REALLY WENT TO WORK ON THEM.
"CHEMICAL EXCISION OF THE CONSCIENCE. PSYCHE EROSION. SYNTHETIC PERSONALITY GRAFTING. IMPLANTED MEMORIES.
"HYDRA REPROGRAMMED THEM WITH SPY NARRATIVES AND ARCHETYPES. THEN THEY SET THEM ON MISSION."
HELICARRIER GYGES, OVER THE STRAIT OF GIBRALTAR.
CASUALTIES: 143.
S.H.I.E.L.D. SAFE HOUSE A107, APPALACHIA.
CASUALTIES: 11.
A.I.M. MANUFACTORY, TEHRAN.
CASUALTIES: 168.

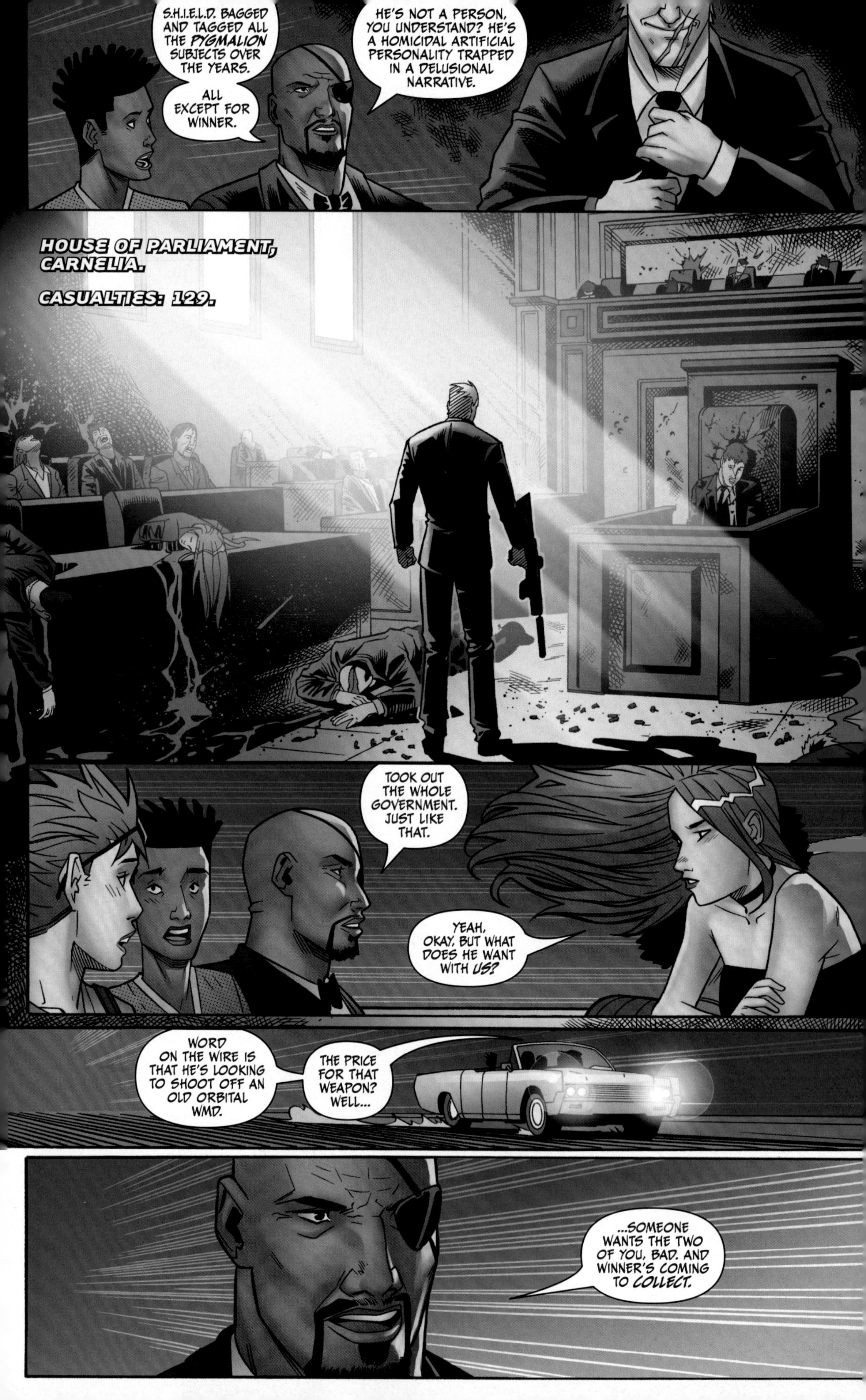
S.H.I.E.L.D. BAGGED AND TAGGED ALL THE PYGMALION SUBJECTS OVER THE YEARS.
ALL EXCEPT FOR WINNER.
HE'S NOT A PERSON, YOU UNDERSTAND? HE'S A HOMICIDAL ARTIFICIAL PERSONALITY TRAPPED IN A DELUSIONAL NARRATIVE.
HOUSE OF PARLIAMENT, CARNELIA.
CASUALTIES: 129.
TOOK OUT THE WHOLE GOVERNMENT. JUST LIKE THAT.
YEAH, OKAY, BUT WHAT DOES HE WANT WITH US?
WORD ON THE WIRE IS THAT HE'S LOOKING TO SHOOT OFF AN OLD ORBITAL WMD.
THE PRICE FOR THAT WEAPON? WELL...
...SOMEONE WANTS THE TWO OF YOU, BAD. AND WINNER'S COMING TO COLLECT.

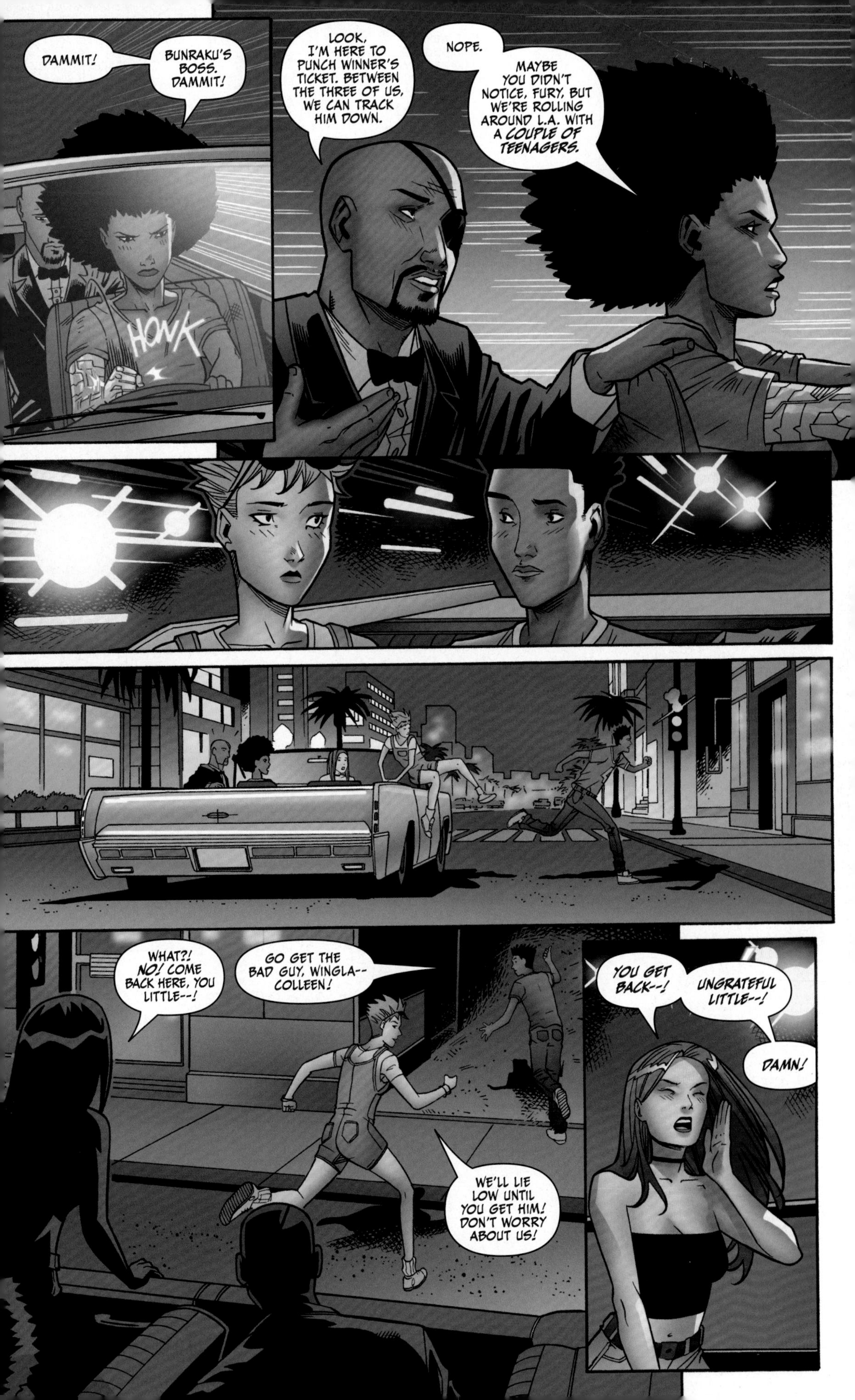
DAMMIT!
BUNRAKU'S BOSS. DAMMIT!
LOOK, I'M HERE TO PUNCH WINNER'S TICKET. BETWEEN THE THREE OF US, WE CAN TRACK HIM DOWN.
NOPE.
MAYBE YOU DIDN'T NOTICE, FURY, BUT WE'RE ROLLING AROUND L.A. WITH A COUPLE OF TEENAGERS.
HONK
WHAT?! NO! COME BACK HERE, YOU LITTLE--!
GO GET THE BAD GUY, WINGLA-- COLLEEN!
WE'LL LIE LOW UNTIL YOU GET HIM! DON'T WORRY ABOUT US!
YOU GET BACK--!
UNGRATEFUL LITTLE--!
DAMN!

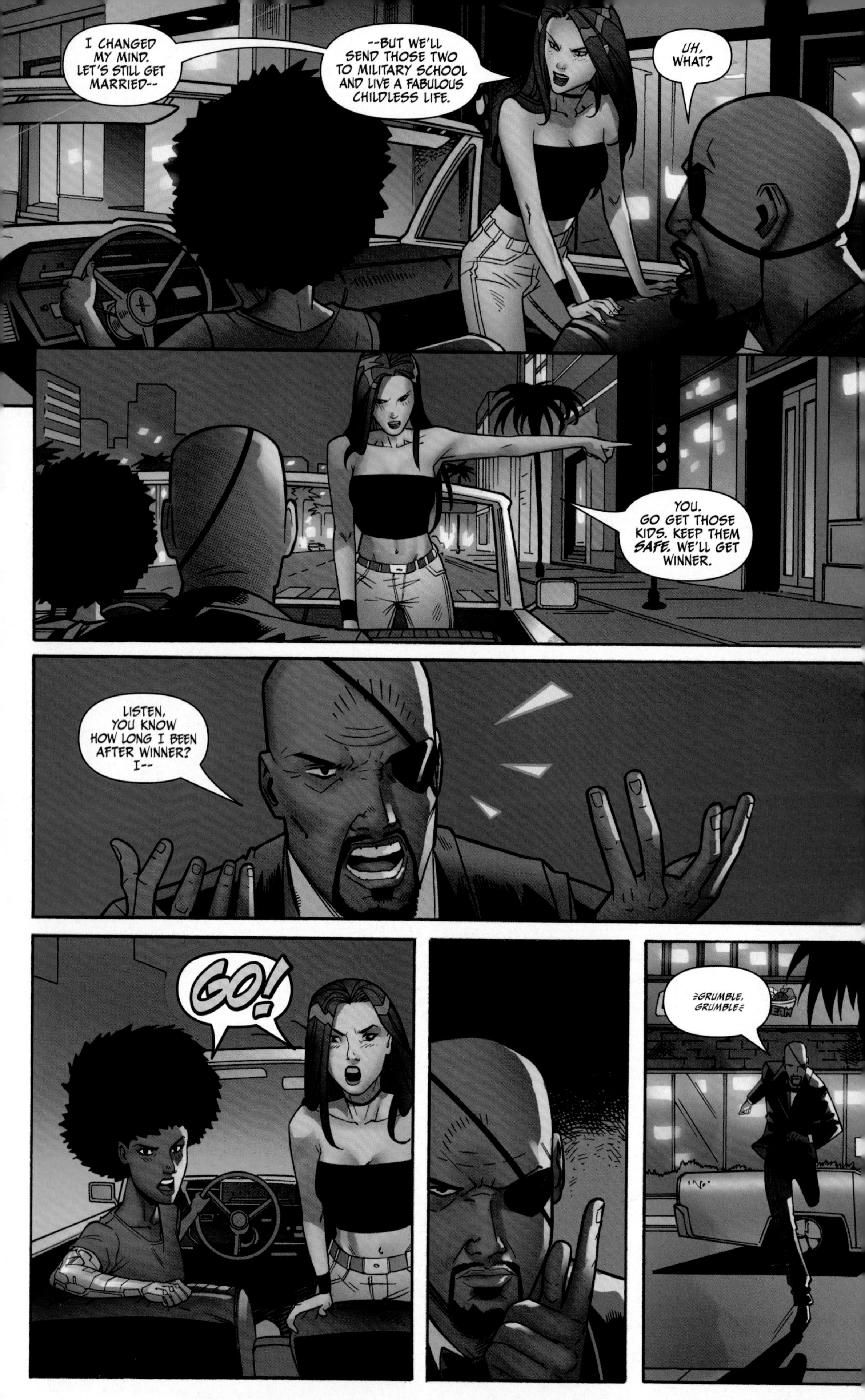
I CHANGED MY MIND. LET'S STILL GET MARRIED--
--BUT WE'LL SEND THOSE TWO TO MILITARY SCHOOL AND LIVE A FABULOUS CHILDLESS LIFE.
UH, WHAT?
YOU. GO GET THOSE KIDS. KEEP THEM SAFE. WE'LL GET WINNER.
LISTEN, YOU KNOW HOW LONG I BEEN AFTER WINNER? I--
GO!
≈GRUMBLE, GRUMBLE≈

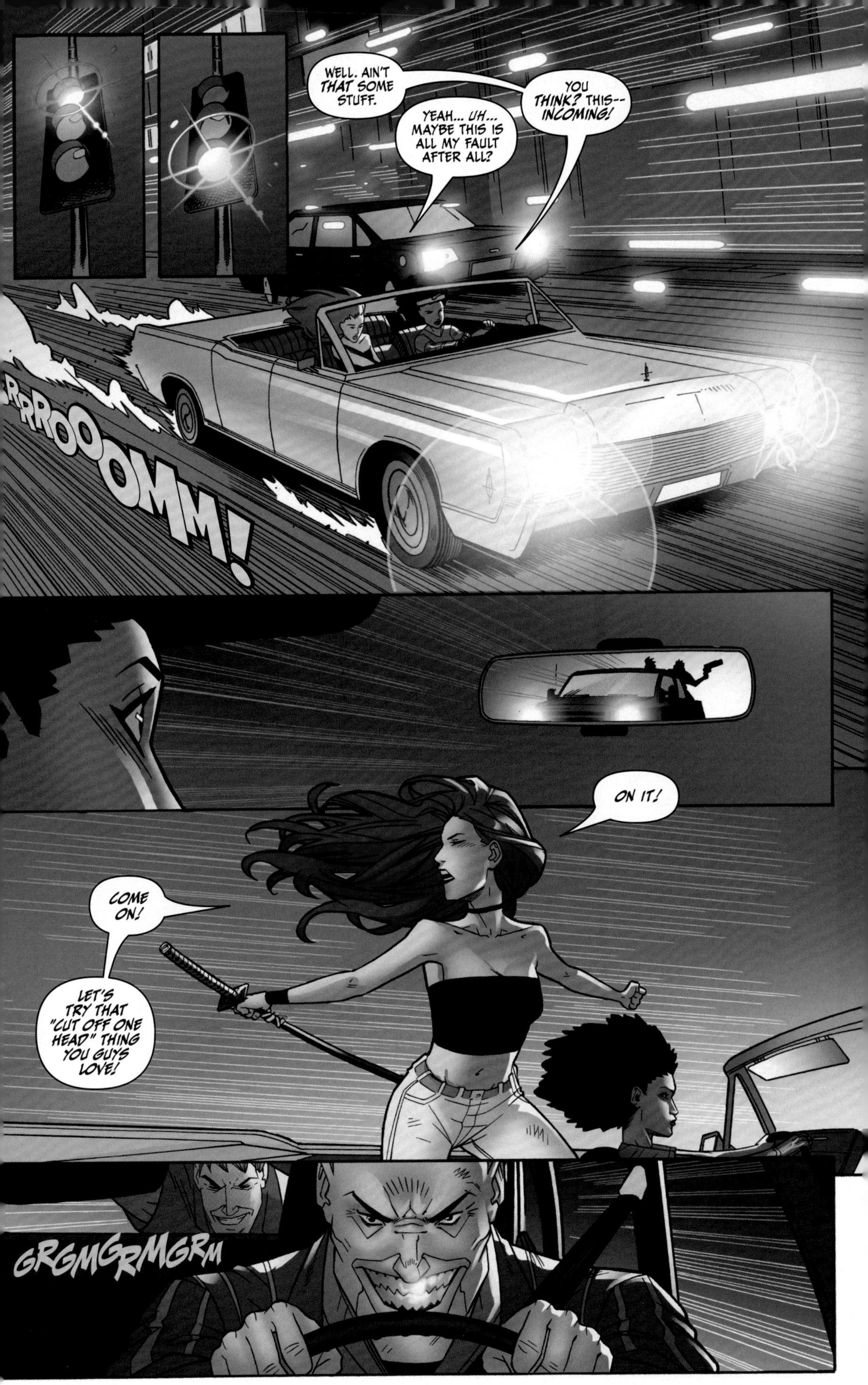
WELL. AIN'T THAT SOME STUFF.
YEAH... UH... MAYBE THIS IS ALL MY FAULT AFTER ALL?
YOU THINK? THIS-- INCOMING!
RRROOOOMM!
ON IT!
COME ON!
LET'S TRY THAT "CUT OFF ONE HEAD" THING YOU GUYS LOVE!
GRGMGRMGRM

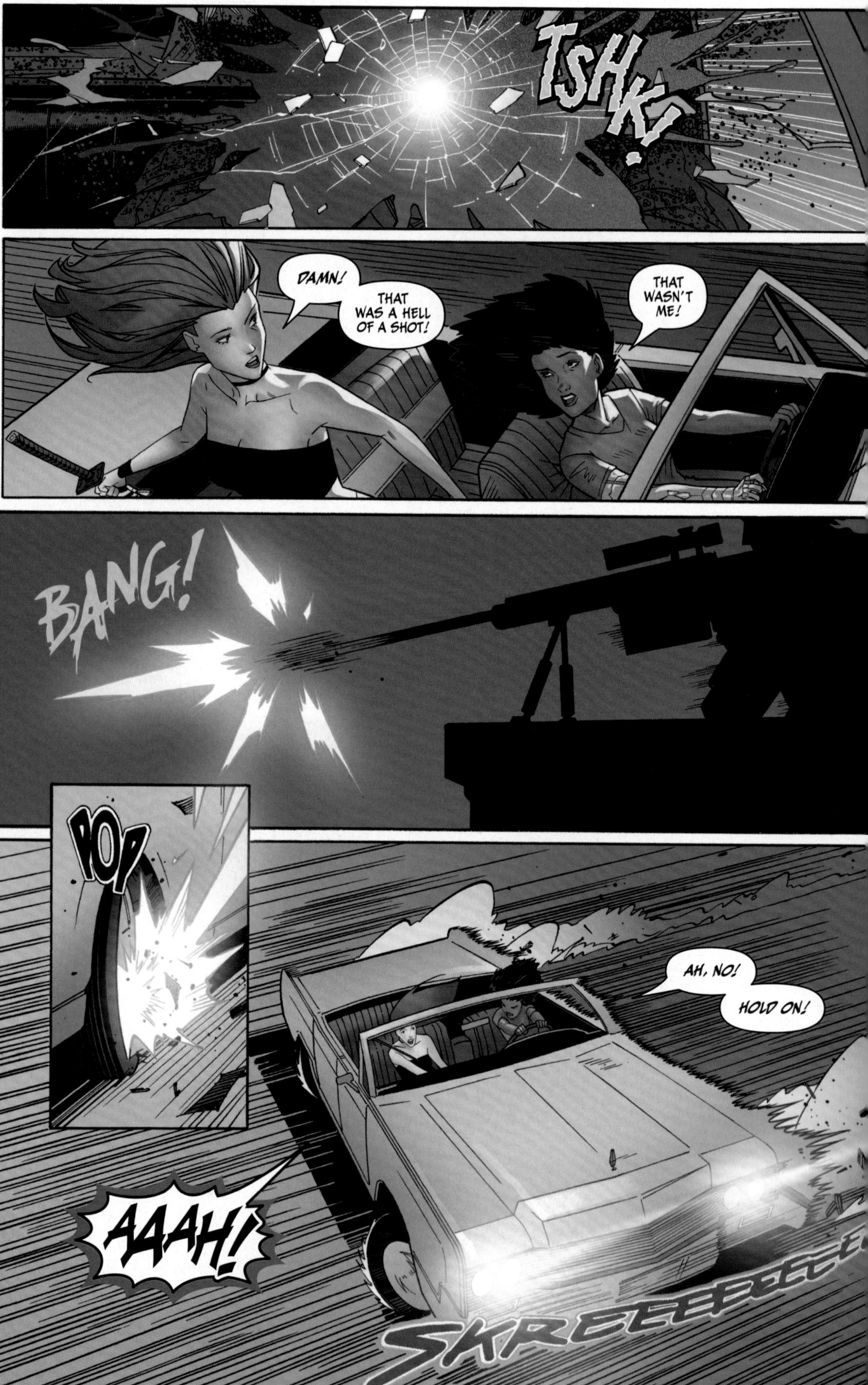
TSHK!
DAMN!
THAT WAS A HELL OF A SHOT!
THAT WASN'T ME!
BANG!
POP
AH, NO!
HOLD ON!
AAAH!
SKREEEEEEEE

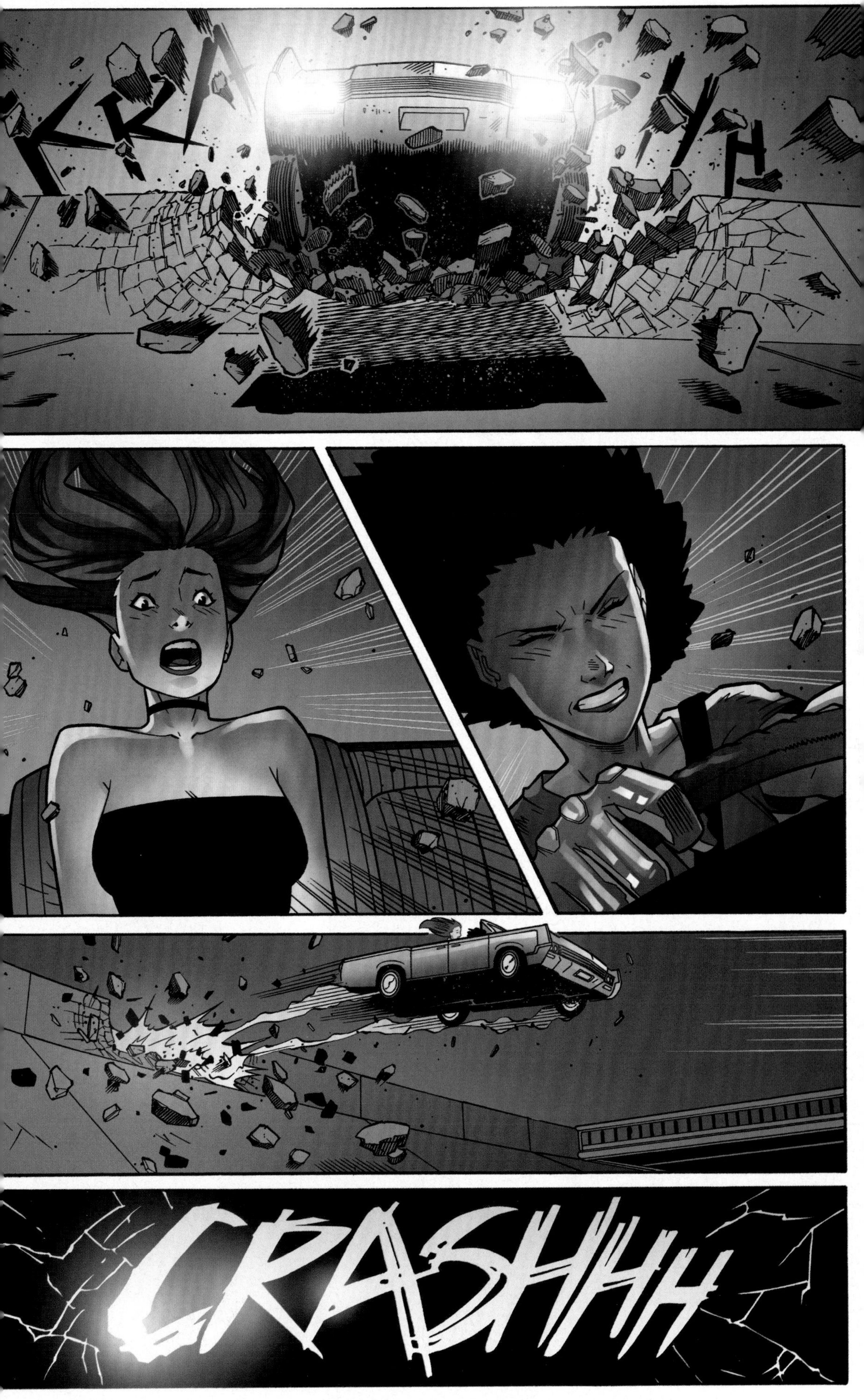
KRA
CRASHHH

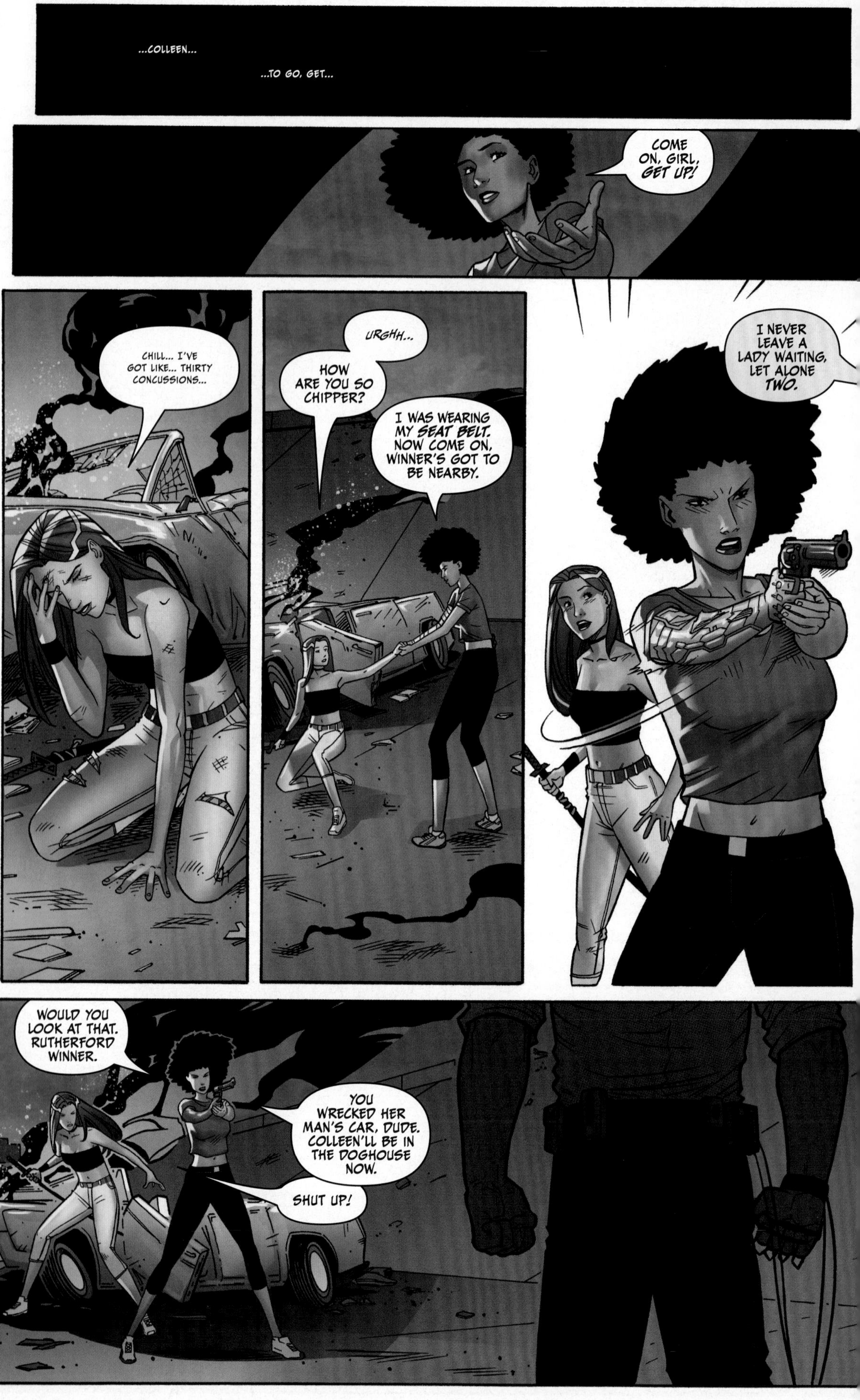
...COLLEEN...
...TO GO, GET...
COME ON, GIRL, GET UP!
CHILL... I'VE GOT LIKE... THIRTY CONCUSSIONS...
URGHH...
HOW ARE YOU SO CHIPPER?
I WAS WEARING MY SEAT BELT. NOW COME ON, WINNER'S GOT TO BE NEARBY.
I NEVER LEAVE A LADY WAITING, LET ALONE TWO.
WOULD YOU LOOK AT THAT. RUTHERFORD WINNER.
YOU WRECKED HER MAN'S CAR, DUDE. COLLEEN'LL BE IN THE DOGHOUSE NOW.
SHUT UP!

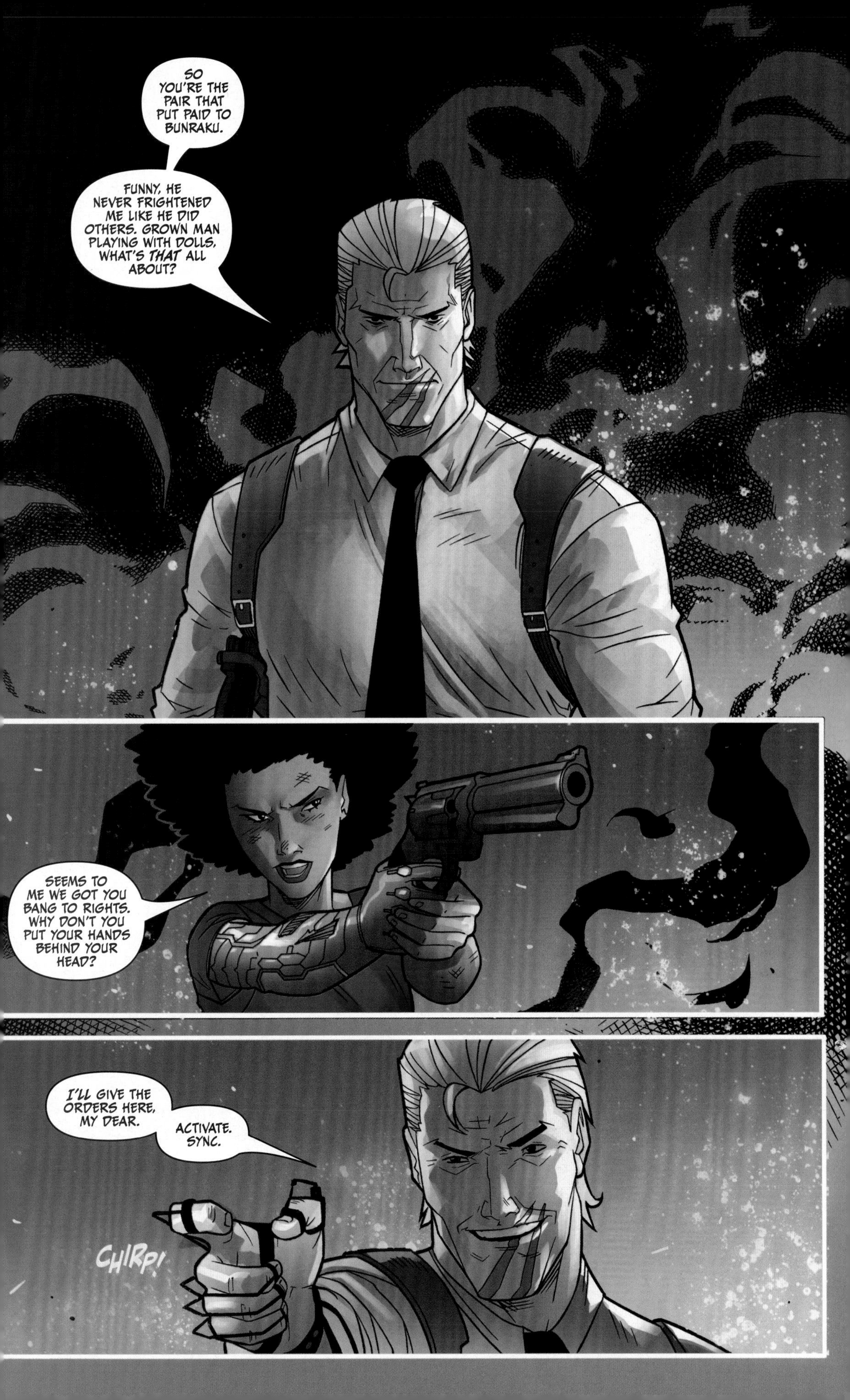
SO YOU'RE THE PAIR THAT PUT PAID TO BUNRAKU.
FUNNY, HE NEVER FRIGHTENED ME LIKE HE DID OTHERS. GROWN MAN PLAYING WITH DOLLS, WHAT'S *THAT* ALL ABOUT?
SEEMS TO ME WE GOT YOU BANG TO RIGHTS. WHY DON'T YOU PUT YOUR HANDS BEHIND YOUR HEAD?
I'LL GIVE THE ORDERS HERE, MY DEAR.
ACTIVATE. SYNC.
CHIRP!

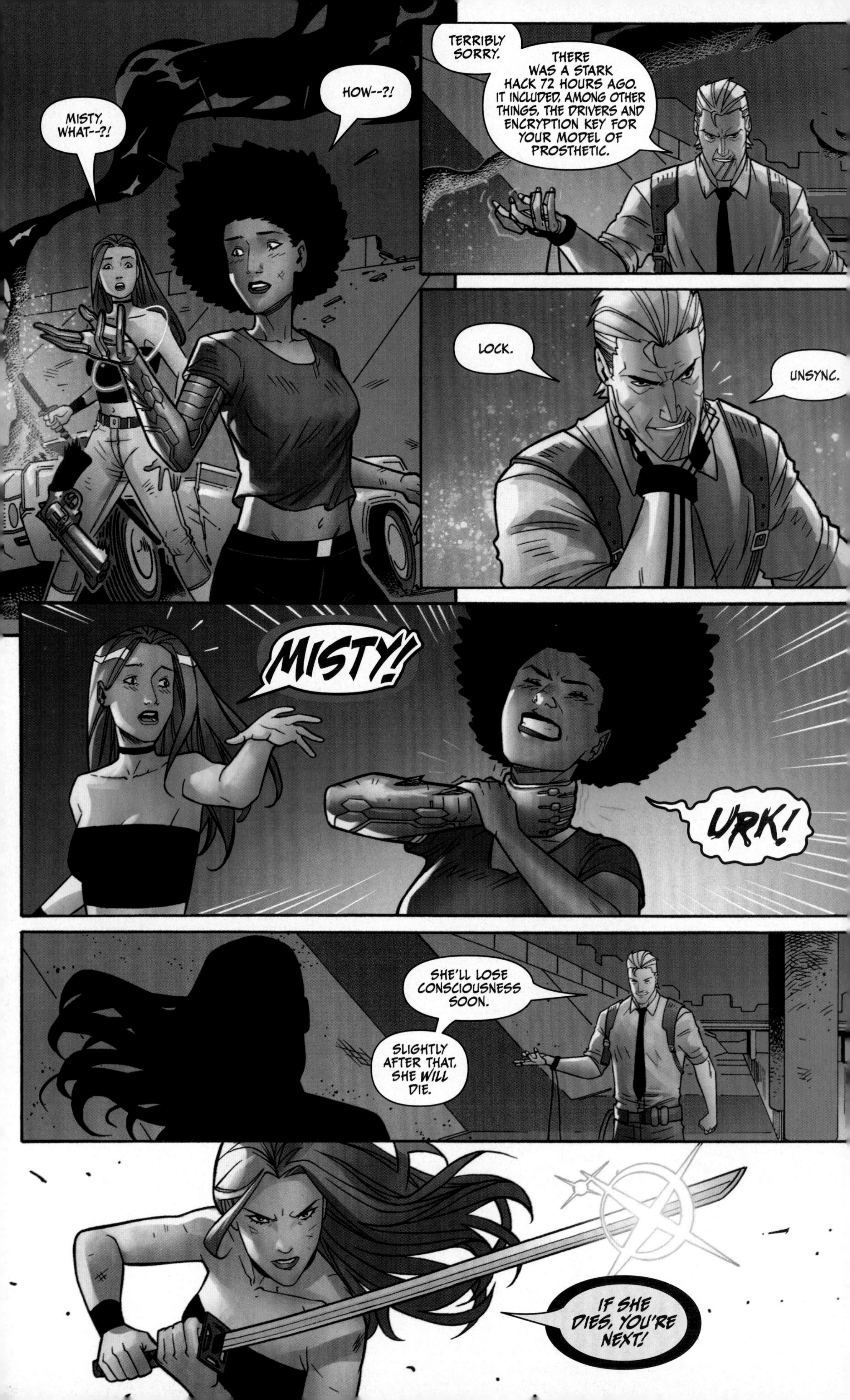
MISTY, WHAT--?!
HOW--?!
TERRIBLY SORRY.
THERE WAS A STARK HACK 72 HOURS AGO. IT INCLUDED, AMONG OTHER THINGS, THE DRIVERS AND ENCRYPTION KEY FOR YOUR MODEL OF PROSTHETIC.
LOCK.
UNSYNC.
MISTY!
URK!
SHE'LL LOSE CONSCIOUSNESS SOON.
SLIGHTLY AFTER THAT, SHE *WILL* DIE.
IF SHE DIES, YOU'RE NEXT!

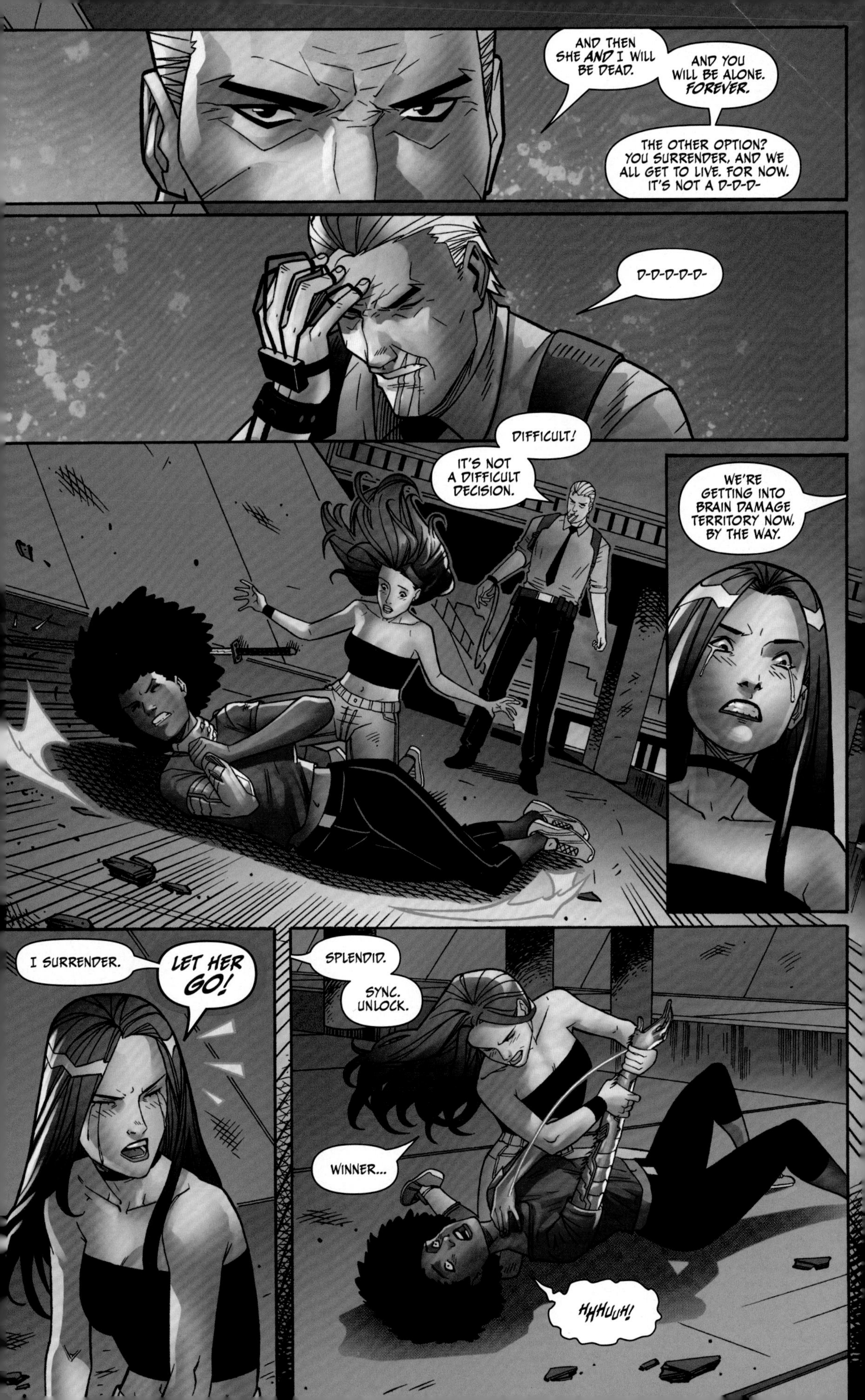
AND THEN SHE AND I WILL BE DEAD.
AND YOU WILL BE ALONE. FOREVER.
THE OTHER OPTION? YOU SURRENDER, AND WE ALL GET TO LIVE. FOR NOW. IT'S NOT A D-D-D-
D-D-D-D-D-
DIFFICULT!
IT'S NOT A DIFFICULT DECISION.
WE'RE GETTING INTO BRAIN DAMAGE TERRITORY NOW, BY THE WAY.
I SURRENDER.
LET HER GO!
SPLENDID.
SYNC. UNLOCK.
WINNER...
HHHUUH!

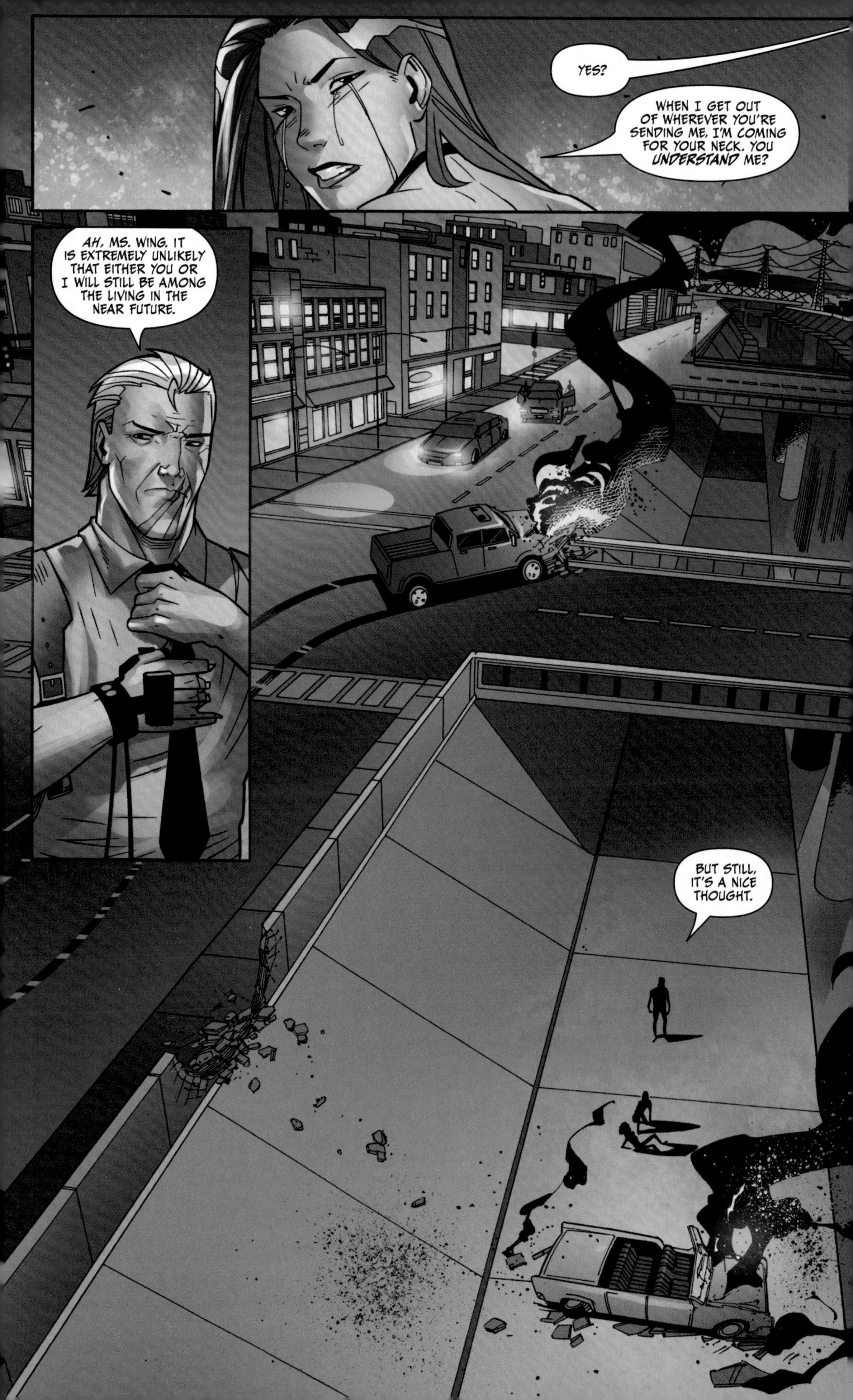
YES?
WHEN I GET OUT OF WHEREVER YOU'RE SENDING ME, I'M COMING FOR YOUR NECK. YOU UNDERSTAND ME?
AH, MS. WING. IT IS EXTREMELY UNLIKELY THAT EITHER YOU OR I WILL STILL BE AMONG THE LIVING IN THE NEAR FUTURE.
BUT STILL, IT'S A NICE THOUGHT.

CHAPTER
4

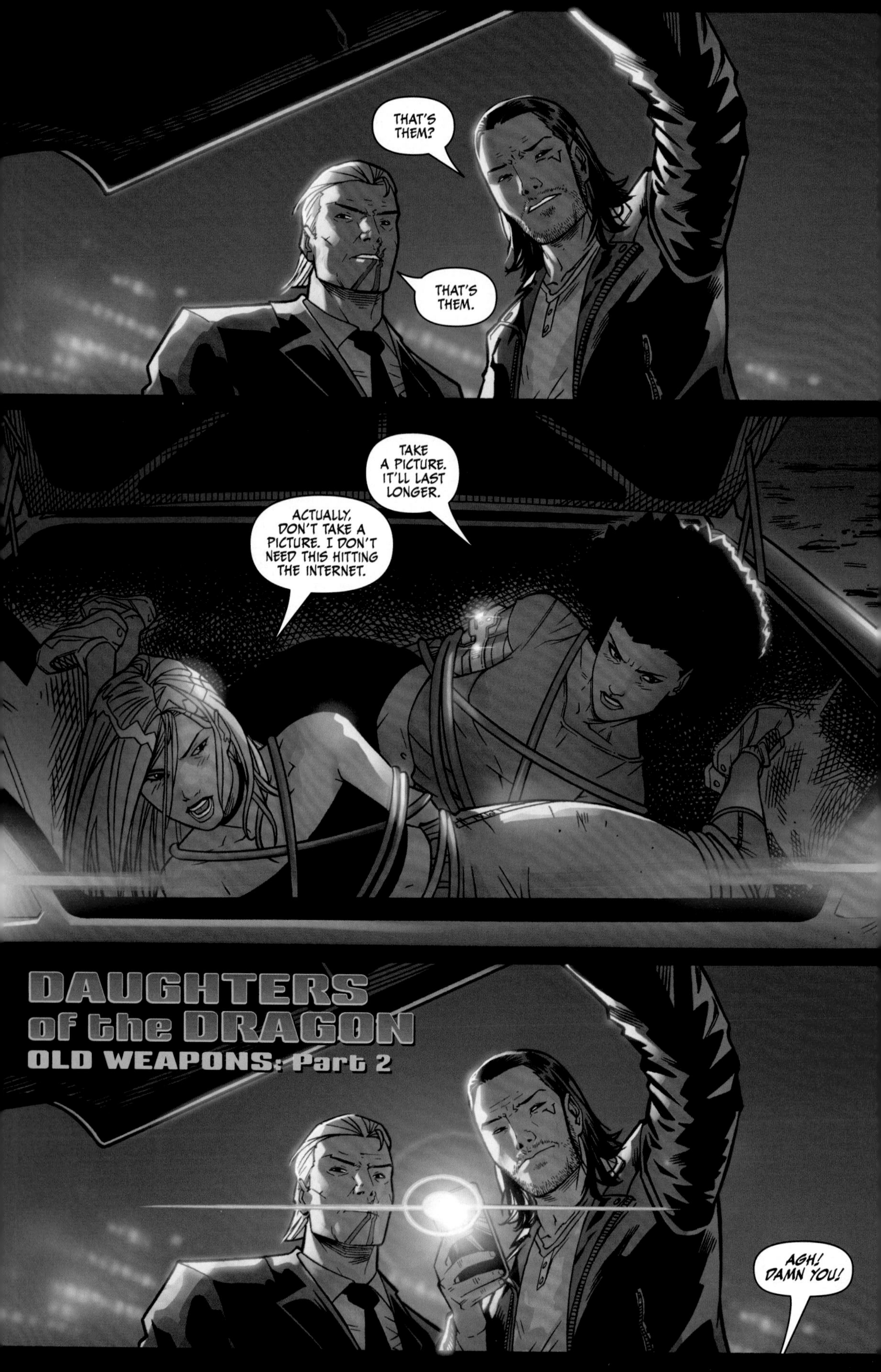
THAT'S THEM?
THAT'S THEM.
TAKE A PICTURE. IT'LL LAST LONGER.
ACTUALLY, DON'T TAKE A PICTURE. I DON'T NEED THIS HITTING THE INTERNET.
DAUGHTERS of the DRAGON
OLD WEAPONS: Part 2
AGH! DAMN YOU!

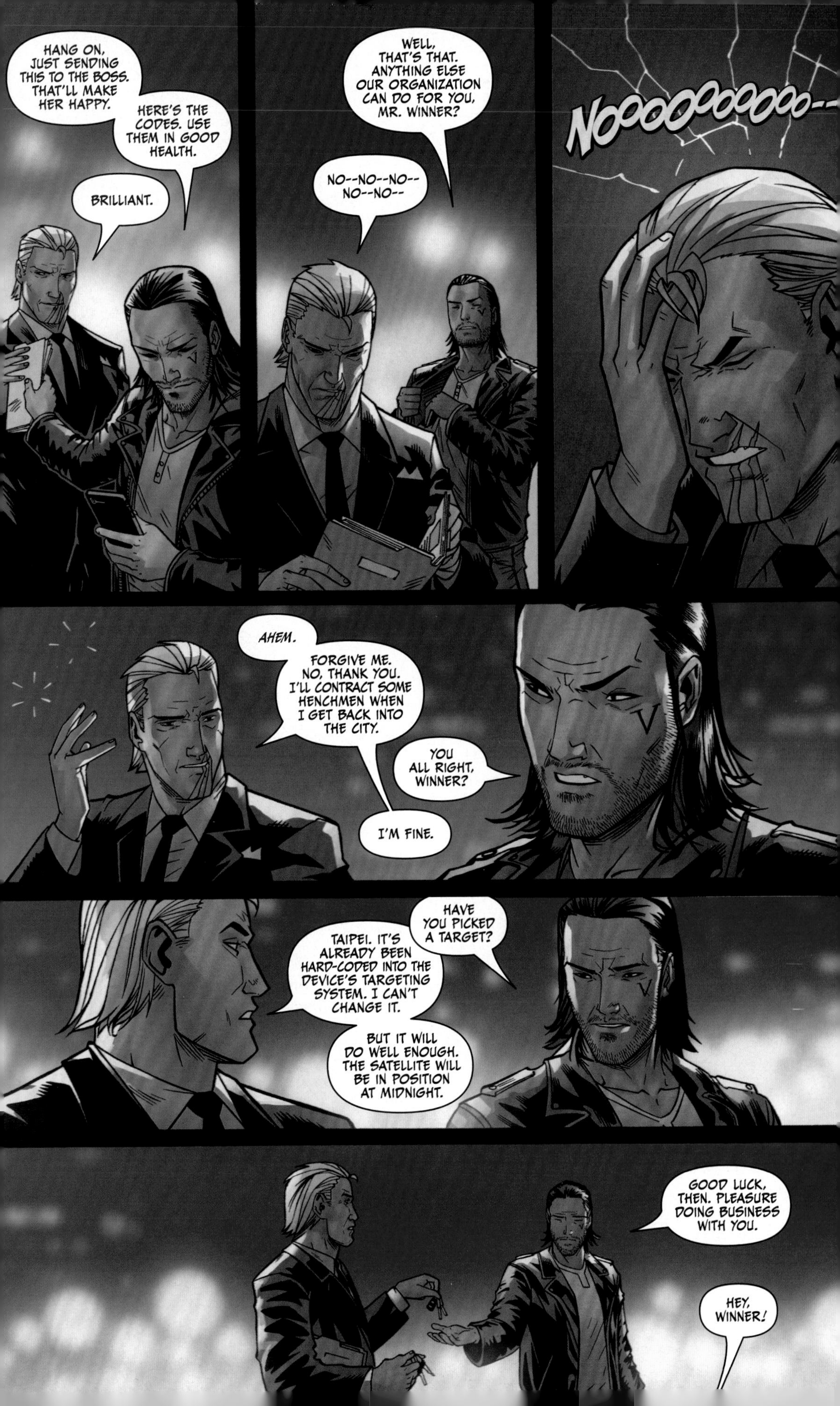
HANG ON, JUST SENDING THIS TO THE BOSS. THAT'LL MAKE HER HAPPY.
HERE'S THE CODES. USE THEM IN GOOD HEALTH.
BRILLIANT.
WELL, THAT'S THAT. ANYTHING ELSE OUR ORGANIZATION CAN DO FOR YOU, MR. WINNER?
NO--NO--NO-- NO--NO--
NOOOOOOOOOO--
AHEM.
FORGIVE ME. NO, THANK YOU. I'LL CONTRACT SOME HENCHMEN WHEN I GET BACK INTO THE CITY.
YOU ALL RIGHT, WINNER?
I'M FINE.
HAVE YOU PICKED A TARGET?
TAIPEI. IT'S ALREADY BEEN HARD-CODED INTO THE DEVICE'S TARGETING SYSTEM. I CAN'T CHANGE IT.
BUT IT WILL DO WELL ENOUGH. THE SATELLITE WILL BE IN POSITION AT MIDNIGHT.
GOOD LUCK, THEN. PLEASURE DOING BUSINESS WITH YOU.
HEY, WINNER!

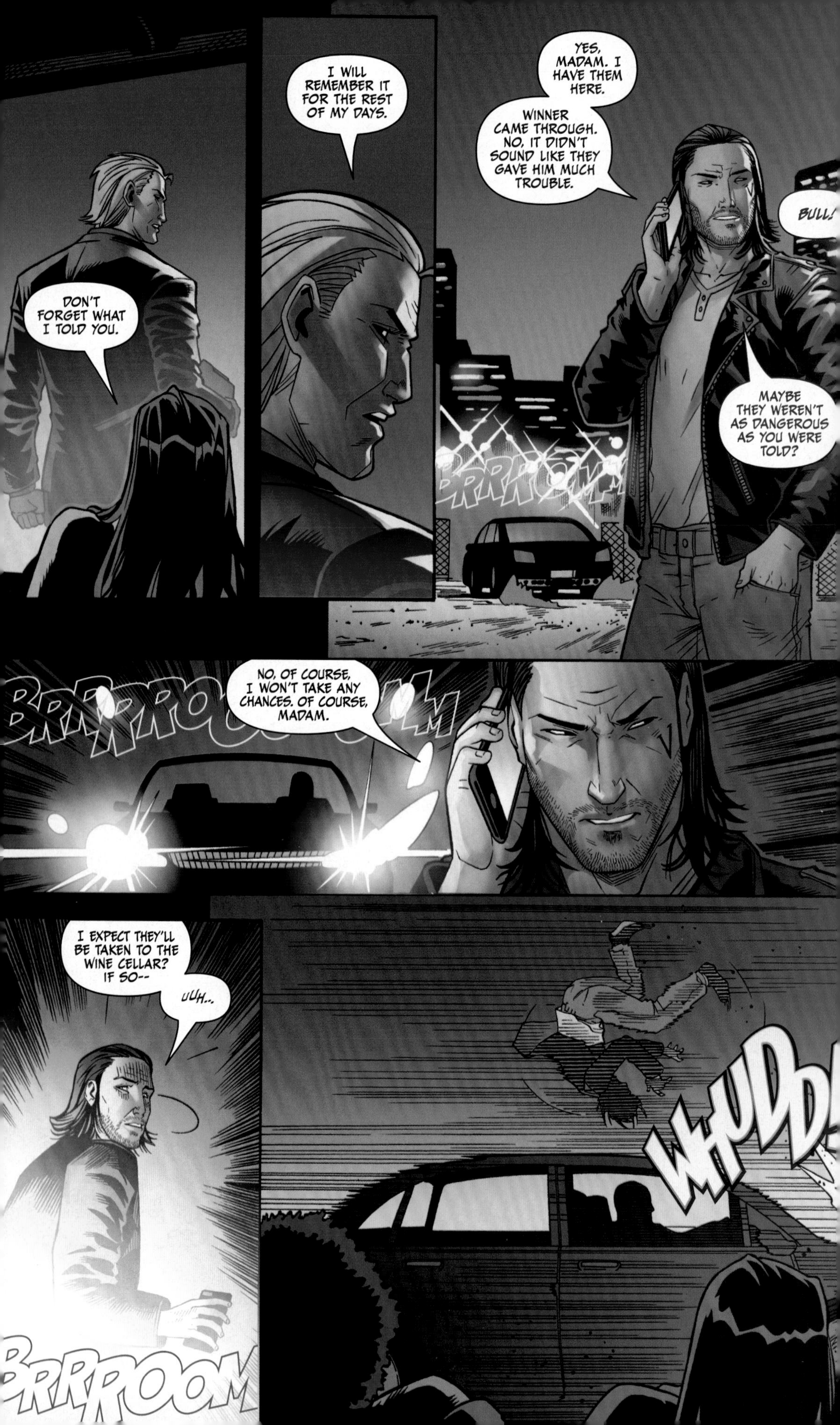
DON'T FORGET WHAT I TOLD YOU.
I WILL REMEMBER IT FOR THE REST OF MY DAYS.
YES, MADAM. I HAVE THEM HERE.
WINNER CAME THROUGH. NO, IT DIDN'T SOUND LIKE THEY GAVE HIM MUCH TROUBLE.
BULL!
MAYBE THEY WEREN'T AS DANGEROUS AS YOU WERE TOLD?
BRRROOM
BRRROOOOOOM
NO, OF COURSE, I WON'T TAKE ANY CHANCES. OF COURSE, MADAM.
I EXPECT THEY'LL BE TAKEN TO THE WINE CELLAR? IF SO--
UUH...
BRRROOM

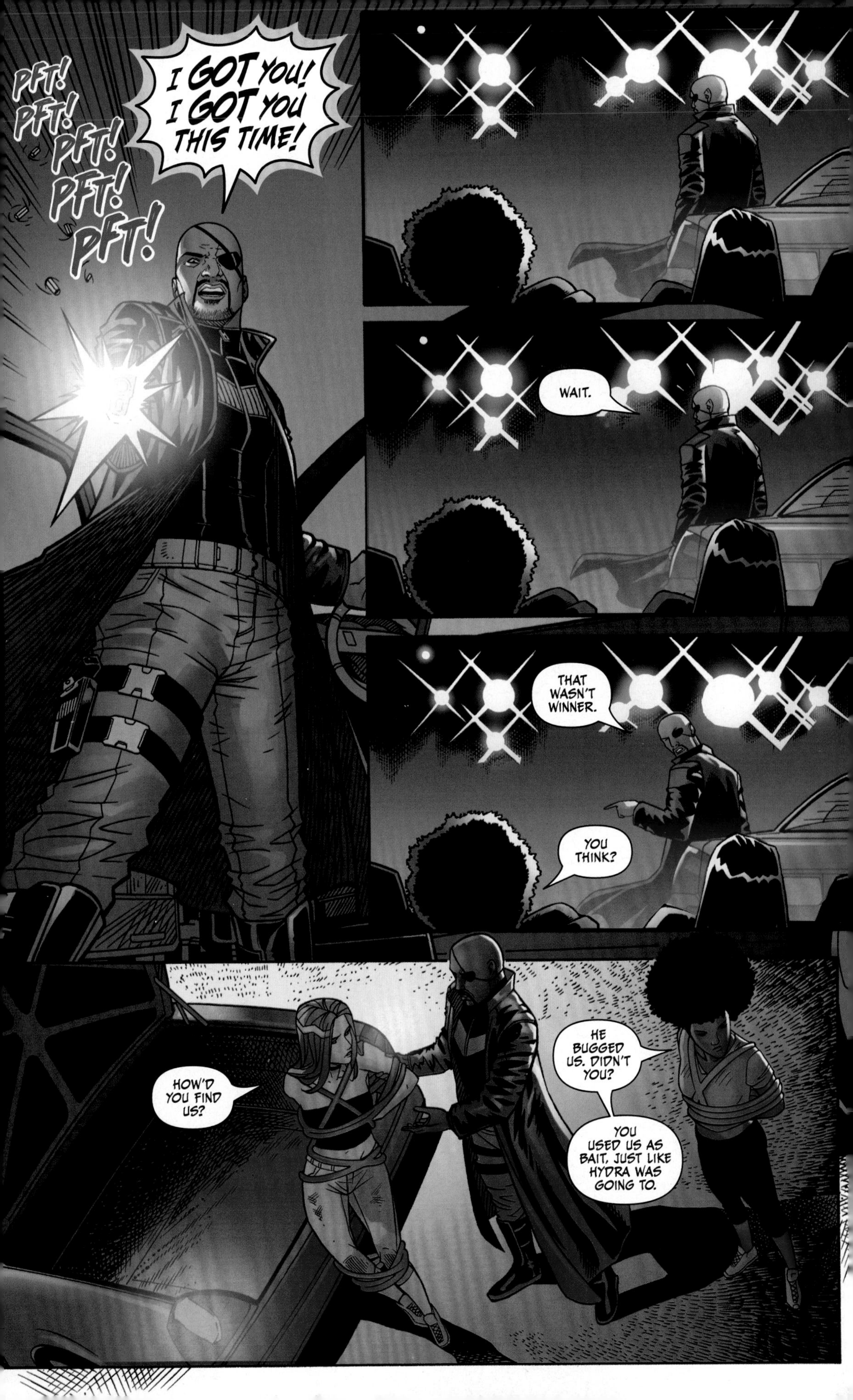
PFT!
PFT!
PFT!
PFT!
PFT!
I GOT YOU! I GOT YOU THIS TIME!
WAIT.
THAT WASN'T WINNER.
YOU THINK?
HOW'D YOU FIND US?
HE BUGGED US. DIDN'T YOU?
YOU USED US AS BAIT, JUST LIKE HYDRA WAS GOING TO.

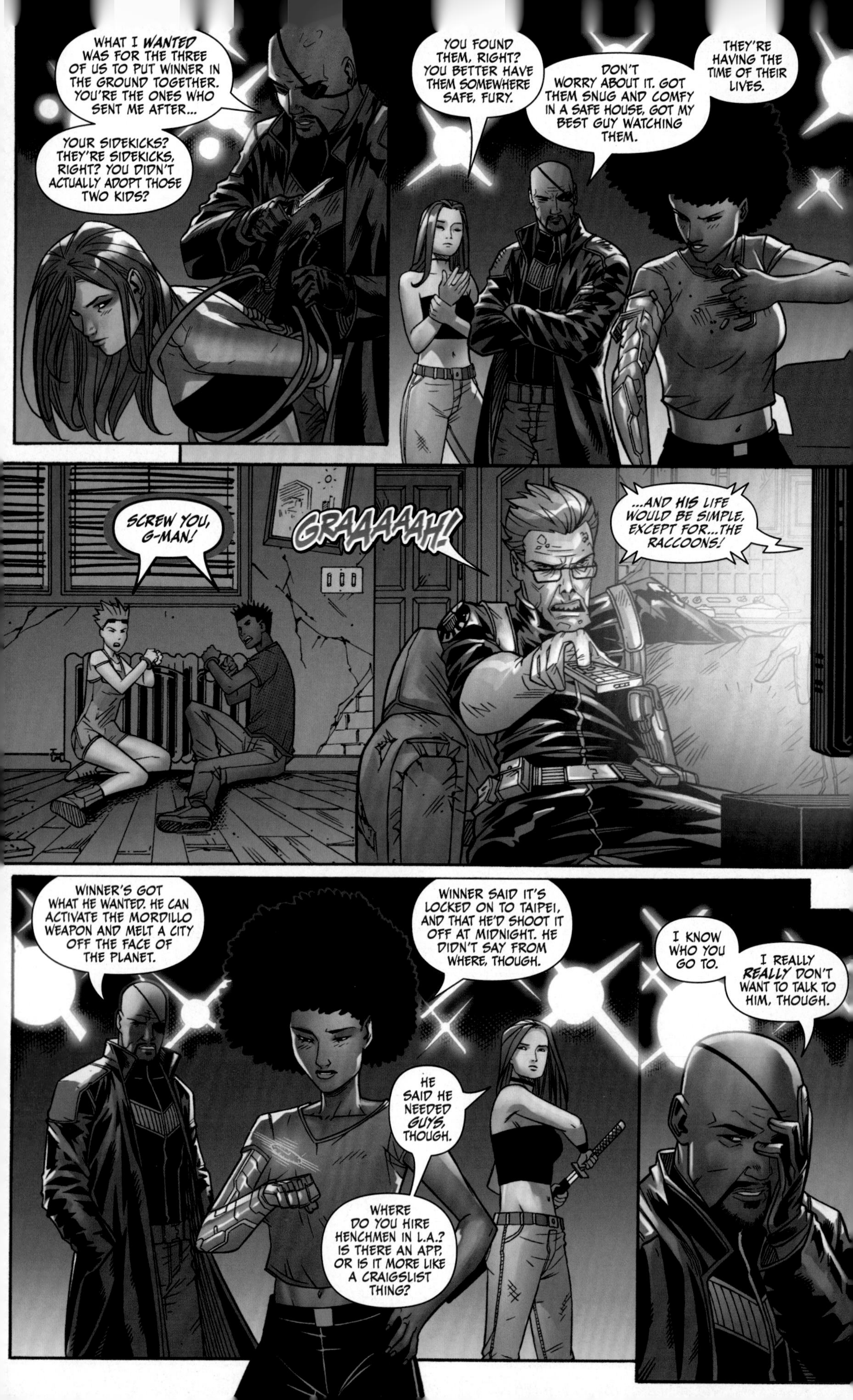
WHAT I *WANTED* WAS FOR THE THREE OF US TO PUT WINNER IN THE GROUND TOGETHER. YOU'RE THE ONES WHO SENT ME AFTER...
YOUR SIDEKICKS? THEY'RE SIDEKICKS, RIGHT? YOU DIDN'T ACTUALLY ADOPT THOSE TWO KIDS?
YOU FOUND THEM, RIGHT? YOU BETTER HAVE THEM SOMEWHERE SAFE, FURY.
DON'T WORRY ABOUT IT. GOT THEM SNUG AND COMFY IN A SAFE HOUSE, GOT MY BEST GUY WATCHING THEM.
THEY'RE HAVING THE TIME OF THEIR LIVES.
SCREW YOU, G-MAN!
GRAAAAAH!
...AND HIS LIFE WOULD BE SIMPLE, EXCEPT FOR...THE RACCOONS!
WINNER'S GOT WHAT HE WANTED. HE CAN ACTIVATE THE MORDILLO WEAPON AND MELT A CITY OFF THE FACE OF THE PLANET.
WINNER SAID IT'S LOCKED ON TO TAIPEI, AND THAT HE'D SHOOT IT OFF AT MIDNIGHT. HE DIDN'T SAY FROM WHERE, THOUGH.
HE SAID HE NEEDED *GUYS*, THOUGH.
WHERE DO YOU HIRE HENCHMEN IN L.A.? IS THERE AN APP, OR IS IT MORE LIKE A CRAIGSLIST THING?
I KNOW WHO YOU GO TO.
I REALLY *REALLY* DON'T WANT TO TALK TO HIM, THOUGH.

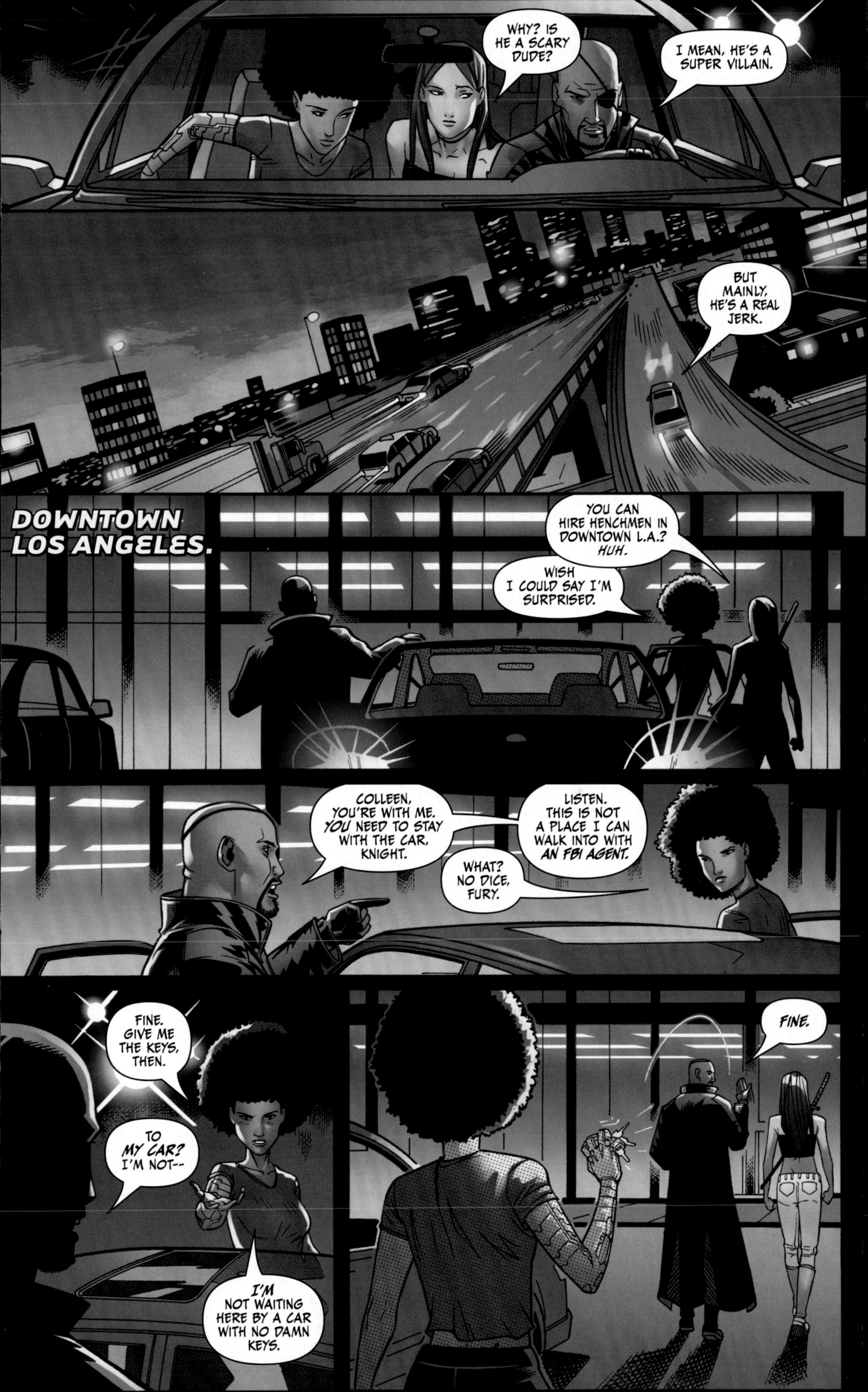
WHY? IS HE A SCARY DUDE?
I MEAN, HE'S A SUPER VILLAIN.
BUT MAINLY, HE'S A REAL JERK.
DOWNTOWN LOS ANGELES.
YOU CAN HIRE HENCHMEN IN DOWNTOWN L.A.? HUH.
WISH I COULD SAY I'M SURPRISED.
COLLEEN, YOU'RE WITH ME. YOU NEED TO STAY WITH THE CAR, KNIGHT.
WHAT? NO DICE, FURY.
LISTEN. THIS IS NOT A PLACE I CAN WALK INTO WITH AN FBI AGENT.
FINE. GIVE ME THE KEYS, THEN.
TO MY CAR? I'M NOT--
I'M NOT WAITING HERE BY A CAR WITH NO DAMN KEYS.
FINE.

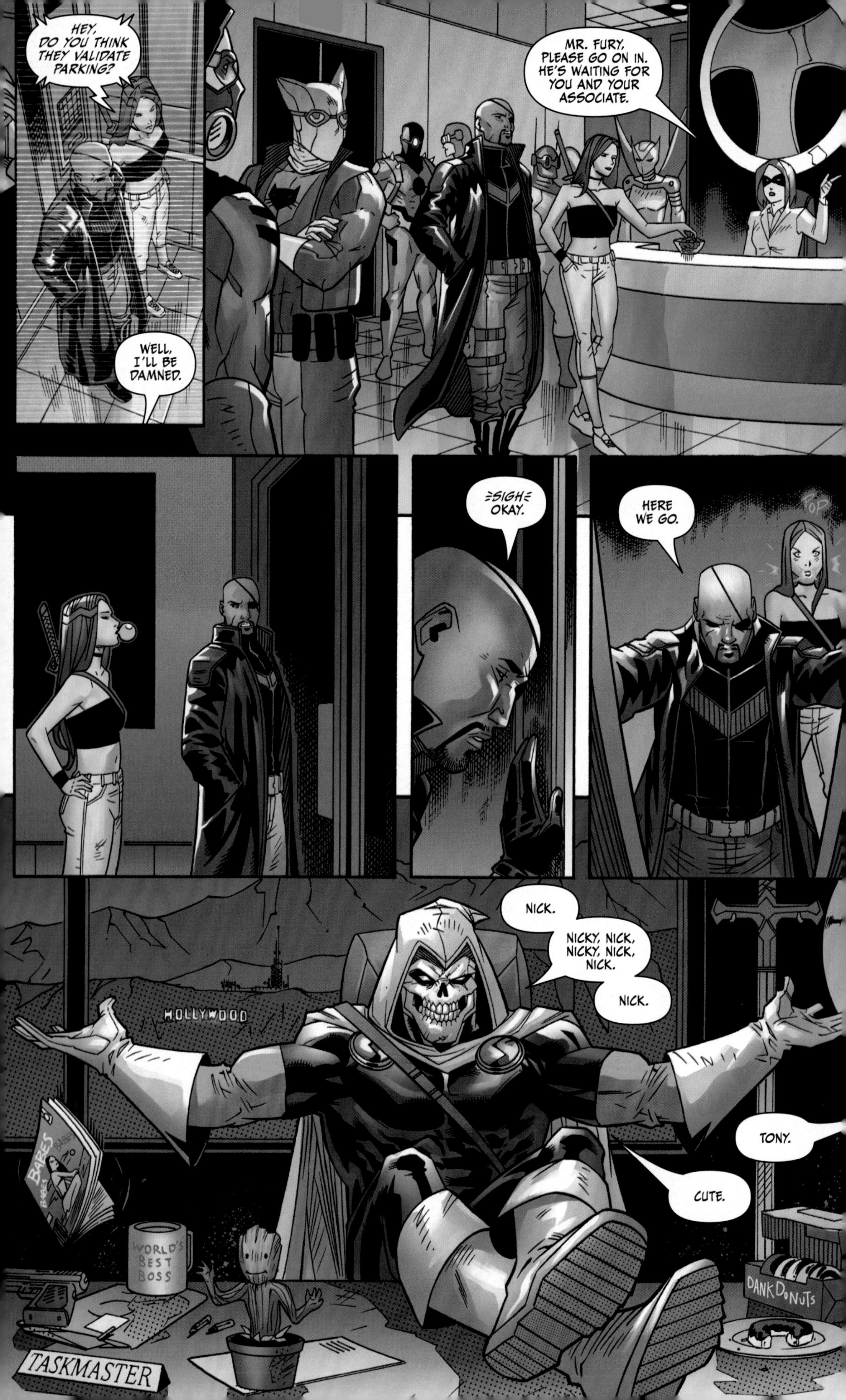
HEY, DO YOU THINK THEY VALIDATE PARKING?
WELL, I'LL BE DAMNED.
MR. FURY, PLEASE GO ON IN. HE'S WAITING FOR YOU AND YOUR ASSOCIATE.
SIGH OKAY.
HERE WE GO.
POP
NICK.
NICKY, NICK, NICKY, NICK, NICK.
NICK.
HOLLYWOOD
TONY.
CUTE.
BABES
WORLD'S BEST BOSS
DANK DONUTS
TASKMASTER

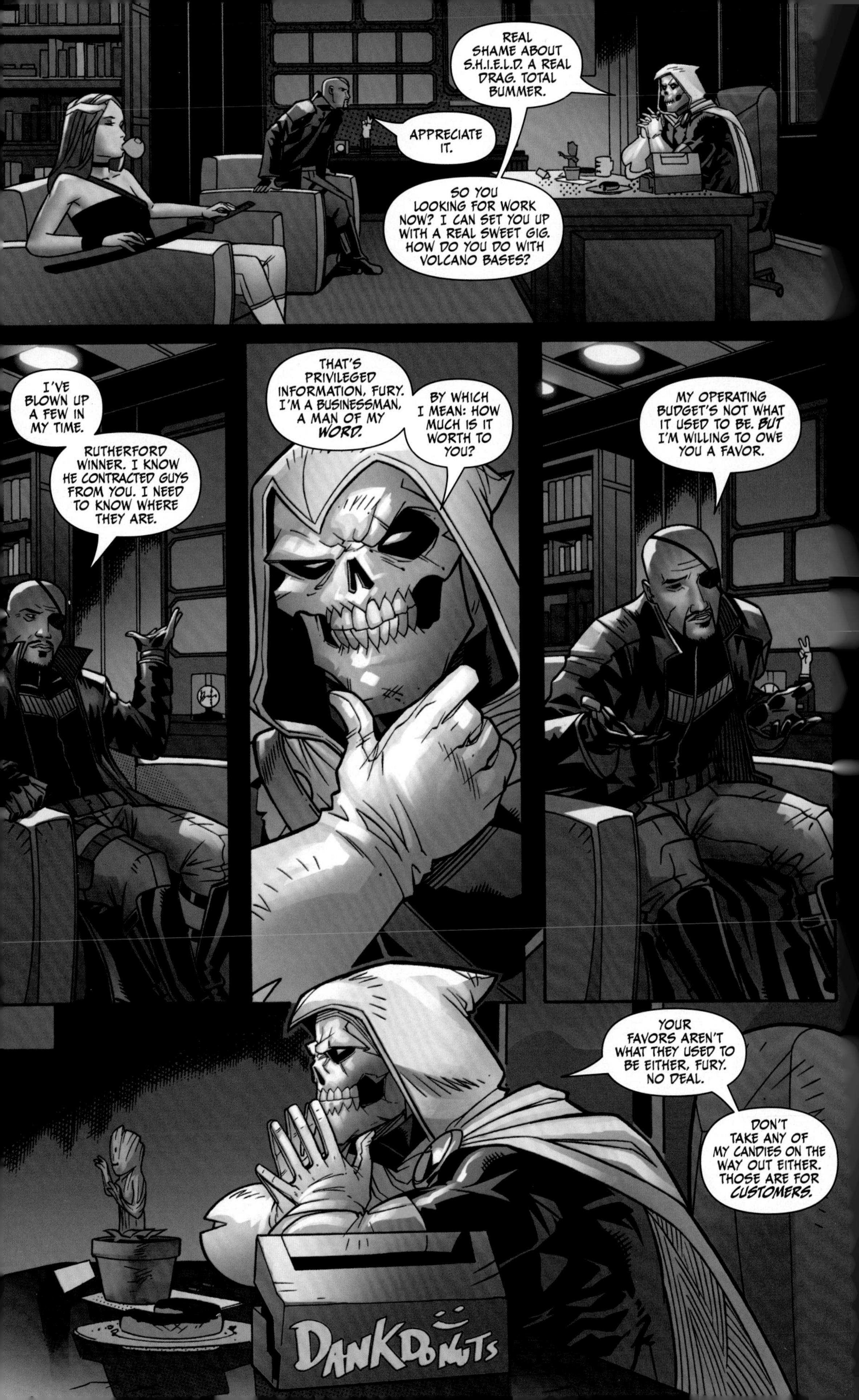
REAL SHAME ABOUT S.H.I.E.L.D. A REAL DRAG. TOTAL BUMMER.
APPRECIATE IT.
SO YOU LOOKING FOR WORK NOW? I CAN SET YOU UP WITH A REAL SWEET GIG. HOW DO YOU DO WITH VOLCANO BASES?
I'VE BLOWN UP A FEW IN MY TIME.
RUTHERFORD WINNER. I KNOW HE CONTRACTED GUYS FROM YOU. I NEED TO KNOW WHERE THEY ARE.
THAT'S PRIVILEGED INFORMATION, FURY. I'M A BUSINESSMAN, A MAN OF MY *WORD.*
BY WHICH I MEAN: HOW MUCH IS IT WORTH TO YOU?
MY OPERATING BUDGET'S NOT WHAT IT USED TO BE. *BUT* I'M WILLING TO OWE YOU A FAVOR.
YOUR FAVORS AREN'T WHAT THEY USED TO BE EITHER, FURY. NO DEAL.
DON'T TAKE ANY OF MY CANDIES ON THE WAY OUT EITHER. THOSE ARE FOR *CUSTOMERS.*
DANKDONUTS

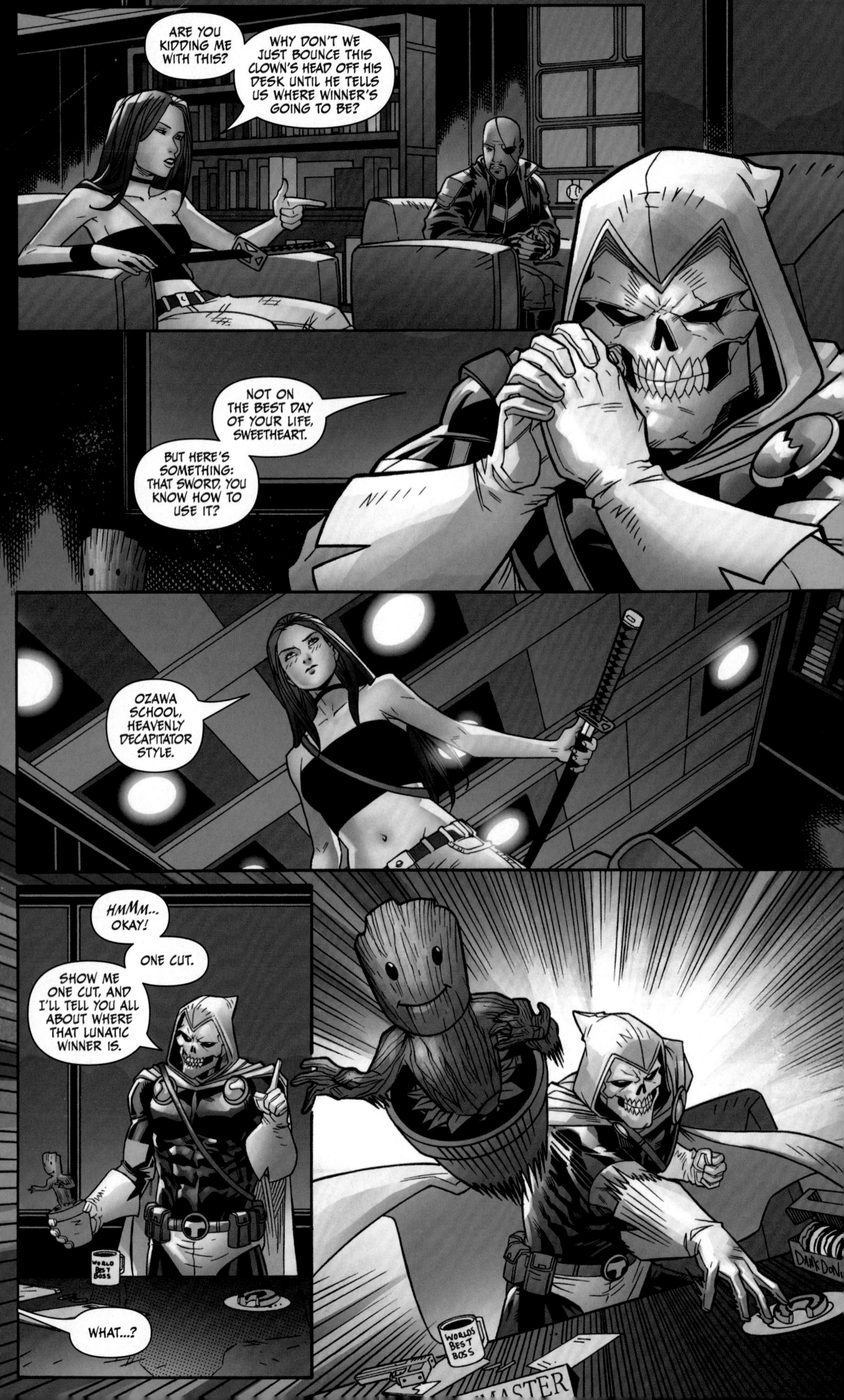

ARE YOU KIDDING ME WITH THIS?
WHY DON'T WE JUST BOUNCE THIS CLOWN'S HEAD OFF HIS DESK UNTIL HE TELLS US WHERE WINNER'S GOING TO BE?
NOT ON THE BEST DAY OF YOUR LIFE, SWEETHEART.
BUT HERE'S SOMETHING: THAT SWORD, YOU KNOW HOW TO USE IT?
OZAWA SCHOOL, HEAVENLY DECAPITATOR STYLE.
HMMM... OKAY!
ONE CUT.
SHOW ME ONE CUT, AND I'LL TELL YOU ALL ABOUT WHERE THAT LUNATIC WINNER IS.
WORLDS BEST BOSS
WHAT...?
WORLDS BEST BOSS
MASTER

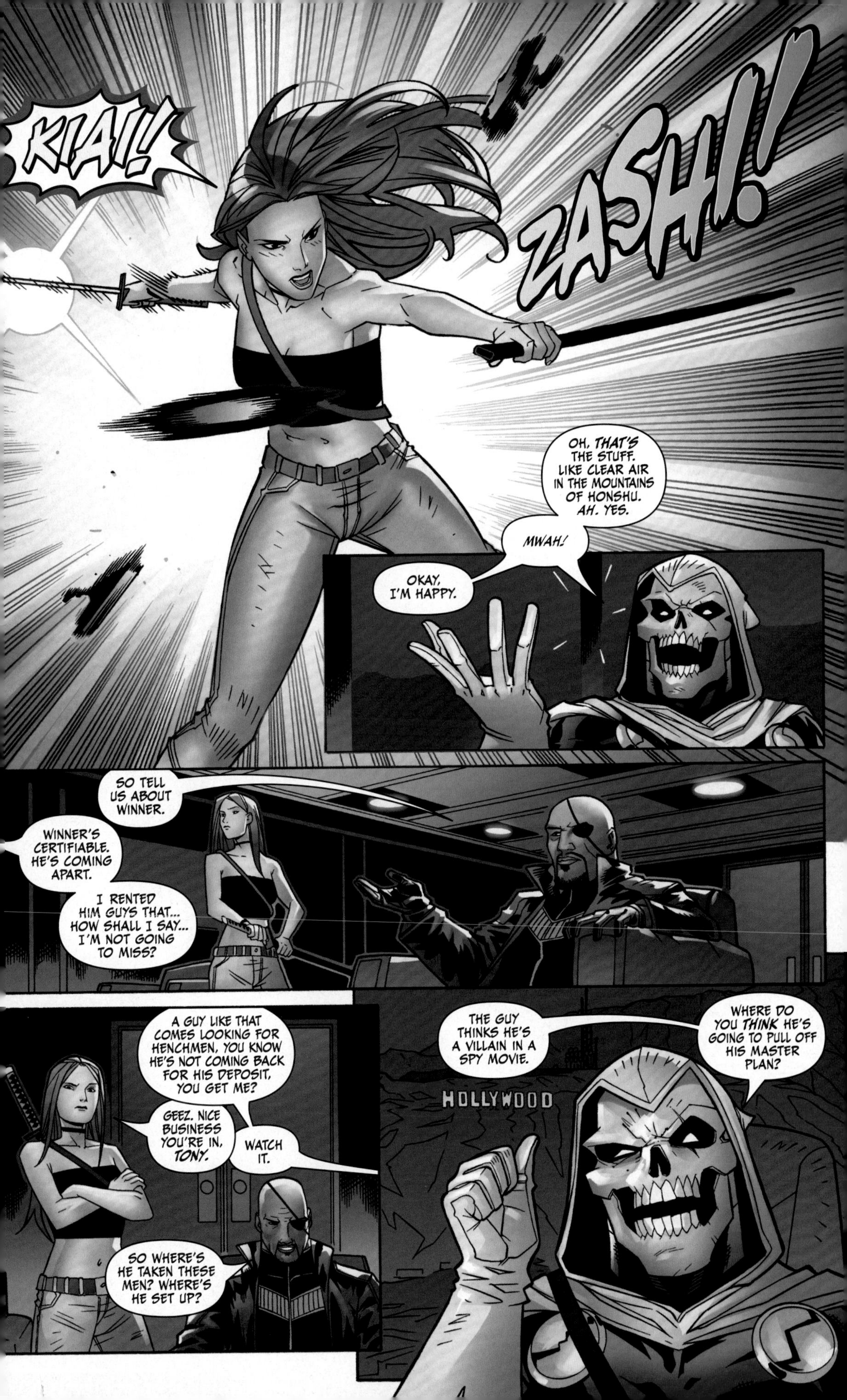
KIAI!!
ZASH!!
OH, THAT'S THE STUFF. LIKE CLEAR AIR IN THE MOUNTAINS OF HONSHU. AH. YES.
MWAH!
OKAY, I'M HAPPY.
SO TELL US ABOUT WINNER.
WINNER'S CERTIFIABLE. HE'S COMING APART.
I RENTED HIM GUYS THAT... HOW SHALL I SAY... I'M NOT GOING TO MISS?
A GUY LIKE THAT COMES LOOKING FOR HENCHMEN, YOU KNOW HE'S NOT COMING BACK FOR HIS DEPOSIT, YOU GET ME?
GEEZ. NICE BUSINESS YOU'RE IN, TONY.
WATCH IT.
SO WHERE'S HE TAKEN THESE MEN? WHERE'S HE SET UP?
THE GUY THINKS HE'S A VILLAIN IN A SPY MOVIE.
HOLLYWOOD
WHERE DO YOU THINK HE'S GOING TO PULL OFF HIS MASTER PLAN?

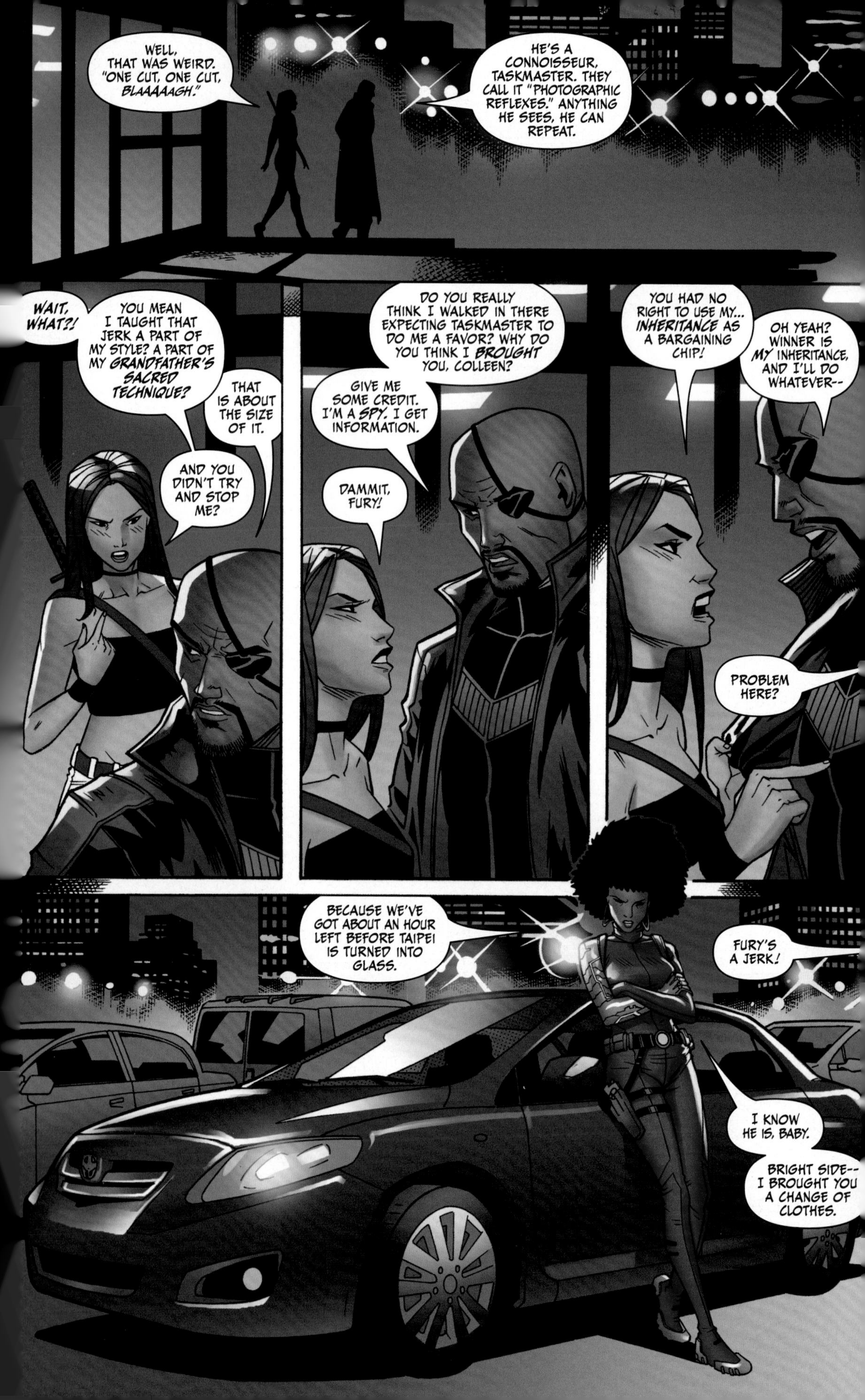
WELL, THAT WAS WEIRD. "ONE CUT, ONE CUT, BLAAAAAGH."
HE'S A CONNOISSEUR, TASKMASTER. THEY CALL IT "PHOTOGRAPHIC REFLEXES." ANYTHING HE SEES, HE CAN REPEAT.
WAIT, WHAT?!
YOU MEAN I TAUGHT THAT JERK A PART OF MY STYLE? A PART OF MY GRANDFATHER'S SACRED TECHNIQUE?
THAT IS ABOUT THE SIZE OF IT.
AND YOU DIDN'T TRY AND STOP ME?
DO YOU REALLY THINK I WALKED IN THERE EXPECTING TASKMASTER TO DO ME A FAVOR? WHY DO YOU THINK I BROUGHT YOU, COLLEEN?
GIVE ME SOME CREDIT. I'M A SPY. I GET INFORMATION.
DAMMIT, FURY!
YOU HAD NO RIGHT TO USE MY... INHERITANCE AS A BARGAINING CHIP!
OH YEAH? WINNER IS MY INHERITANCE, AND I'LL DO WHATEVER--
PROBLEM HERE?
BECAUSE WE'VE GOT ABOUT AN HOUR LEFT BEFORE TAIPEI IS TURNED INTO GLASS.
FURY'S A JERK!
I KNOW HE IS, BABY.
BRIGHT SIDE-- I BROUGHT YOU A CHANGE OF CLOTHES.

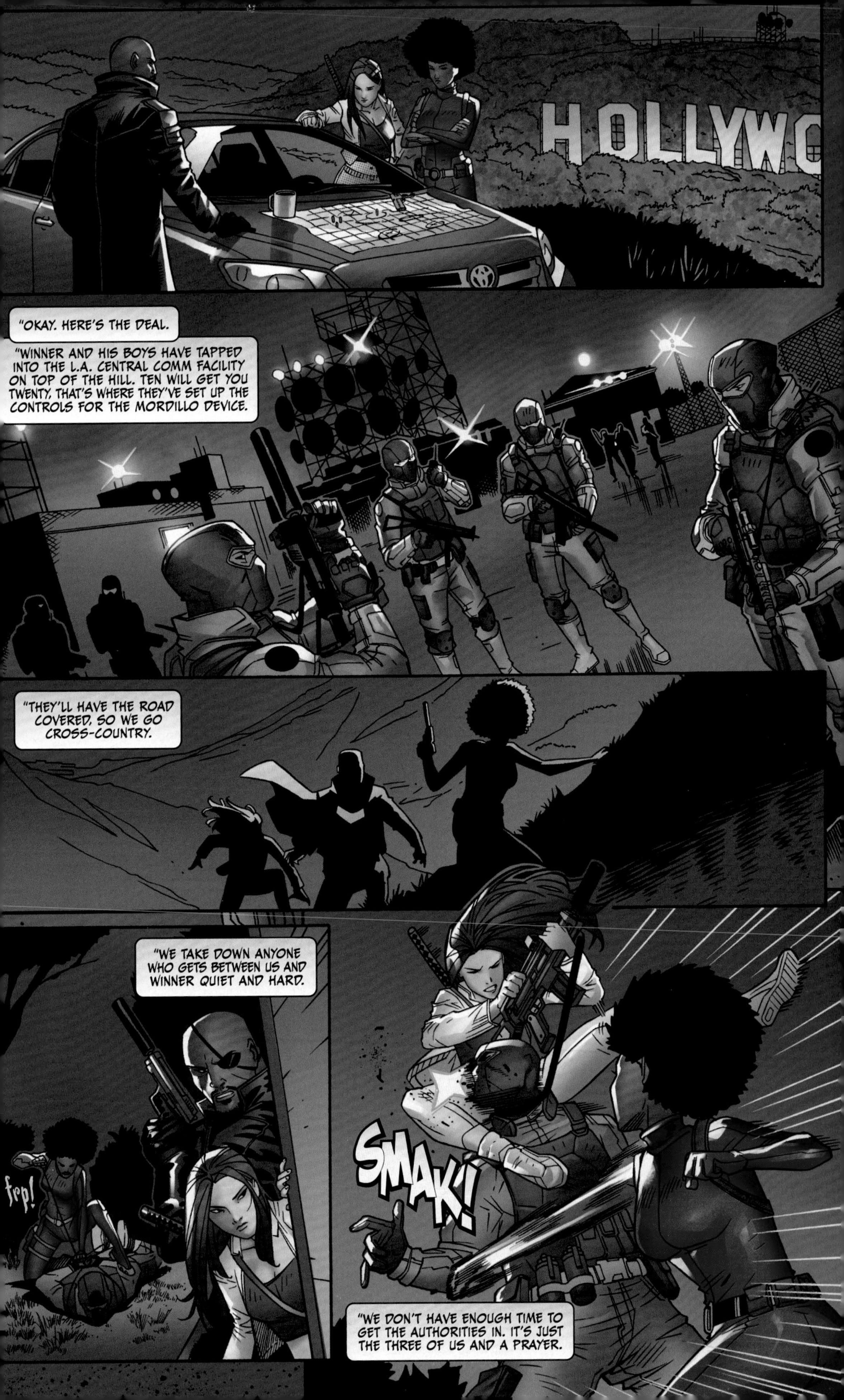
HOLLYWO
"OKAY. HERE'S THE DEAL.
"WINNER AND HIS BOYS HAVE TAPPED INTO THE L.A. CENTRAL COMM FACILITY ON TOP OF THE HILL. TEN WILL GET YOU TWENTY, THAT'S WHERE THEY'VE SET UP THE CONTROLS FOR THE MORDILLO DEVICE.
"THEY'LL HAVE THE ROAD COVERED, SO WE GO CROSS-COUNTRY.
"WE TAKE DOWN ANYONE WHO GETS BETWEEN US AND WINNER QUIET AND HARD.
frp!
SMAK!
"WE DON'T HAVE ENOUGH TIME TO GET THE AUTHORITIES IN. IT'S JUST THE THREE OF US AND A PRAYER.

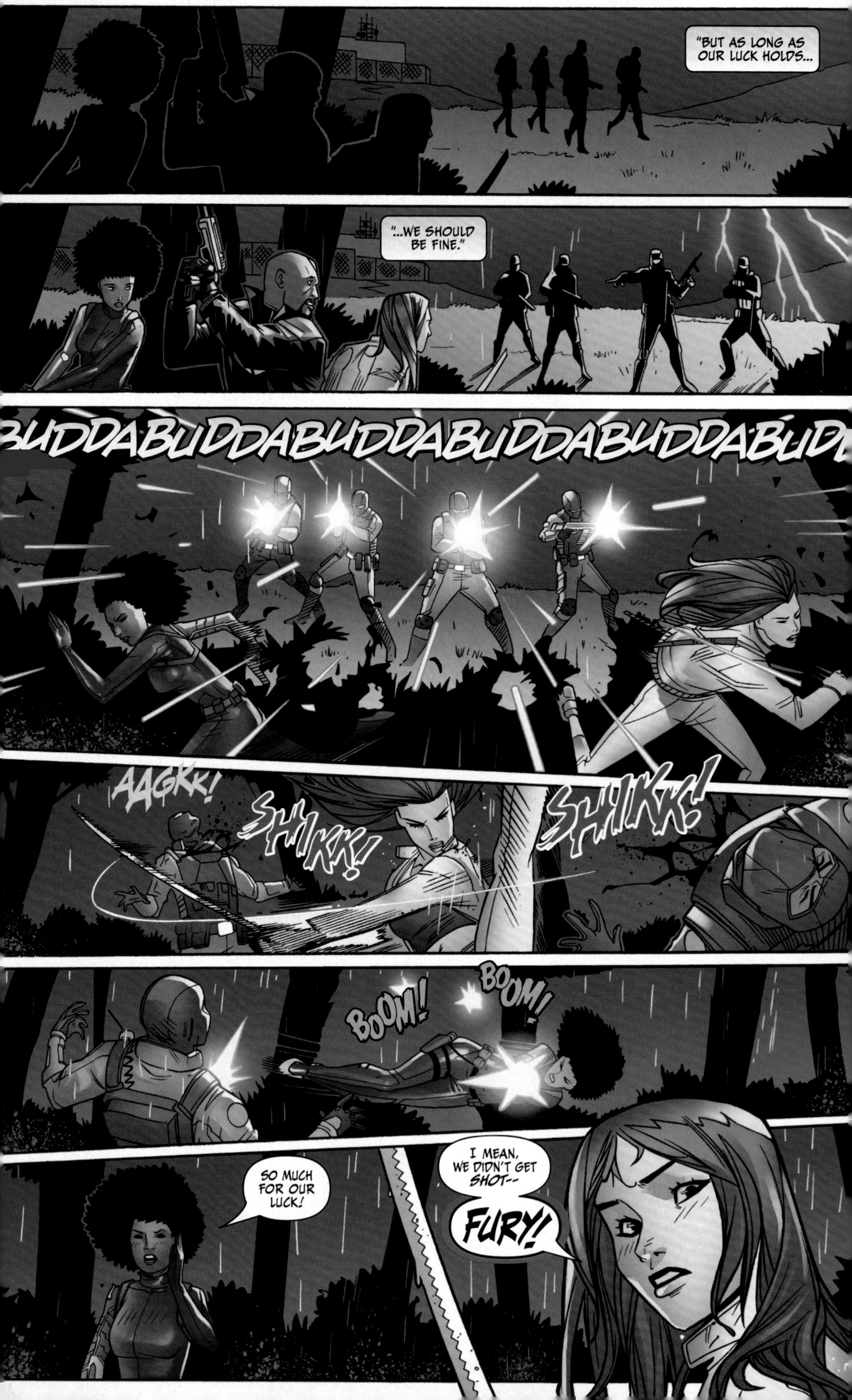
"BUT AS LONG AS OUR LUCK HOLDS...
"...WE SHOULD BE FINE."
BUDDABUDDABUDDABUDDABUDDABUD
AAGKK!
SHIKK!
SHIKK!
BOOM!
BOOM!
SO MUCH FOR OUR LUCK!
I MEAN, WE DIDN'T GET SHOT--
FURY!

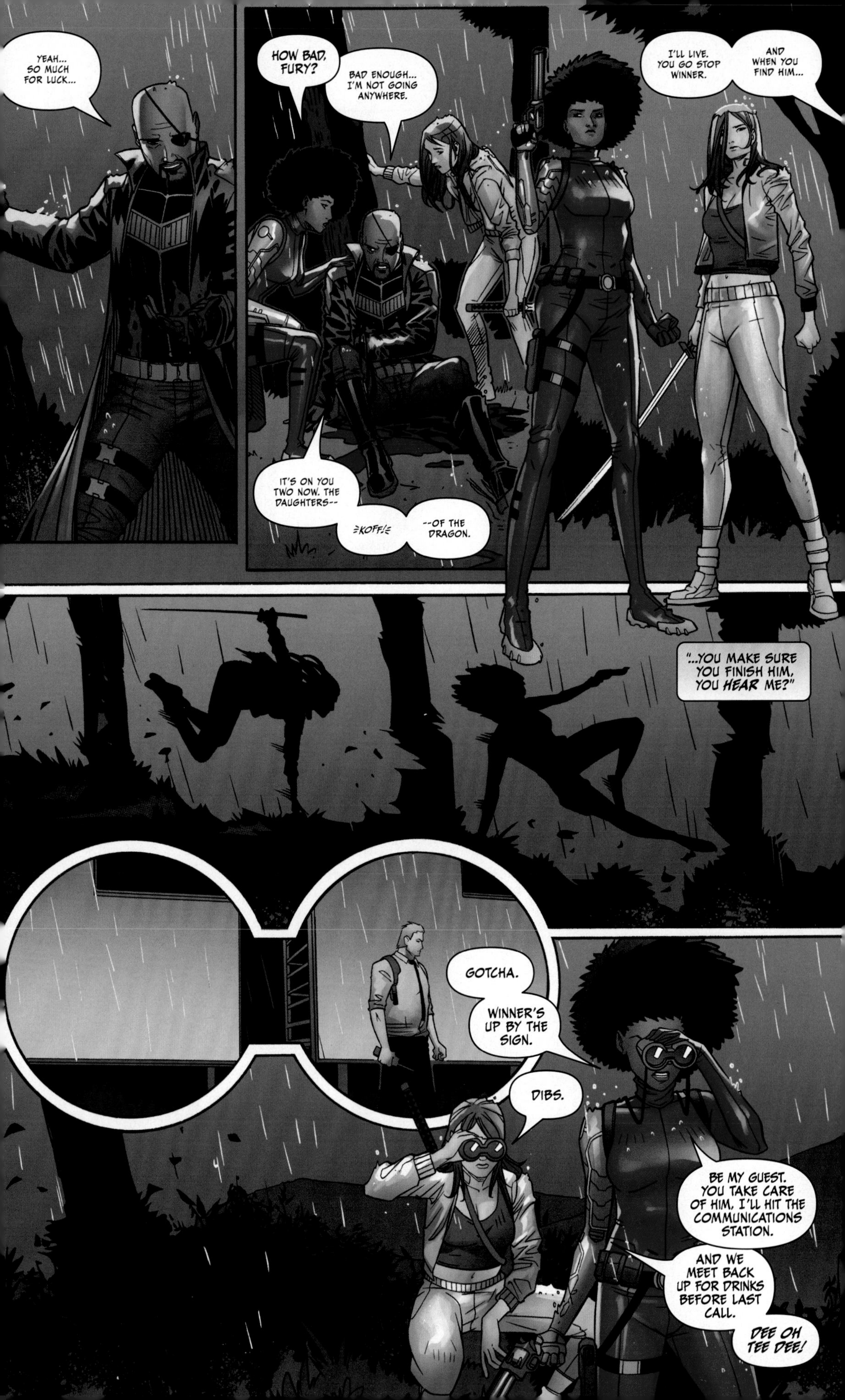
YEAH... SO MUCH FOR LUCK...
HOW BAD, FURY?
BAD ENOUGH... I'M NOT GOING ANYWHERE.
IT'S ON YOU TWO NOW. THE DAUGHTERS--
KOFF!
--OF THE DRAGON.
I'LL LIVE. YOU GO STOP WINNER.
AND WHEN YOU FIND HIM...
"...YOU MAKE SURE YOU FINISH HIM, YOU HEAR ME?"
GOTCHA.
WINNER'S UP BY THE SIGN.
DIBS.
BE MY GUEST. YOU TAKE CARE OF HIM, I'LL HIT THE COMMUNICATIONS STATION.
AND WE MEET BACK UP FOR DRINKS BEFORE LAST CALL.
DEE OH TEE DEE!

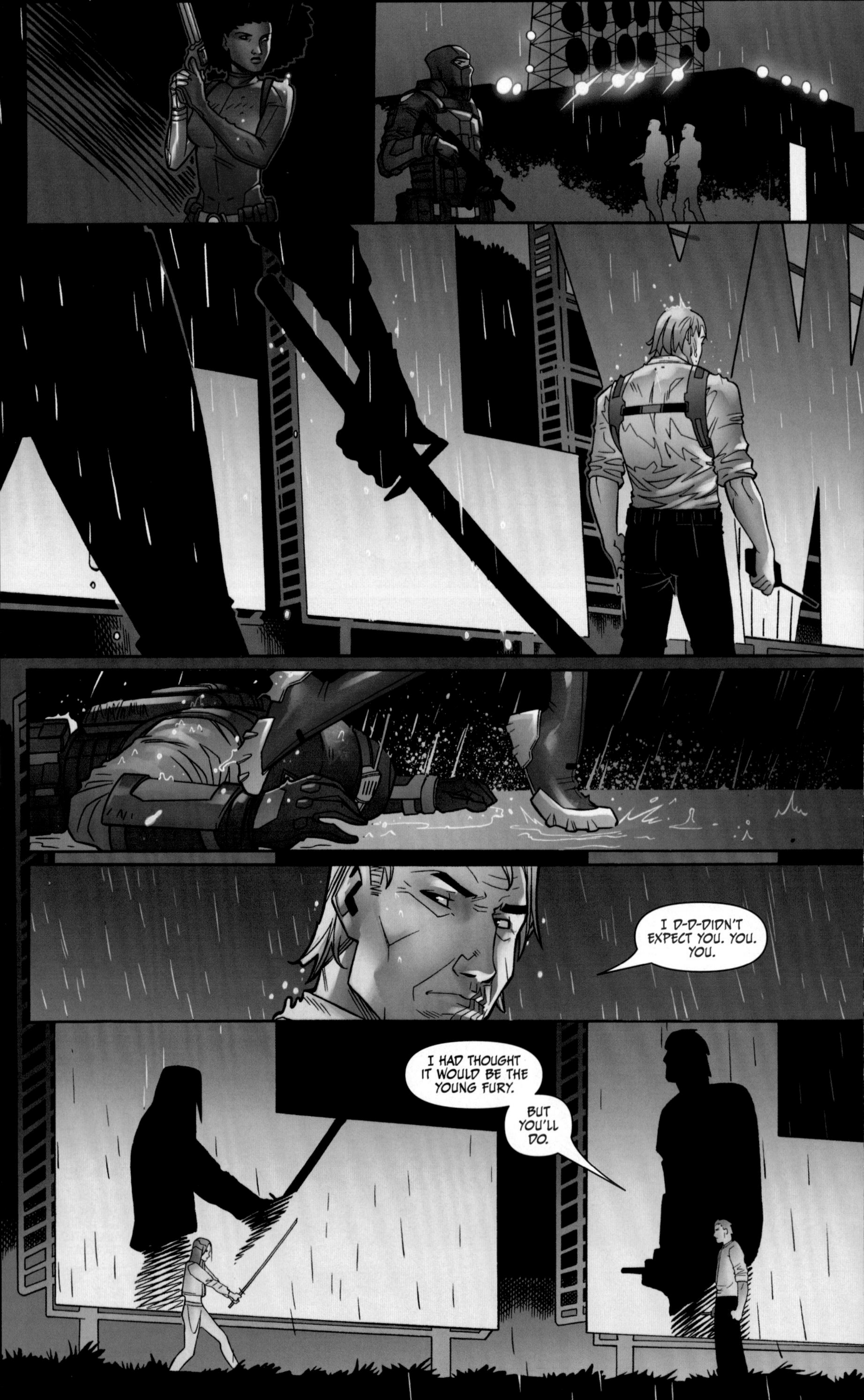
I D-D-DIDN'T EXPECT YOU. YOU. YOU.
I HAD THOUGHT IT WOULD BE THE YOUNG FURY.
BUT YOU'LL DO.

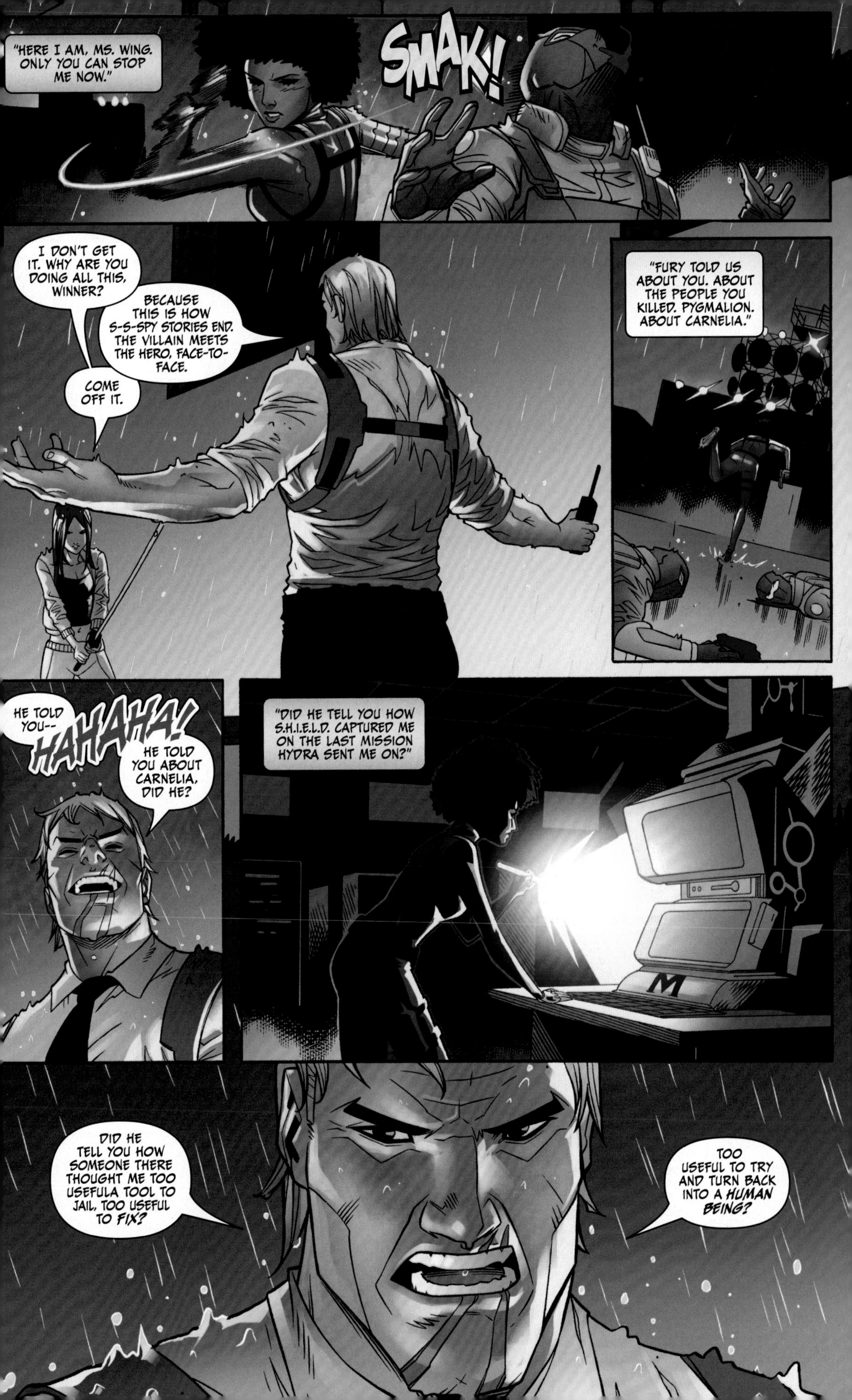
"HERE I AM, MS. WING. ONLY YOU CAN STOP ME NOW."
SMAK!
I DON'T GET IT. WHY ARE YOU DOING ALL THIS, WINNER?
BECAUSE THIS IS HOW S-S-SPY STORIES END. THE VILLAIN MEETS THE HERO, FACE-TO-FACE.
COME OFF IT.
"FURY TOLD US ABOUT YOU. ABOUT THE PEOPLE YOU KILLED. PYGMALION. ABOUT CARNELIA."
HE TOLD YOU--
HAHAHA!
HE TOLD YOU ABOUT CARNELIA, DID HE?
"DID HE TELL YOU HOW S.H.I.E.L.D. CAPTURED ME ON THE LAST MISSION HYDRA SENT ME ON?"
M
DID HE TELL YOU HOW SOMEONE THERE THOUGHT ME TOO USEFULA TOOL TO JAIL, TOO USEFUL TO *FIX*?
TOO USEFUL TO TRY AND TURN BACK INTO A *HUMAN BEING*?

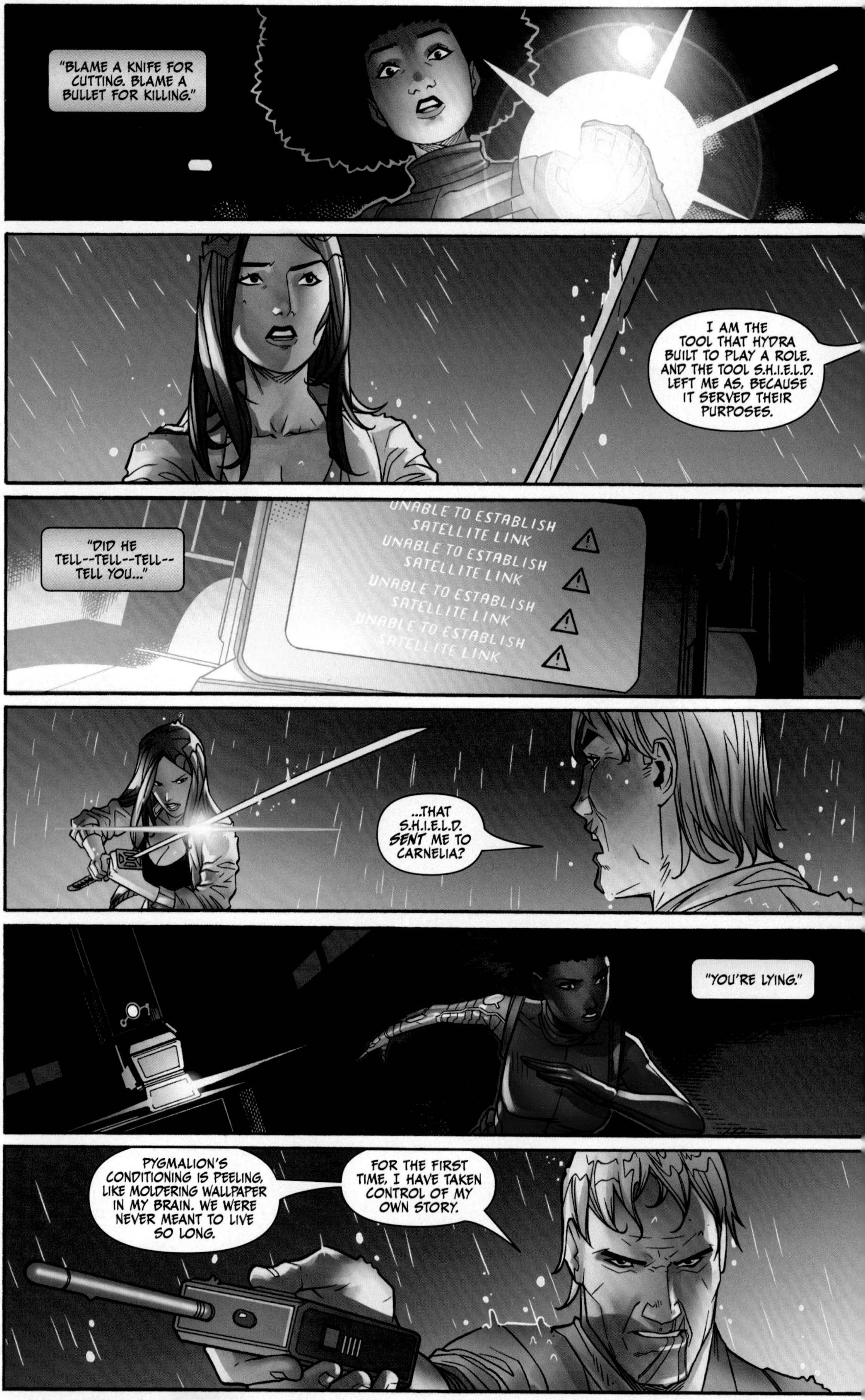
"BLAME A KNIFE FOR CUTTING. BLAME A BULLET FOR KILLING."
I AM THE TOOL THAT HYDRA BUILT TO PLAY A ROLE. AND THE TOOL S.H.I.E.L.D. LEFT ME AS, BECAUSE IT SERVED THEIR PURPOSES.
"DID HE TELL--TELL--TELL--TELL YOU..."
UNABLE TO ESTABLISH SATELLITE LINK
UNABLE TO ESTABLISH SATELLITE LINK
UNABLE TO ESTABLISH SATELLITE LINK
UNABLE TO ESTABLISH SATELLITE LINK
...THAT S.H.I.E.L.D. SENT ME TO CARNELIA?
"YOU'RE LYING."
PYGMALION'S CONDITIONING IS PEELING, LIKE MOLDERING WALLPAPER IN MY BRAIN. WE WERE NEVER MEANT TO LIVE SO LONG.
FOR THE FIRST TIME, I HAVE TAKEN CONTROL OF MY OWN STORY.

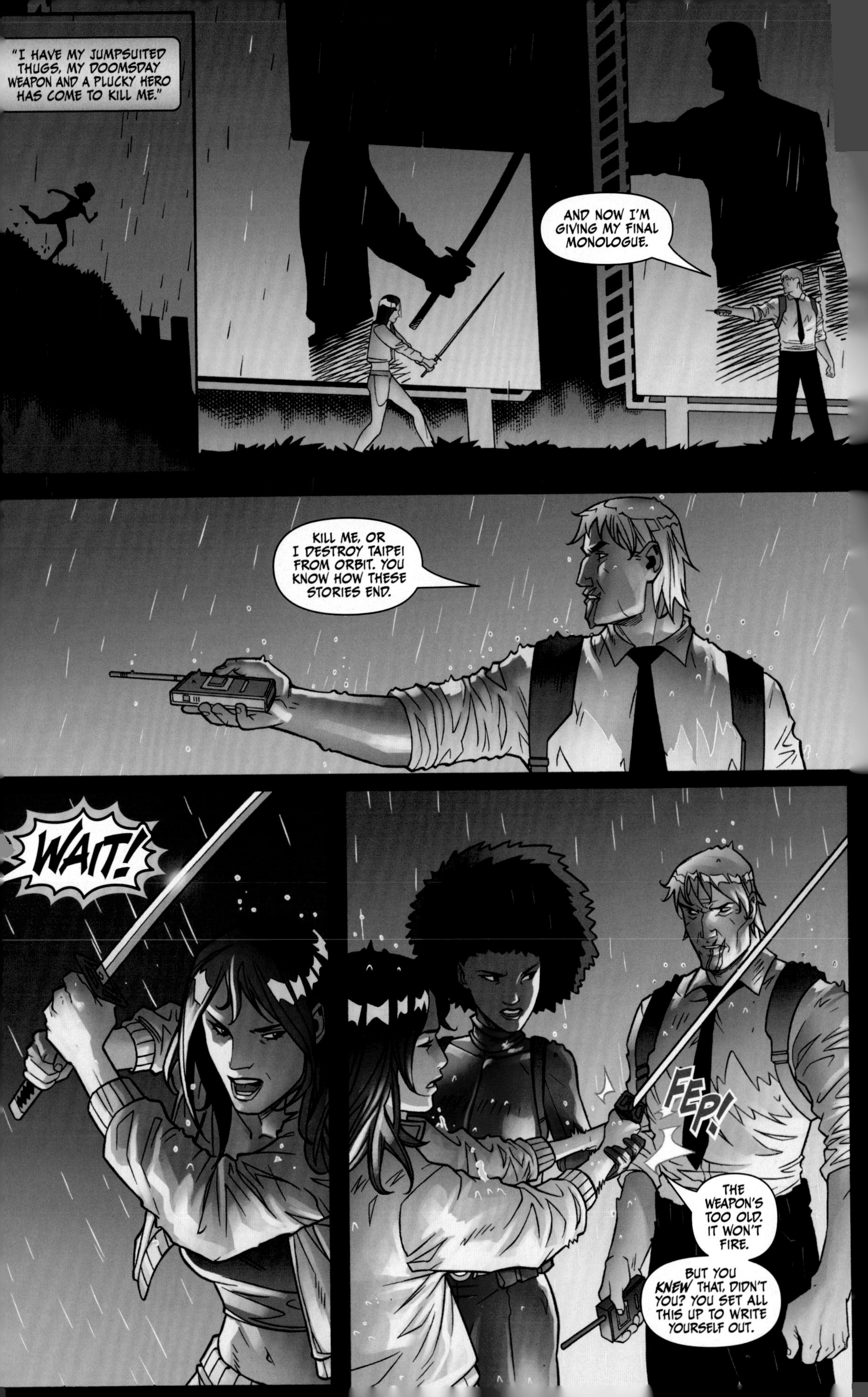
"I HAVE MY JUMPSUITED THUGS, MY DOOMSDAY WEAPON AND A PLUCKY HERO HAS COME TO KILL ME."
AND NOW I'M GIVING MY FINAL MONOLOGUE.
KILL ME, OR I DESTROY TAIPEI FROM ORBIT. YOU KNOW HOW THESE STORIES END.
WAIT!
FEP!
THE WEAPON'S TOO OLD. IT WON'T FIRE.
BUT YOU *KNEW* THAT, DIDN'T YOU? YOU SET ALL THIS UP TO WRITE YOURSELF OUT.

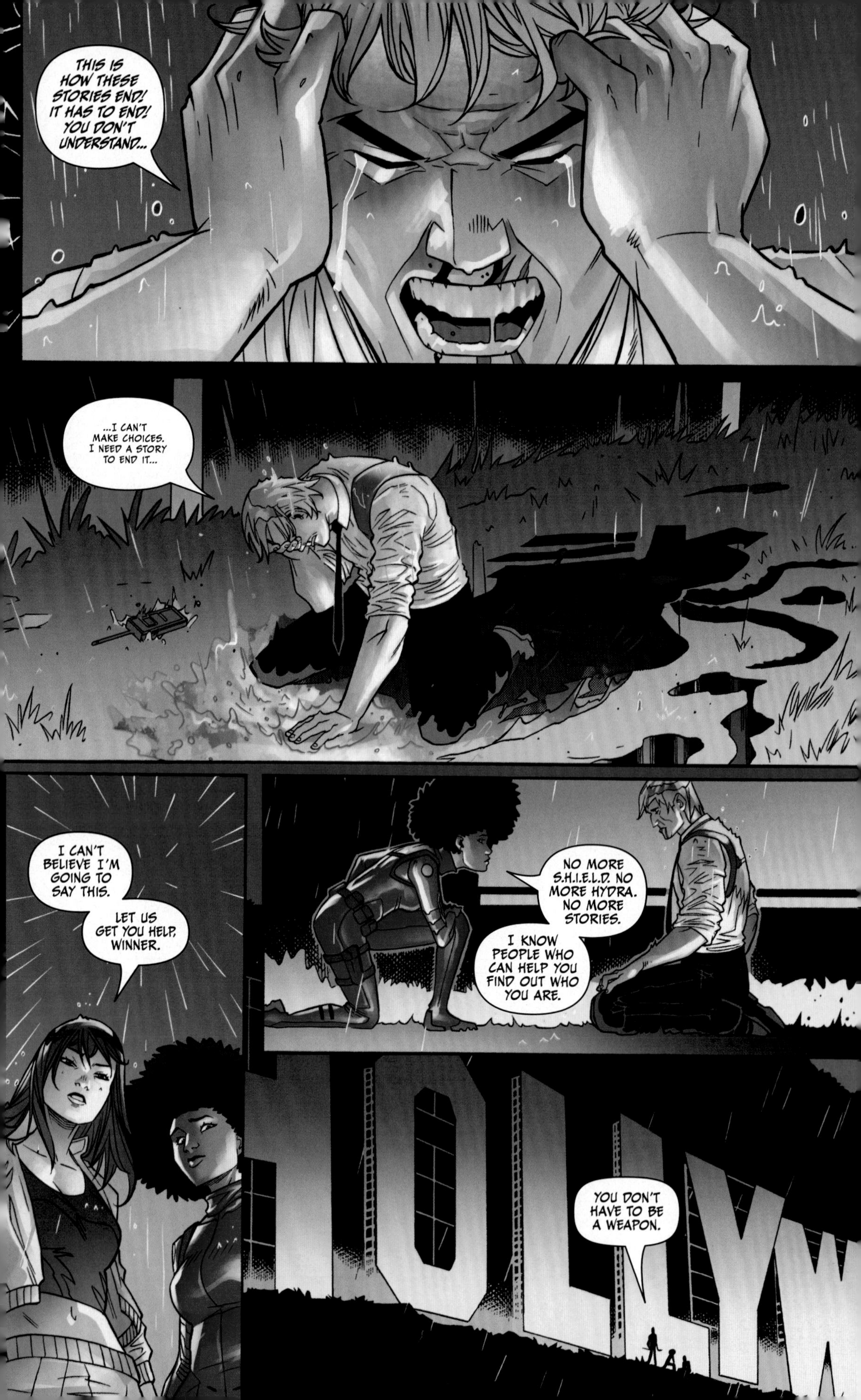
THIS IS HOW THESE STORIES END! IT HAS TO END! YOU DON'T UNDERSTAND...
...I CAN'T MAKE CHOICES. I NEED A STORY TO END IT...
I CAN'T BELIEVE I'M GOING TO SAY THIS.
LET US GET YOU HELP, WINNER.
NO MORE S.H.I.E.L.D. NO MORE HYDRA. NO MORE STORIES.
I KNOW PEOPLE WHO CAN HELP YOU FIND OUT WHO YOU ARE.
YOU DON'T HAVE TO BE A WEAPON.

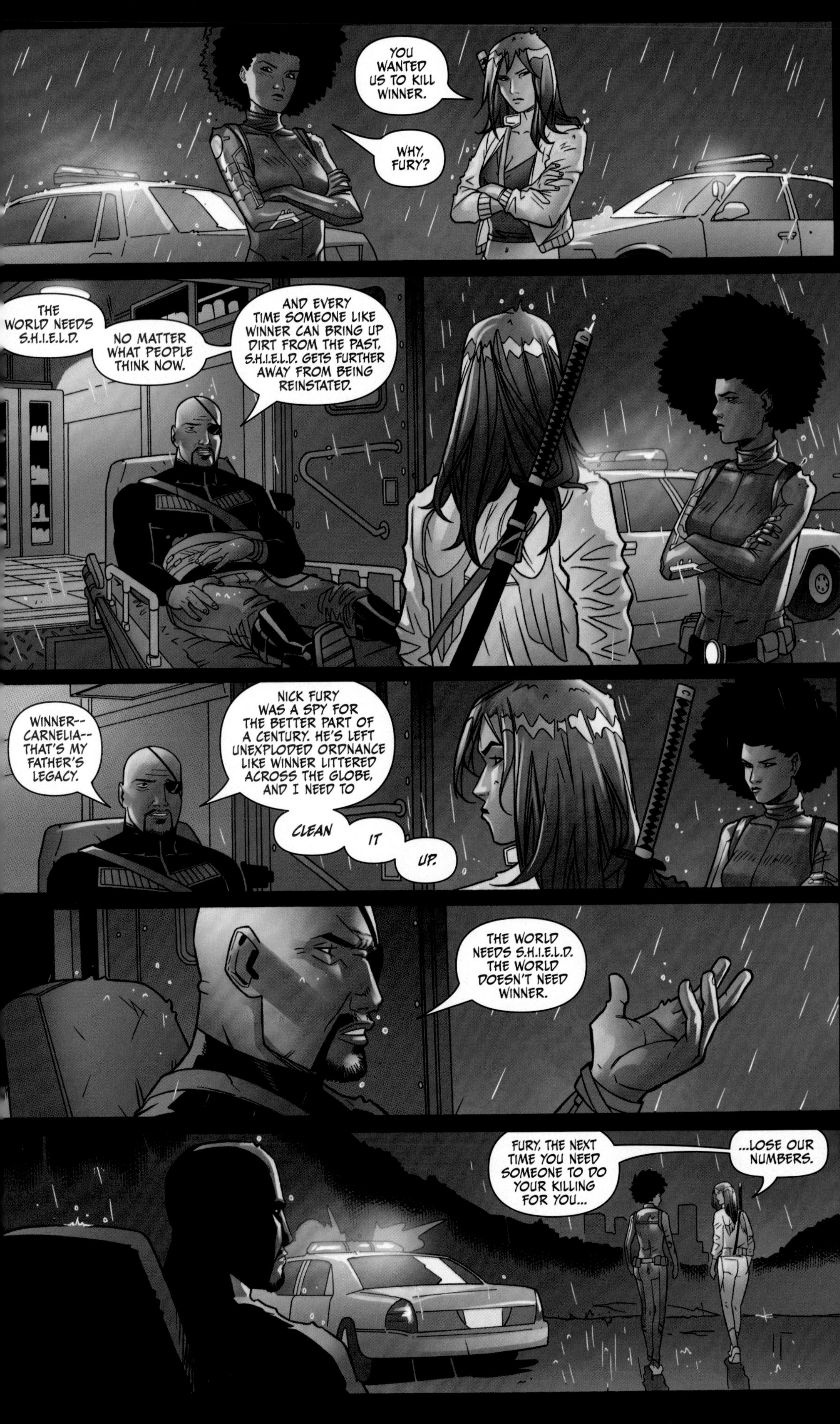
YOU WANTED US TO KILL WINNER.
WHY, FURY?
THE WORLD NEEDS S.H.I.E.L.D.
NO MATTER WHAT PEOPLE THINK NOW.
AND EVERY TIME SOMEONE LIKE WINNER CAN BRING UP DIRT FROM THE PAST, S.H.I.E.L.D. GETS FURTHER AWAY FROM BEING REINSTATED.
WINNER--CARNELIA--THAT'S MY FATHER'S LEGACY.
NICK FURY WAS A SPY FOR THE BETTER PART OF A CENTURY. HE'S LEFT UNEXPLODED ORDNANCE LIKE WINNER LITTERED ACROSS THE GLOBE, AND I NEED TO
CLEAN
IT
UP.
THE WORLD NEEDS S.H.I.E.L.D. THE WORLD DOESN'T NEED WINNER.
FURY, THE NEXT TIME YOU NEED SOMEONE TO DO YOUR KILLING FOR YOU...
...LOSE OUR NUMBERS.

CHAPTER 5

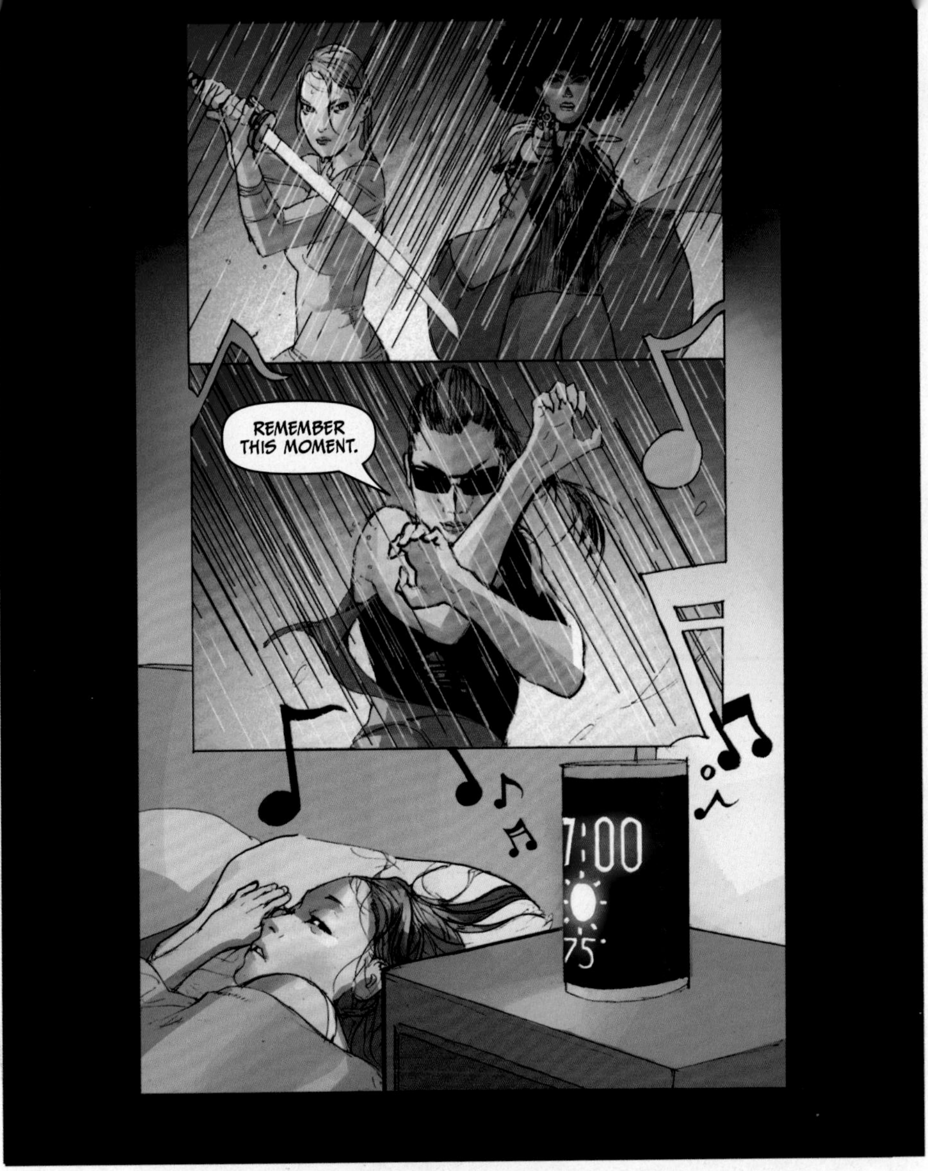
REMEMBER THIS MOMENT.
7:00
75°

MS. CHARDONNAY & MS. PINOT

HOLIDAY: Part 1

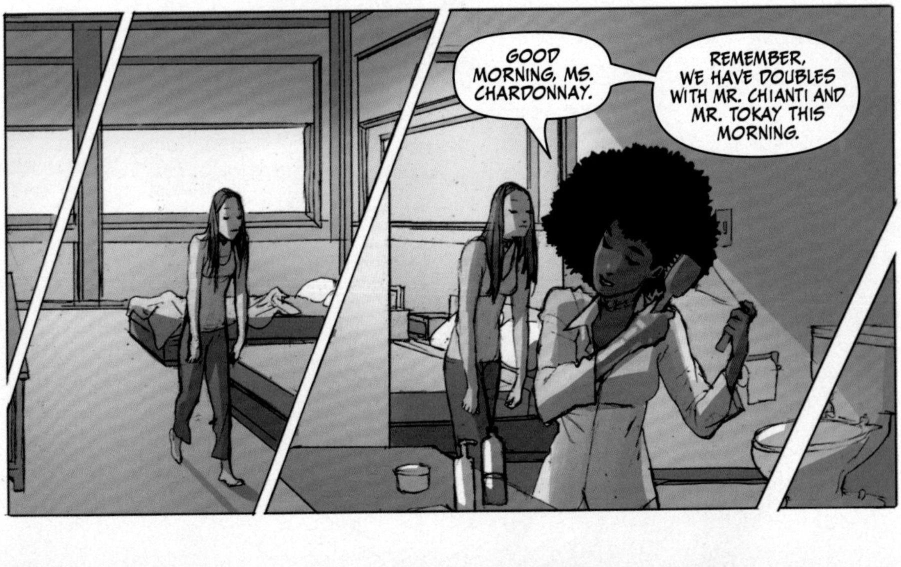
GOOD MORNING, MS. CHARDONNAY.
REMEMBER, WE HAVE DOUBLES WITH MR. CHIANTI AND MR. TOKAY THIS MORNING.

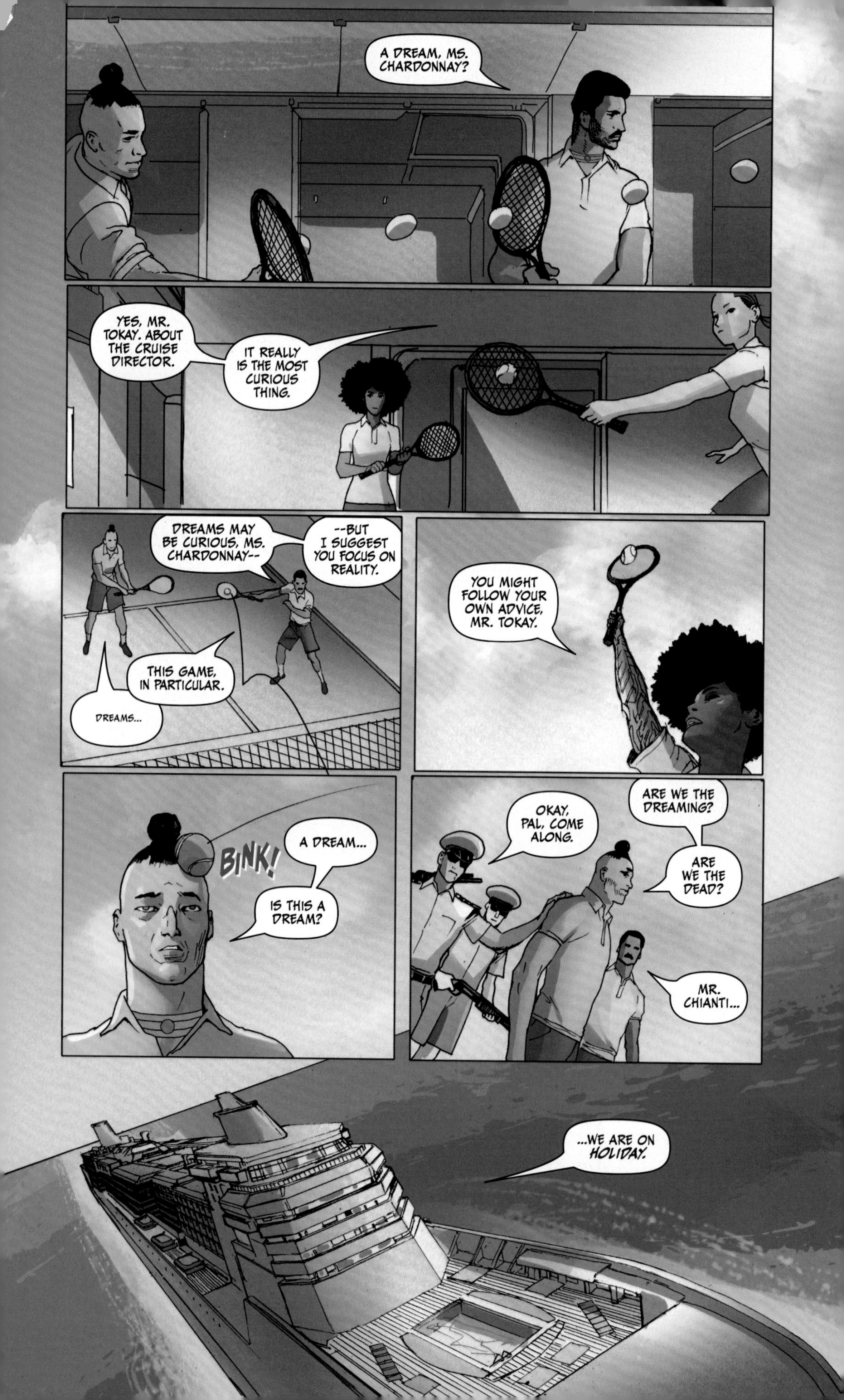
A DREAM, MS. CHARDONNAY?
YES, MR. TOKAY. ABOUT THE CRUISE DIRECTOR.
IT REALLY IS THE MOST CURIOUS THING.
DREAMS MAY BE CURIOUS, MS. CHARDONNAY--
--BUT I SUGGEST YOU FOCUS ON REALITY.
THIS GAME, IN PARTICULAR.
DREAMS...
YOU MIGHT FOLLOW YOUR OWN ADVICE, MR. TOKAY.
BINK!
A DREAM...
IS THIS A DREAM?
OKAY, PAL, COME ALONG.
ARE WE THE DREAMING?
ARE WE THE DEAD?
MR. CHIANTI...
...WE ARE ON *HOLIDAY.*

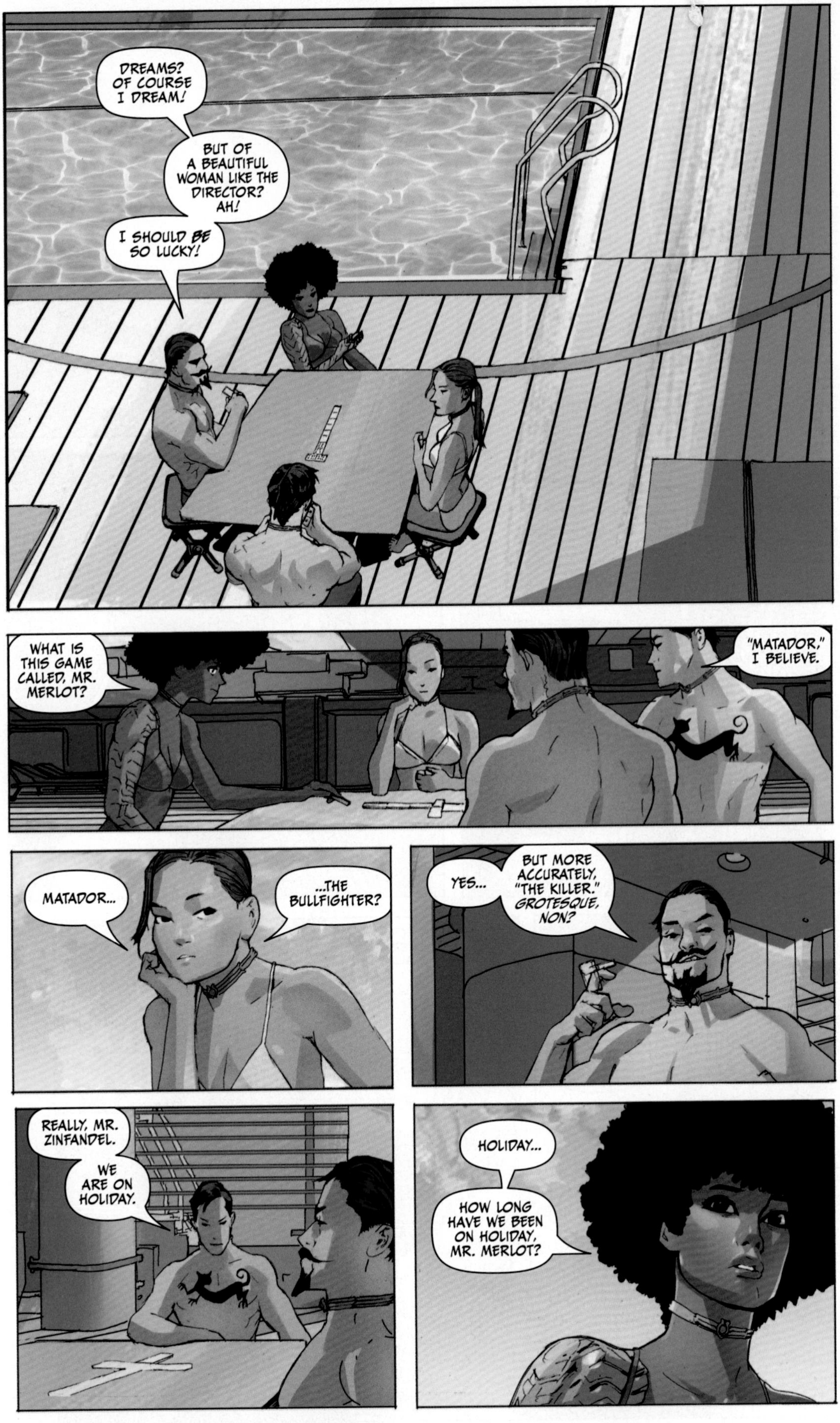
DREAMS? OF COURSE I DREAM!
BUT OF A BEAUTIFUL WOMAN LIKE THE DIRECTOR? AH!
I SHOULD BE SO LUCKY!
WHAT IS THIS GAME CALLED, MR. MERLOT?
"MATADOR," I BELIEVE.
MATADOR...
...THE BULLFIGHTER?
YES...
BUT MORE ACCURATELY, "THE KILLER." GROTESQUE, NON?
REALLY, MR. ZINFANDEL.
WE ARE ON HOLIDAY.
HOLIDAY...
HOW LONG HAVE WE BEEN ON HOLIDAY, MR. MERLOT?

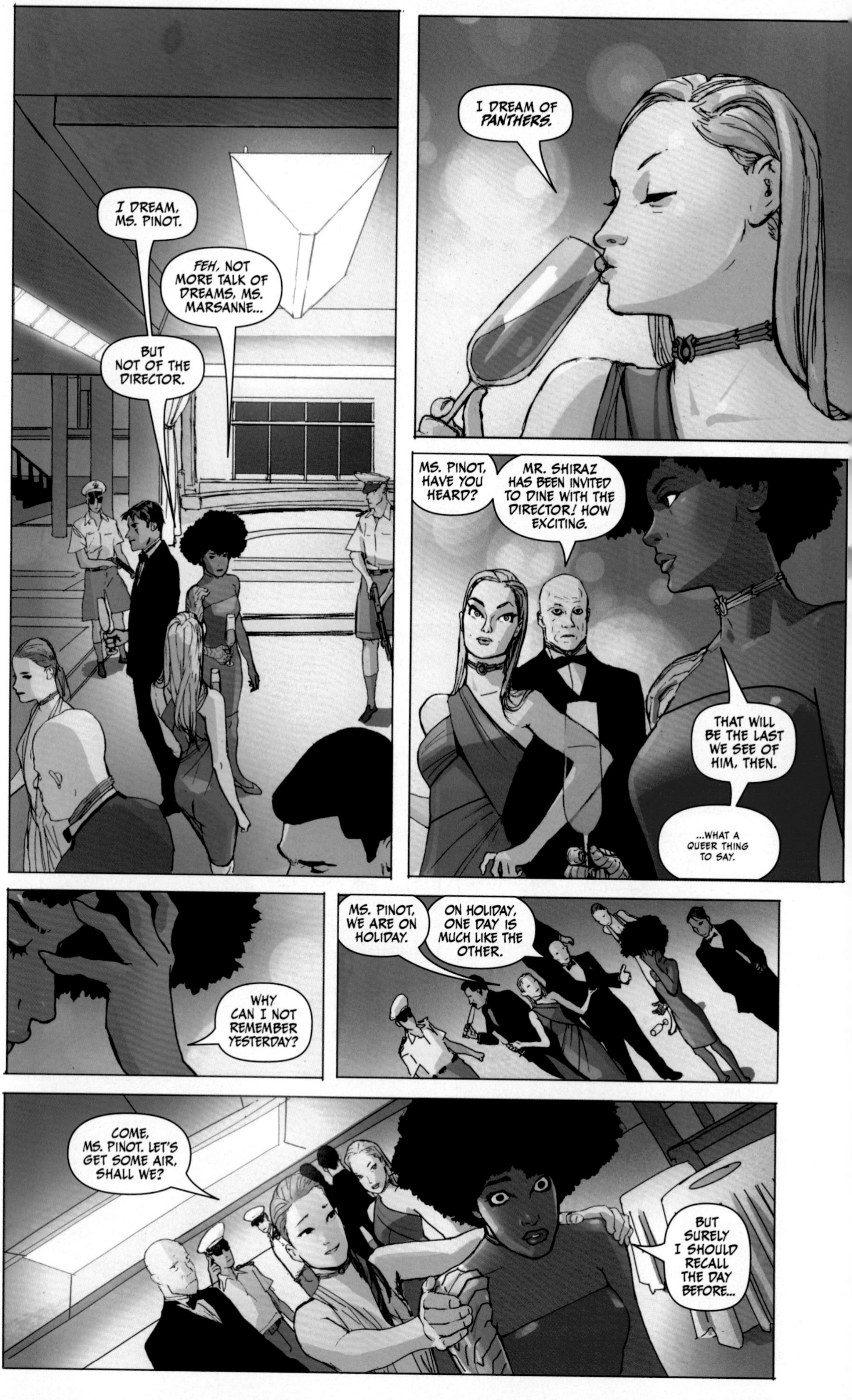
I DREAM, MS. PINOT.
FEH, NOT MORE TALK OF DREAMS, MS. MARSANNE...
BUT NOT OF THE DIRECTOR.
I DREAM OF PANTHERS.
MS. PINOT, HAVE YOU HEARD?
MR. SHIRAZ HAS BEEN INVITED TO DINE WITH THE DIRECTOR! HOW EXCITING.
THAT WILL BE THE LAST WE SEE OF HIM, THEN.
...WHAT A QUEER THING TO SAY.
WHY CAN I NOT REMEMBER YESTERDAY?
MS. PINOT, WE ARE ON HOLIDAY.
ON HOLIDAY, ONE DAY IS MUCH LIKE THE OTHER.
COME, MS. PINOT. LET'S GET SOME AIR, SHALL WE?
BUT SURELY I SHOULD RECALL THE DAY BEFORE...

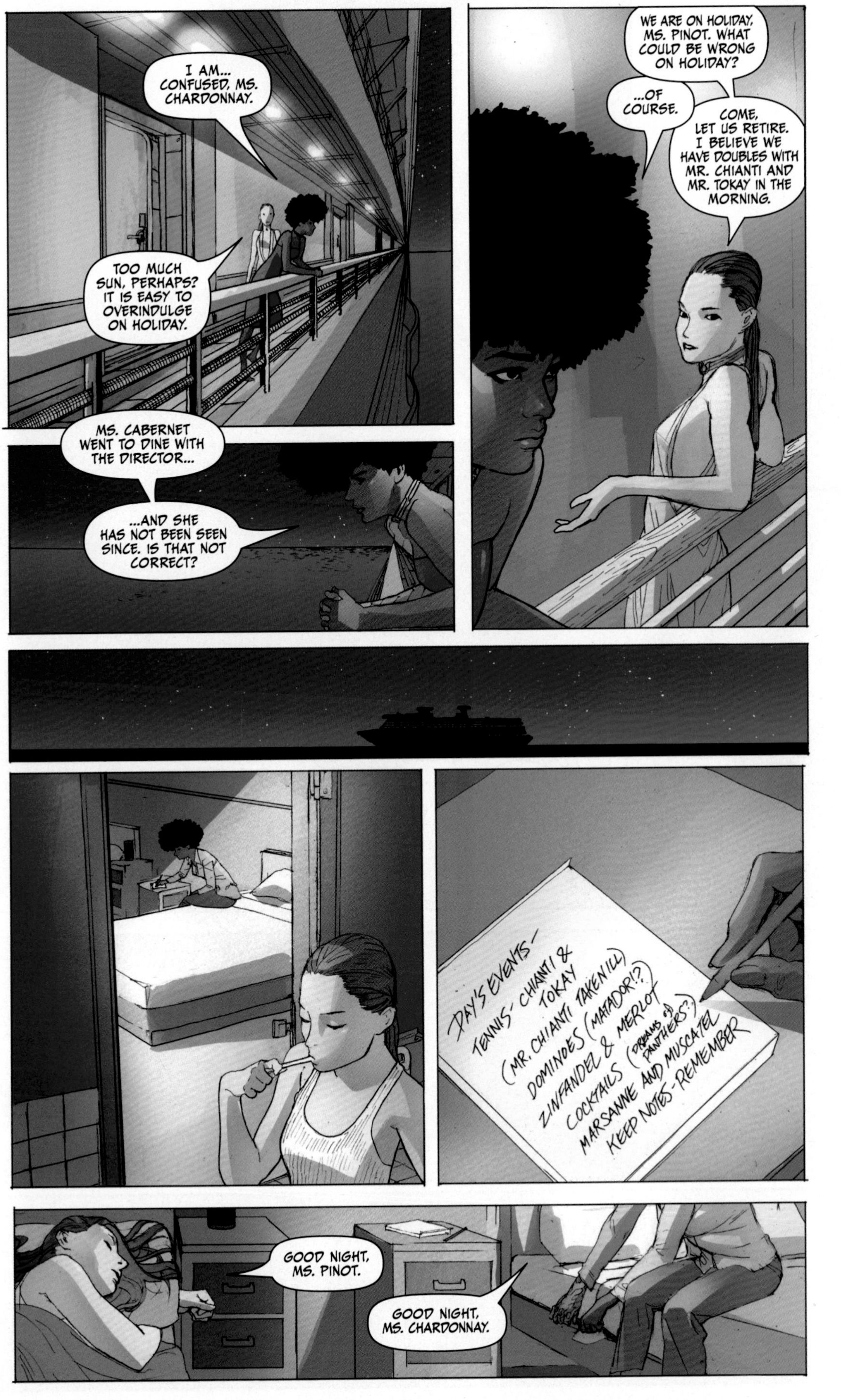
I AM... CONFUSED, MS. CHARDONNAY.
TOO MUCH SUN, PERHAPS? IT IS EASY TO OVERINDULGE ON HOLIDAY.
MS. CABERNET WENT TO DINE WITH THE DIRECTOR...
...AND SHE HAS NOT BEEN SEEN SINCE. IS THAT NOT CORRECT?
WE ARE ON HOLIDAY, MS. PINOT. WHAT COULD BE WRONG ON HOLIDAY?
...OF COURSE.
COME, LET US RETIRE. I BELIEVE WE HAVE DOUBLES WITH MR. CHIANTI AND MR. TOKAY IN THE MORNING.
DAY'S EVENTS -
TENNIS - CHIANTI & TOKAY
(MR. CHIANTI TAKEN ILL)
DOMINOES (MATADOR!?)
ZINFANDEL & MERLOT
COCKTAILS (DREAMS OF PANTHERS?)
MARSANNE AND MUSCATEL
KEEP NOTES - REMEMBER
GOOD NIGHT, MS. PINOT.
GOOD NIGHT, MS. CHARDONNAY.

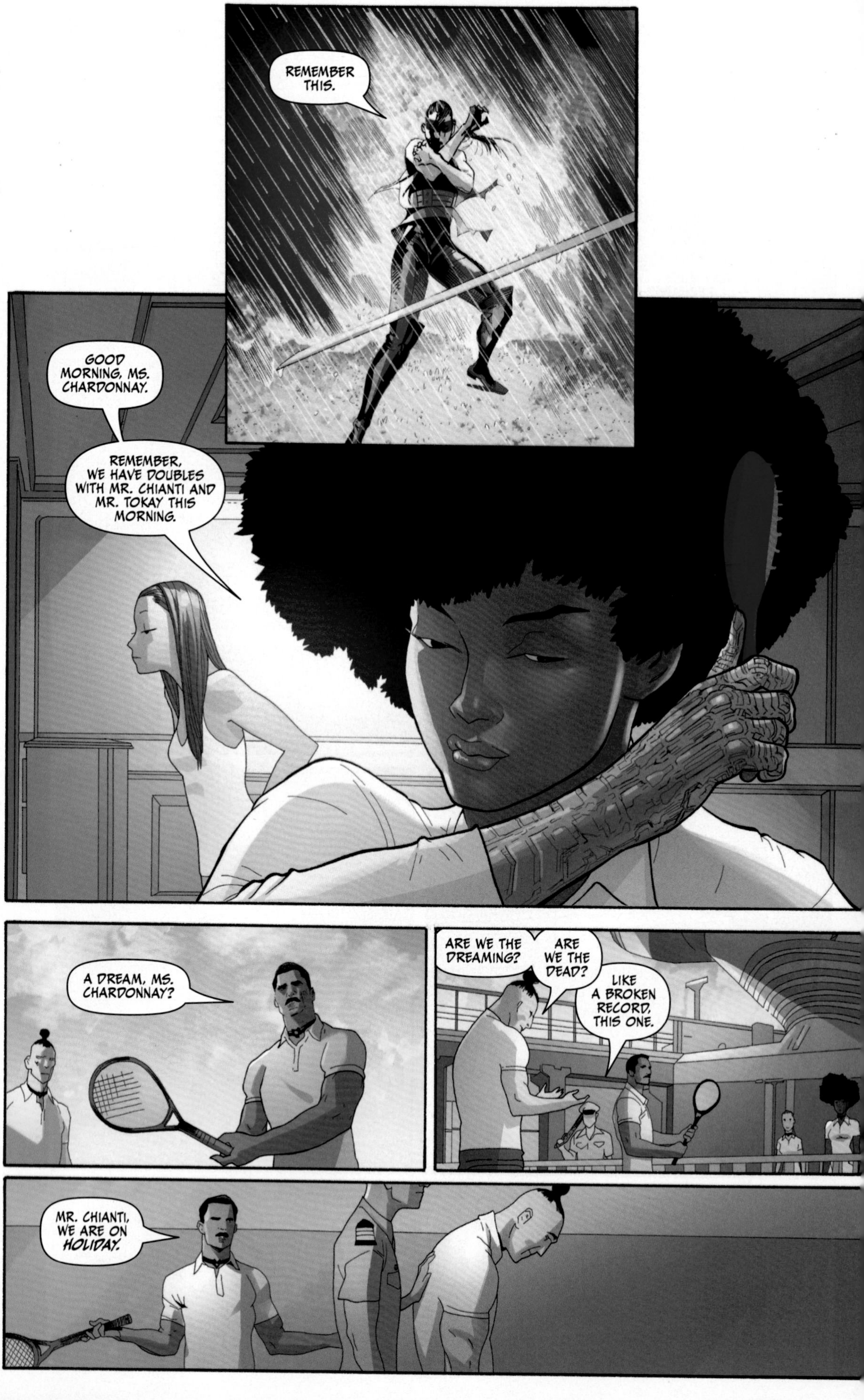
REMEMBER THIS.
GOOD MORNING, MS. CHARDONNAY.
REMEMBER, WE HAVE DOUBLES WITH MR. CHIANTI AND MR. TOKAY THIS MORNING.
A DREAM, MS. CHARDONNAY?
ARE WE THE DREAMING?
ARE WE THE DEAD?
LIKE A BROKEN RECORD, THIS ONE.
MR. CHIANTI, WE ARE ON *HOLIDAY.*

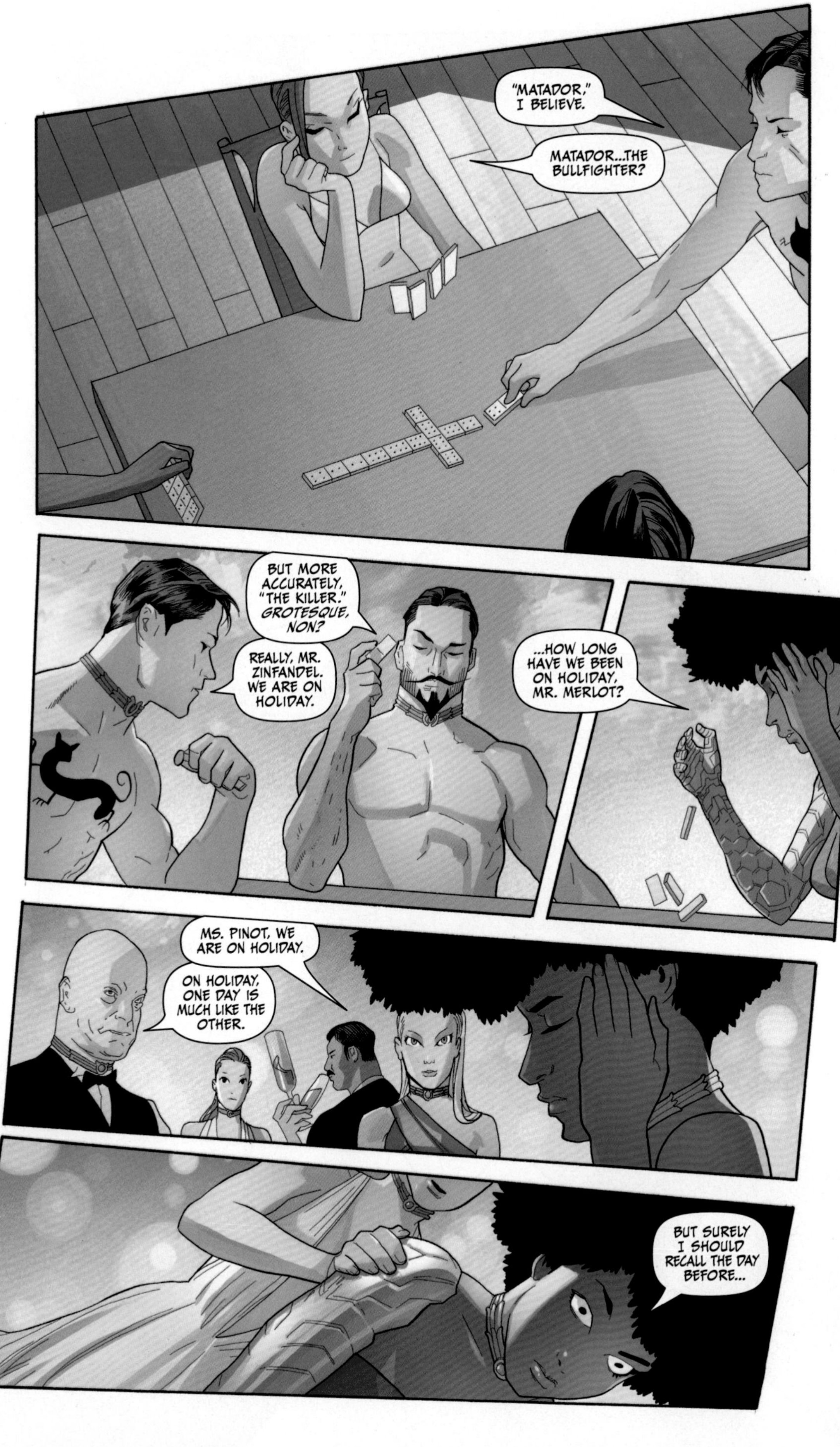
"MATADOR," I BELIEVE.
MATADOR...THE BULLFIGHTER?
BUT MORE ACCURATELY, "THE KILLER." GROTESQUE, NON?
REALLY, MR. ZINFANDEL. WE ARE ON HOLIDAY.
...HOW LONG HAVE WE BEEN ON HOLIDAY, MR. MERLOT?
MS. PINOT, WE ARE ON HOLIDAY.
ON HOLIDAY, ONE DAY IS MUCH LIKE THE OTHER.
BUT SURELY I SHOULD RECALL THE DAY BEFORE...

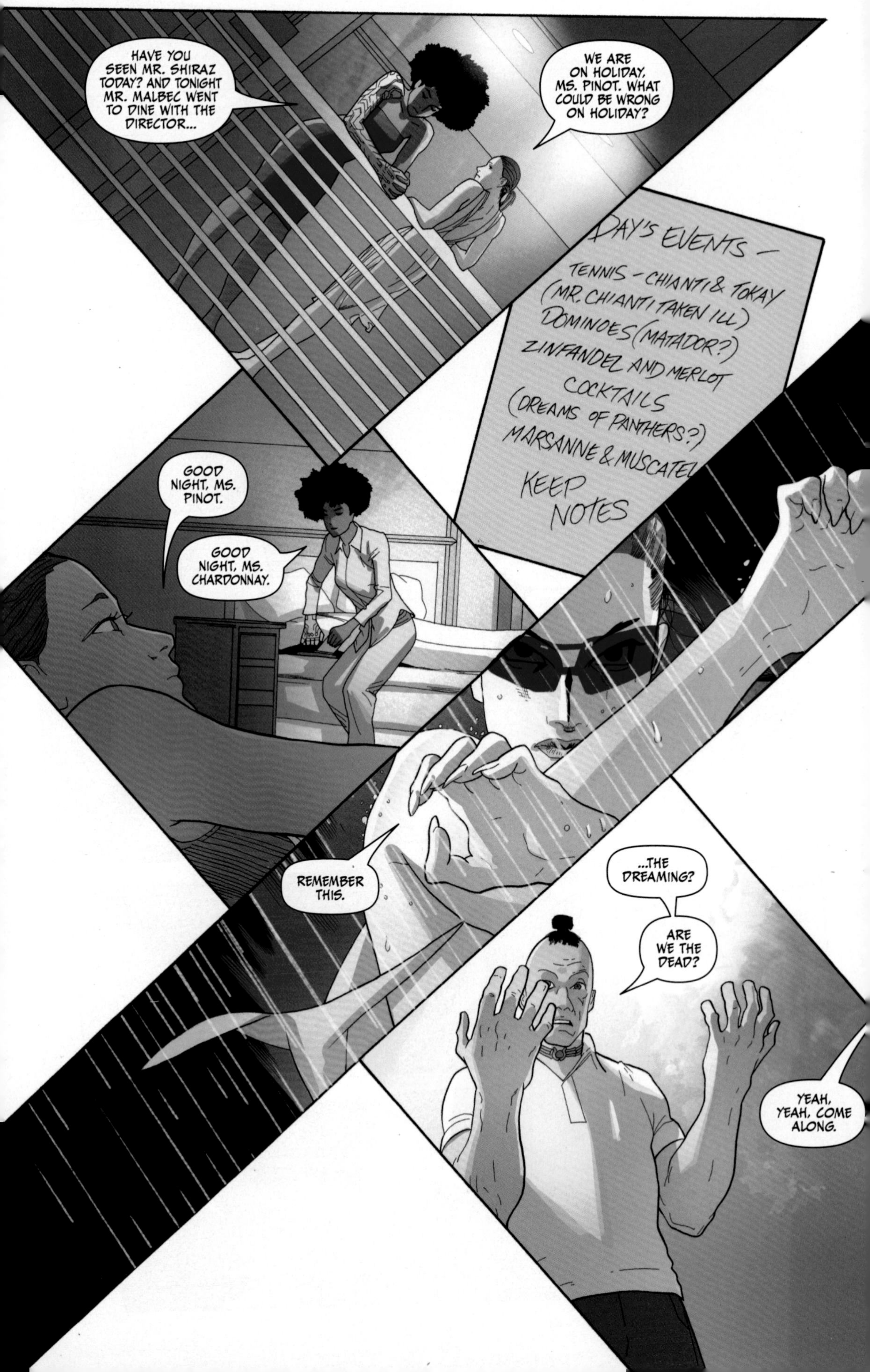
HAVE YOU SEEN MR. SHIRAZ TODAY? AND TONIGHT MR. MALBEC WENT TO DINE WITH THE DIRECTOR...
WE ARE ON HOLIDAY, MS. PINOT. WHAT COULD BE WRONG ON HOLIDAY?
DAY'S EVENTS -
TENNIS - CHIANTI & TOKAY (MR. CHIANTI TAKEN ILL)
DOMINOES (MATADOR?)
ZINFANDEL AND MERLOT COCKTAILS (DREAMS OF PANTHERS?)
MARSANNE & MUSCATEL
KEEP NOTES
GOOD NIGHT, MS. PINOT.
GOOD NIGHT, MS. CHARDONNAY.
REMEMBER THIS.
...THE DREAMING?
ARE WE THE DEAD?
YEAH, YEAH, COME ALONG.

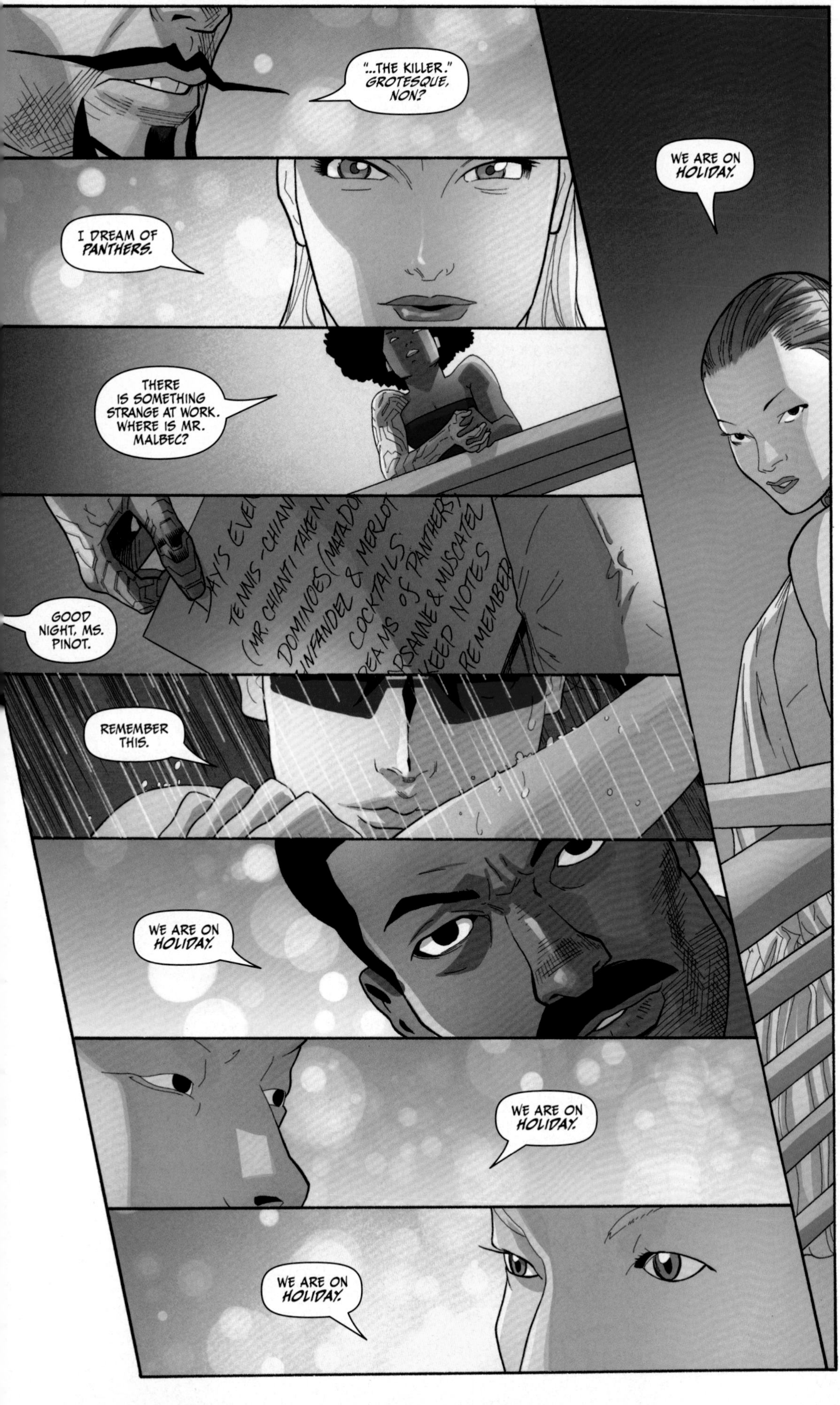
"...THE KILLER." GROTESQUE, NON?
WE ARE ON HOLIDAY.
I DREAM OF PANTHERS.
THERE IS SOMETHING STRANGE AT WORK. WHERE IS MR. MALBEC?
TENNIS
MR. CHIANTI TAKEN
DOMINOES
ZINFANDEL & MERLOT
COCKTAILS
OF PANTHERS
& MUSCATEL
KEEP NOTES
REMEMBER
GOOD NIGHT, MS. PINOT.
REMEMBER THIS.
WE ARE ON HOLIDAY.
WE ARE ON HOLIDAY.
WE ARE ON HOLIDAY.

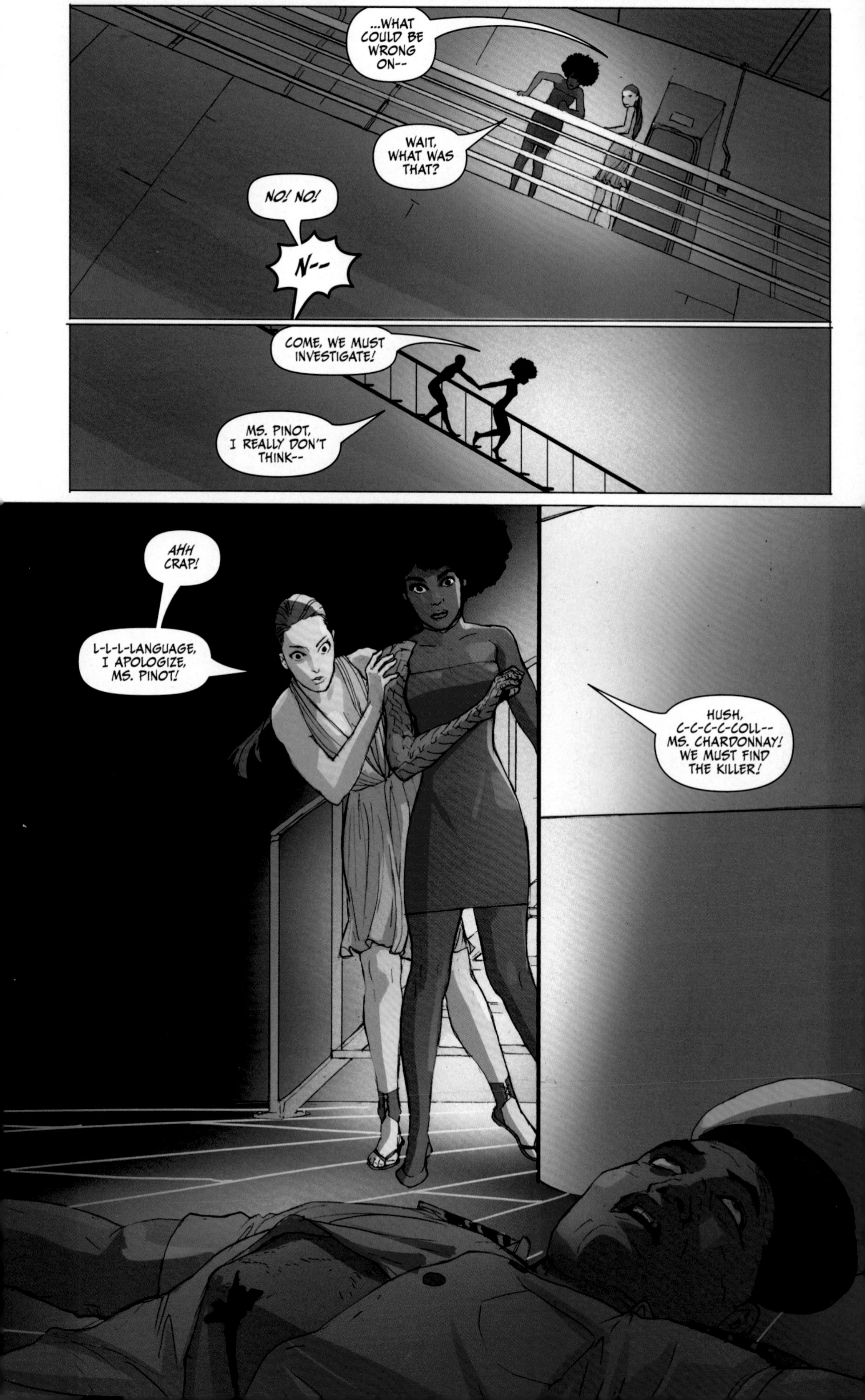
...WHAT COULD BE WRONG ON--
WAIT, WHAT WAS THAT?
NO! NO!
N--
COME, WE MUST INVESTIGATE!
MS. PINOT, I REALLY DON'T THINK--
AHH CRAP!
L-L-L-LANGUAGE, I APOLOGIZE, MS. PINOT!
HUSH, C-C-C-C-COLL-- MS. CHARDONNAY! WE MUST FIND THE KILLER!

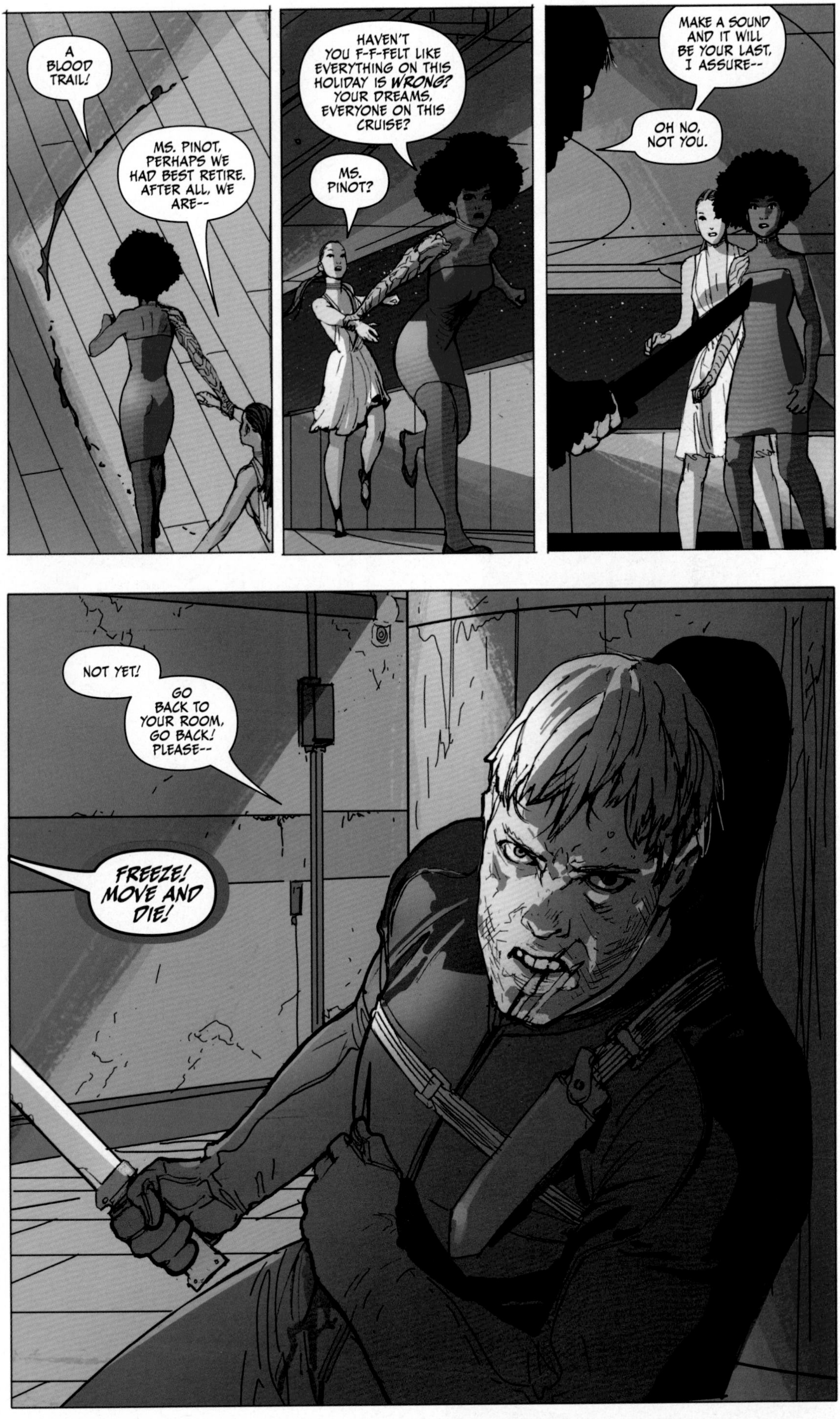
A BLOOD TRAIL!
MS. PINOT, PERHAPS WE HAD BEST RETIRE. AFTER ALL, WE ARE--
HAVEN'T YOU F-F-FELT LIKE EVERYTHING ON THIS HOLIDAY IS WRONG? YOUR DREAMS, EVERYONE ON THIS CRUISE?
MS. PINOT?
MAKE A SOUND AND IT WILL BE YOUR LAST, I ASSURE--
OH NO, NOT YOU.
NOT YET!
GO BACK TO YOUR ROOM, GO BACK! PLEASE--
FREEZE! MOVE AND DIE!

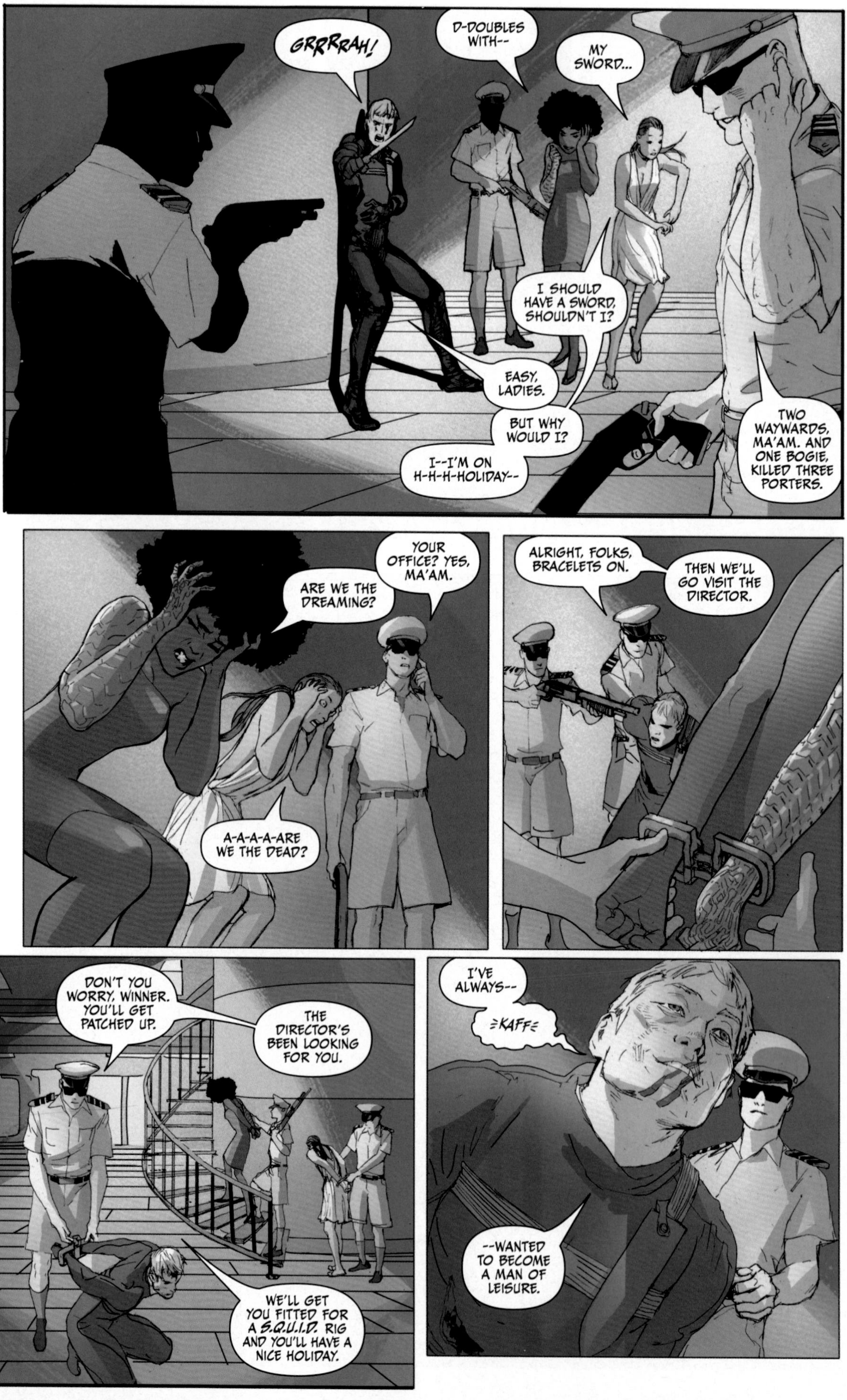

GRRRRAH!
D-DOUBLES WITH--
MY SWORD...
I SHOULD HAVE A SWORD, SHOULDN'T I?
EASY, LADIES.
BUT WHY WOULD I?
I--I'M ON H-H-H-HOLIDAY--
TWO WAYWARDS, MA'AM. AND ONE BOGIE. KILLED THREE PORTERS.
ARE WE THE DREAMING?
YOUR OFFICE? YES, MA'AM.
A-A-A-A-ARE WE THE DEAD?
ALRIGHT, FOLKS, BRACELETS ON.
THEN WE'LL GO VISIT THE DIRECTOR.
DON'T YOU WORRY, WINNER. YOU'LL GET PATCHED UP.
THE DIRECTOR'S BEEN LOOKING FOR YOU.
WE'LL GET YOU FITTED FOR A S.Q.U.I.D. RIG AND YOU'LL HAVE A NICE HOLIDAY.
I'VE ALWAYS--
KAFF
--WANTED TO BECOME A MAN OF LEISURE.

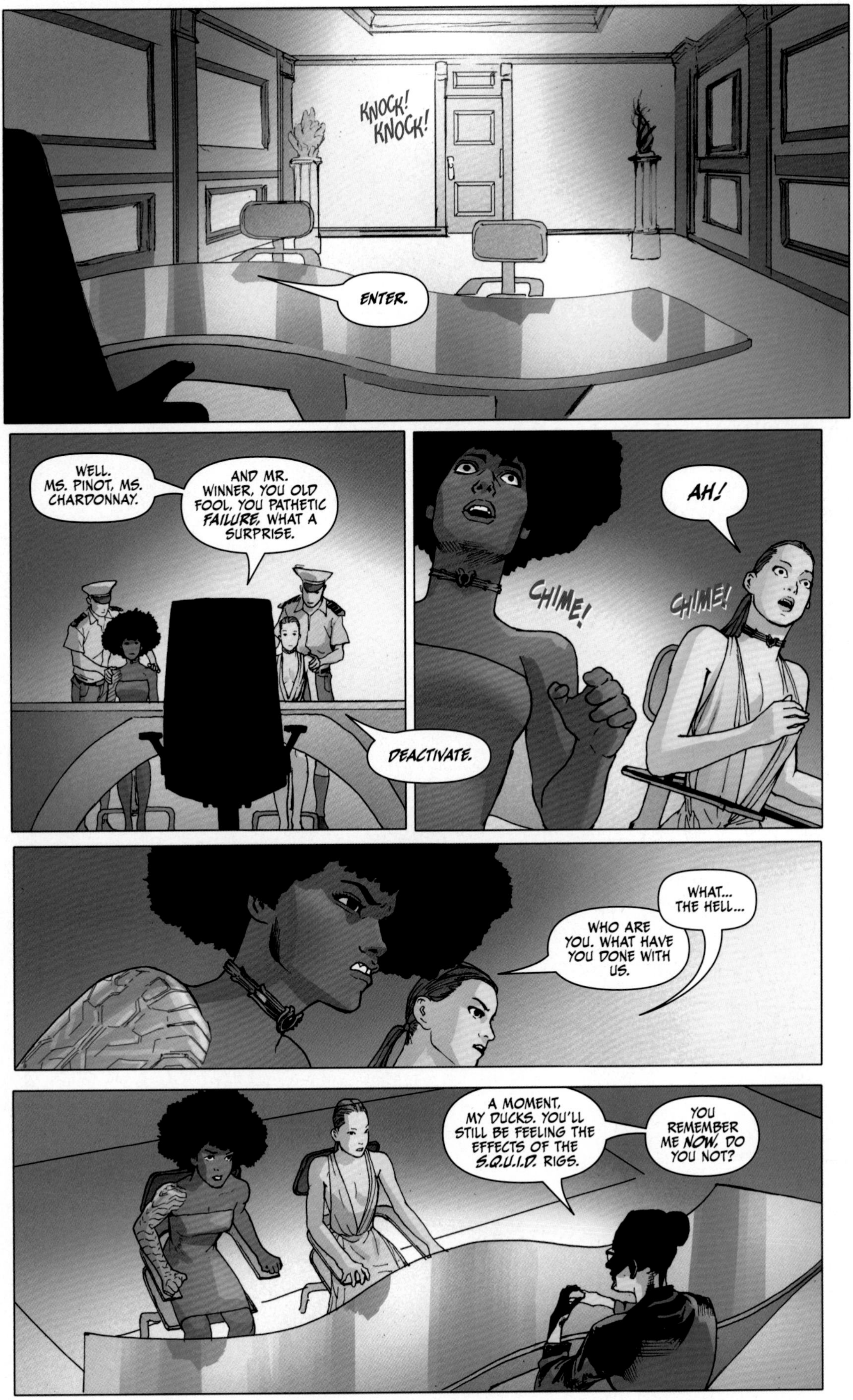
KNOCK! KNOCK!
ENTER.
WELL. MS. PINOT, MS. CHARDONNAY.
AND MR. WINNER, YOU OLD FOOL, YOU PATHETIC FAILURE, WHAT A SURPRISE.
DEACTIVATE.
AH!
CHIME!
CHIME!
WHAT... THE HELL...
WHO ARE YOU. WHAT HAVE YOU DONE WITH US.
A MOMENT, MY DUCKS. YOU'LL STILL BE FEELING THE EFFECTS OF THE S.Q.U.I.D. RIGS.
YOU REMEMBER ME NOW, DO YOU NOT?

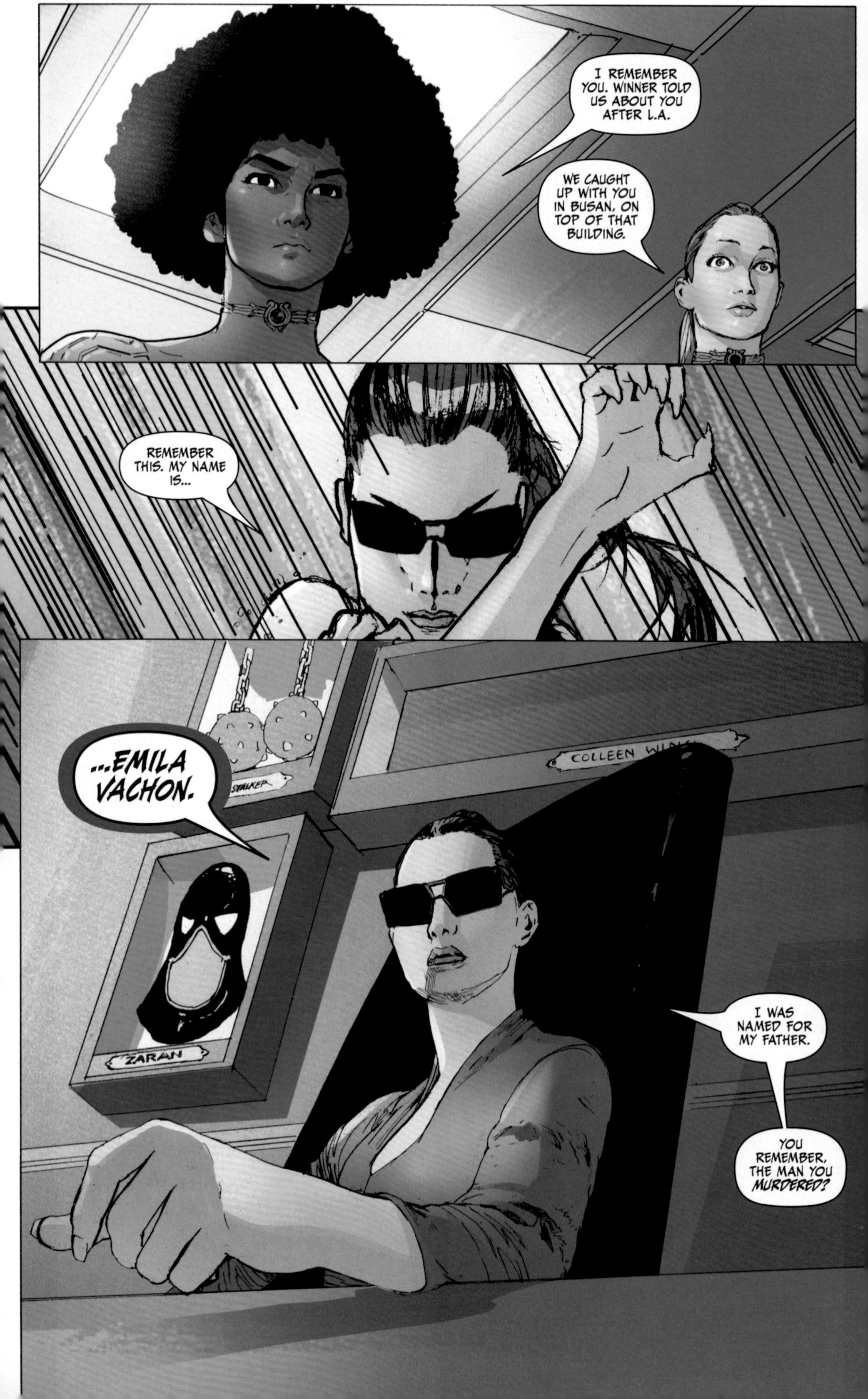
I REMEMBER YOU. WINNER TOLD US ABOUT YOU AFTER L.A.
WE CAUGHT UP WITH YOU IN BUSAN, ON TOP OF THAT BUILDING.
REMEMBER THIS. MY NAME IS...
...EMILA VACHON.
STALKER
ZARAN
I WAS NAMED FOR MY FATHER.
YOU REMEMBER, THE MAN YOU *MURDERED?*

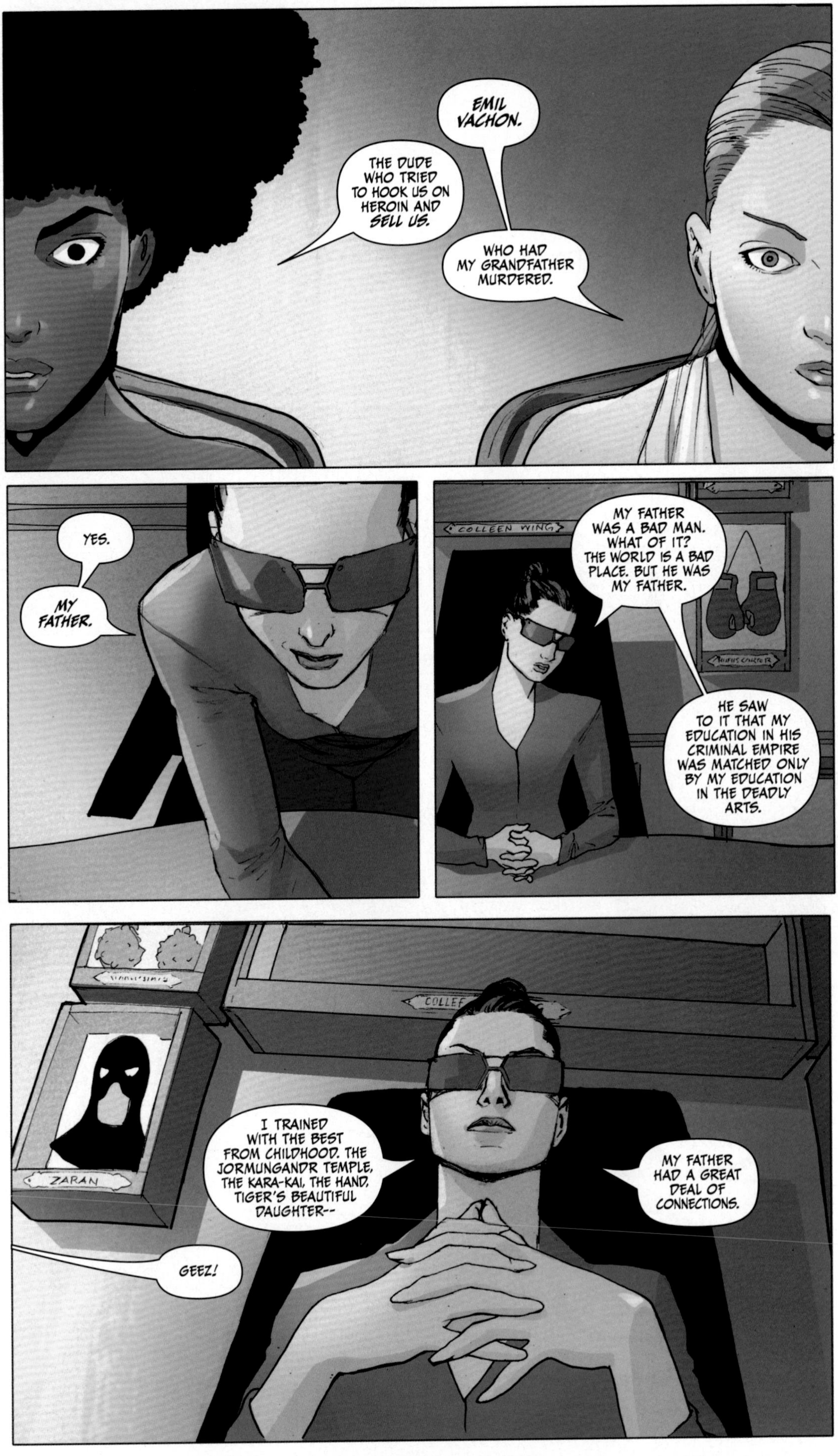
THE DUDE WHO TRIED TO HOOK US ON HEROIN AND SELL US.
EMIL VACHON.
WHO HAD MY GRANDFATHER MURDERED.
YES.
MY FATHER.
COLLEEN WING
MY FATHER WAS A BAD MAN. WHAT OF IT? THE WORLD IS A BAD PLACE. BUT HE WAS MY FATHER.
HE SAW TO IT THAT MY EDUCATION IN HIS CRIMINAL EMPIRE WAS MATCHED ONLY BY MY EDUCATION IN THE DEADLY ARTS.
ZARAN
I TRAINED WITH THE BEST FROM CHILDHOOD. THE JORMUNGANDR TEMPLE, THE KARA-KAI, THE HAND, TIGER'S BEAUTIFUL DAUGHTER--
MY FATHER HAD A GREAT DEAL OF CONNECTIONS.
GEEZ!

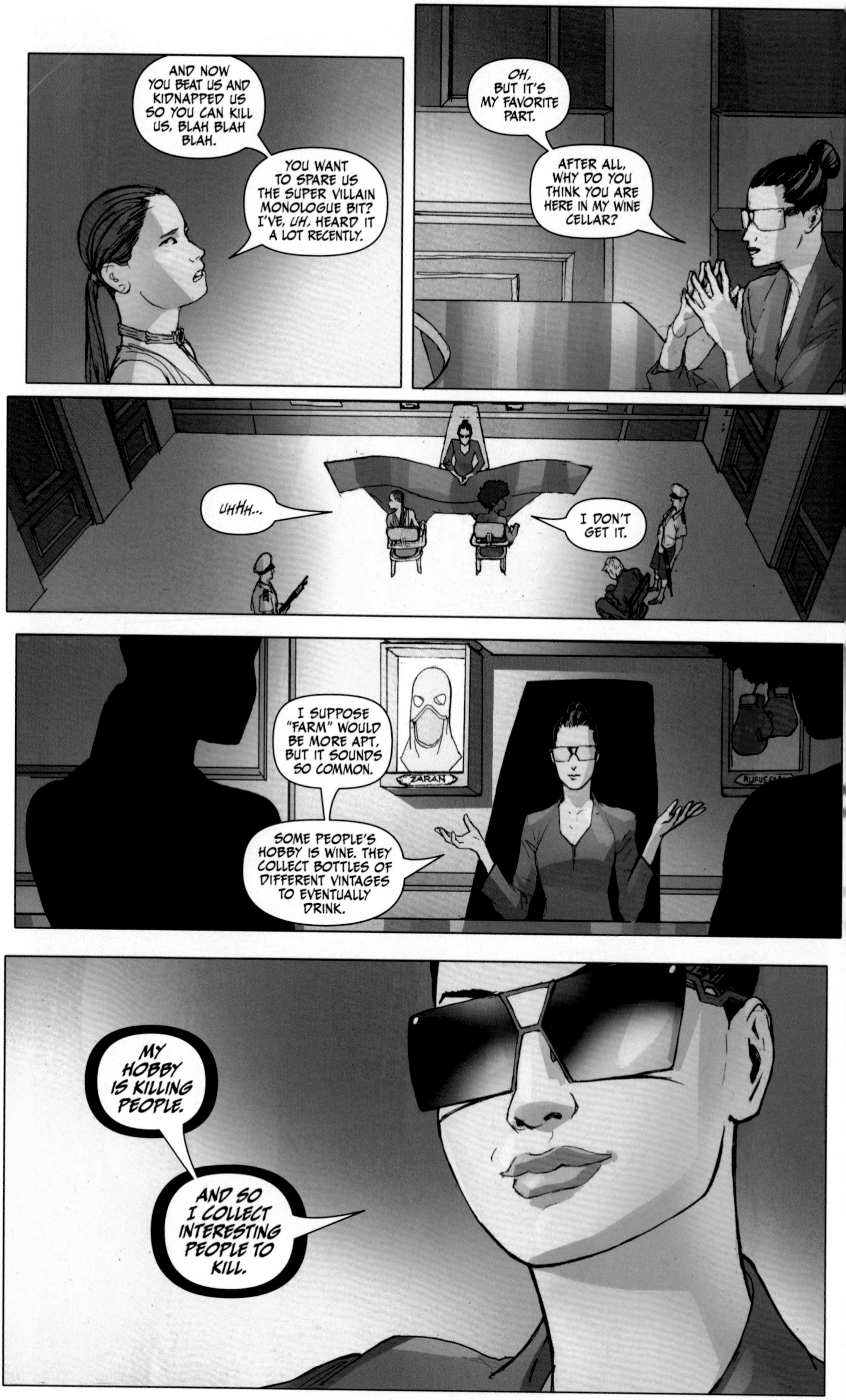
AND NOW YOU BEAT US AND KIDNAPPED US SO YOU CAN KILL US, BLAH BLAH BLAH.
YOU WANT TO SPARE US THE SUPER VILLAIN MONOLOGUE BIT? I'VE, *UH,* HEARD IT A LOT RECENTLY.
OH, BUT IT'S MY FAVORITE PART.
AFTER ALL, WHY DO YOU THINK YOU ARE HERE IN MY WINE CELLAR?
UHHH...
I DON'T GET IT.
I SUPPOSE "FARM" WOULD BE MORE APT, BUT IT SOUNDS SO COMMON.
ZARAN
SOME PEOPLE'S HOBBY IS WINE. THEY COLLECT BOTTLES OF DIFFERENT VINTAGES TO EVENTUALLY DRINK.
MY HOBBY IS KILLING PEOPLE.
AND SO I COLLECT INTERESTING PEOPLE TO KILL.

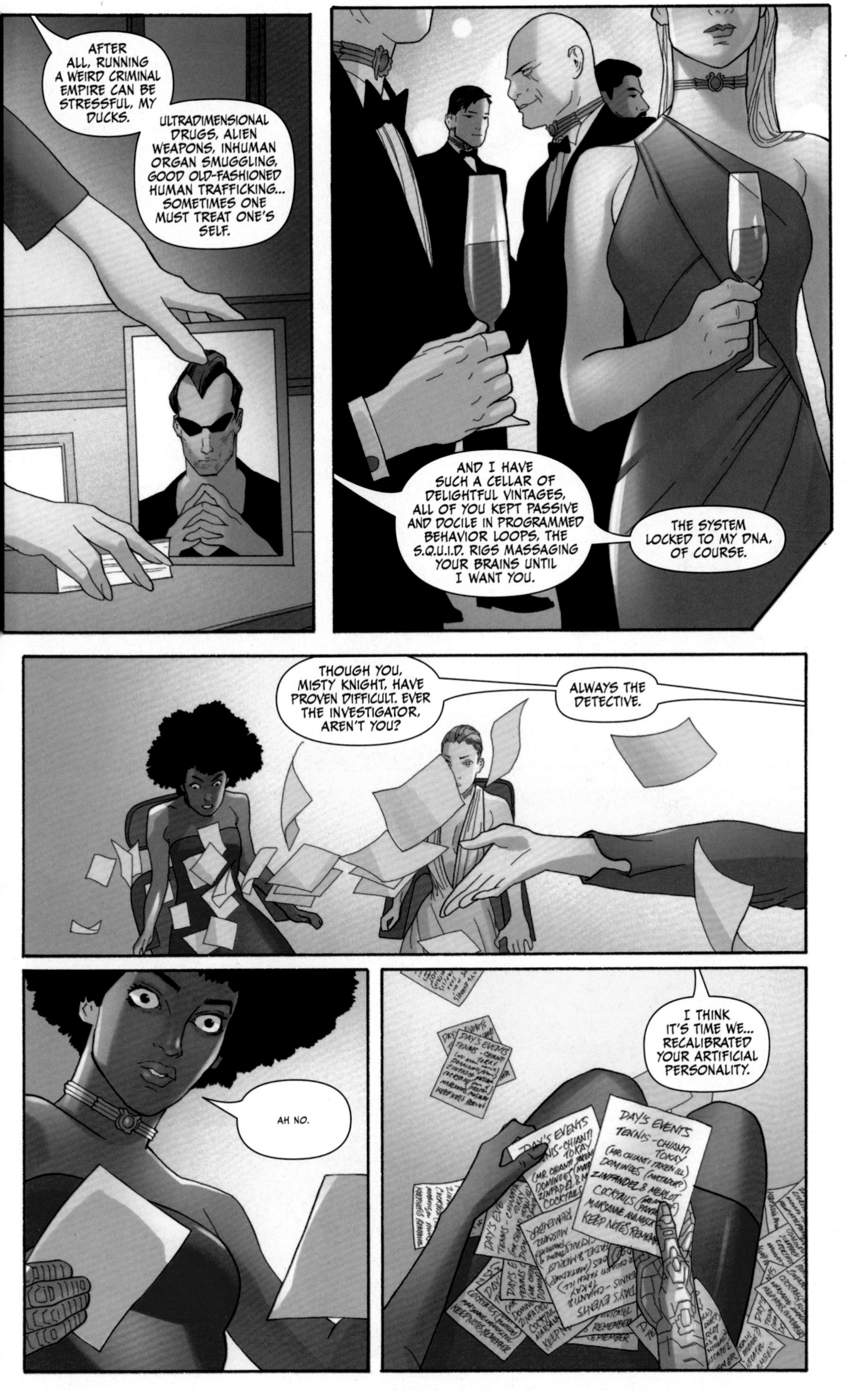

AFTER ALL, RUNNING A WEIRD CRIMINAL EMPIRE CAN BE STRESSFUL, MY DUCKS.
ULTRADIMENSIONAL DRUGS, ALIEN WEAPONS, INHUMAN ORGAN SMUGGLING, GOOD OLD-FASHIONED HUMAN TRAFFICKING... SOMETIMES ONE MUST TREAT ONE'S SELF.
AND I HAVE SUCH A CELLAR OF DELIGHTFUL VINTAGES, ALL OF YOU KEPT PASSIVE AND DOCILE IN PROGRAMMED BEHAVIOR LOOPS, THE S.Q.U.I.D. RIGS MASSAGING YOUR BRAINS UNTIL I WANT YOU.
THE SYSTEM LOCKED TO MY DNA, OF COURSE.
THOUGH YOU, MISTY KNIGHT, HAVE PROVEN DIFFICULT. EVER THE INVESTIGATOR, AREN'T YOU?
ALWAYS THE DETECTIVE.
AH NO.
I THINK IT'S TIME WE... RECALIBRATED YOUR ARTIFICIAL PERSONALITY.

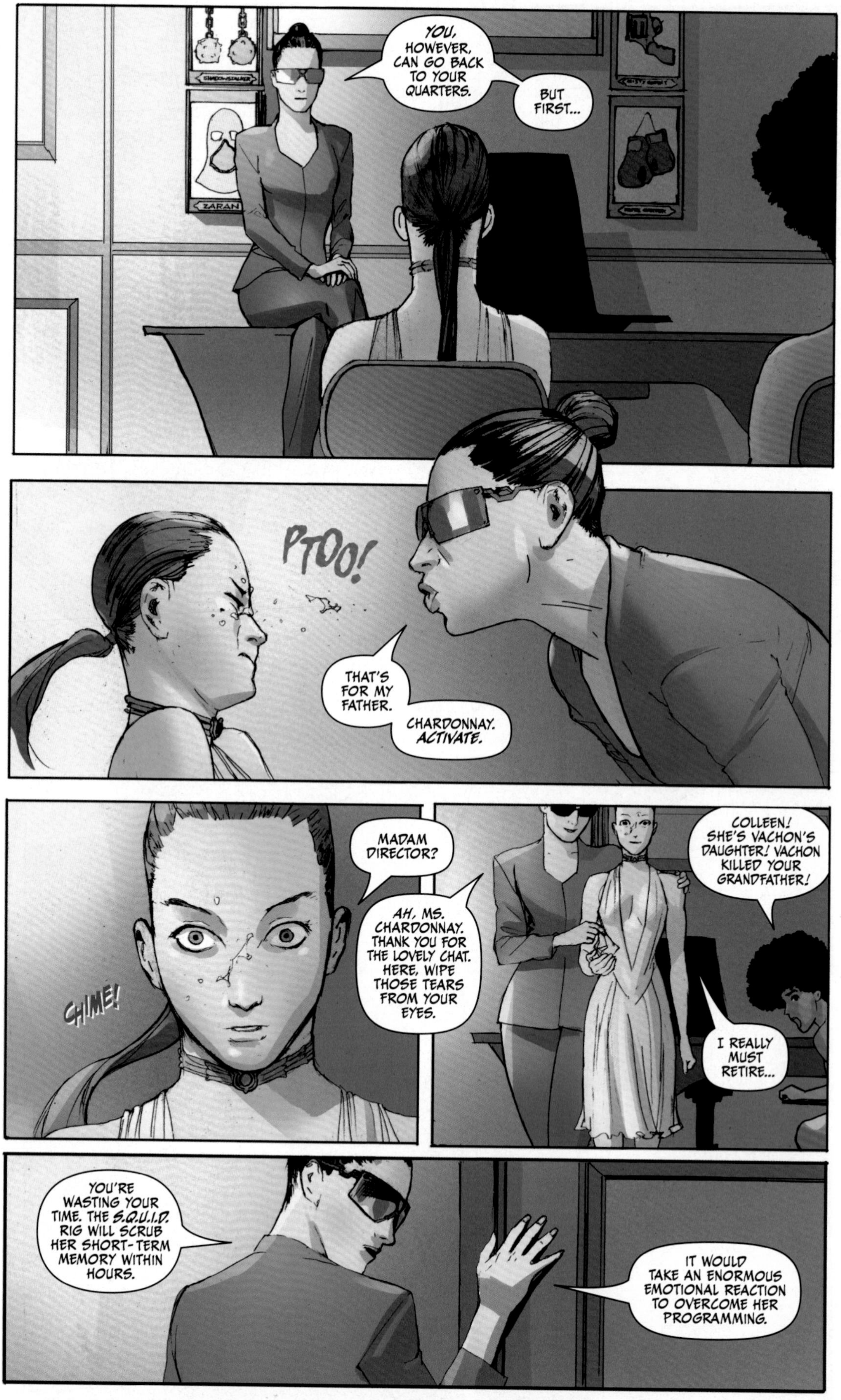

ZARAN
YOU, HOWEVER, CAN GO BACK TO YOUR QUARTERS.
BUT FIRST...
PTOO!
THAT'S FOR MY FATHER.
CHARDONNAY. ACTIVATE.
CHIME!
MADAM DIRECTOR?
AH, MS. CHARDONNAY. THANK YOU FOR THE LOVELY CHAT. HERE, WIPE THOSE TEARS FROM YOUR EYES.
COLLEEN! SHE'S VACHON'S DAUGHTER! VACHON KILLED YOUR GRANDFATHER!
I REALLY MUST RETIRE...
YOU'RE WASTING YOUR TIME. THE S.Q.U.I.D. RIG WILL SCRUB HER SHORT-TERM MEMORY WITHIN HOURS.
IT WOULD TAKE AN ENORMOUS EMOTIONAL REACTION TO OVERCOME HER PROGRAMMING.

"TOMORROW, MS. CHARDONNAY WILL WAKE FOR HER GAME OF DOUBLES WITH MR. CHIANTI AND MR. TOKAY, WITH NO MEMORY OF ANY OF THIS."

AND ONCE I HAVE YOUR ARTIFICIAL PERSONALITY ADJUSTED, YOU WILL JOIN HER. YOU, WINNER, WILL MAKE A FINE ADDITION.

PERHAPS I'LL CALL YOU MR. BORDEAUX.

WINNER? ARE YOU STILL WITH US?

...I'VE PLANTED A BOMB...

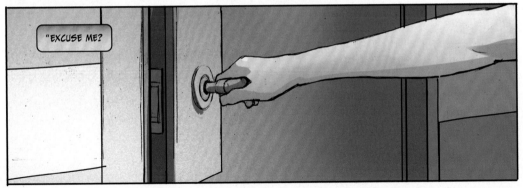

"EXCUSE ME?"

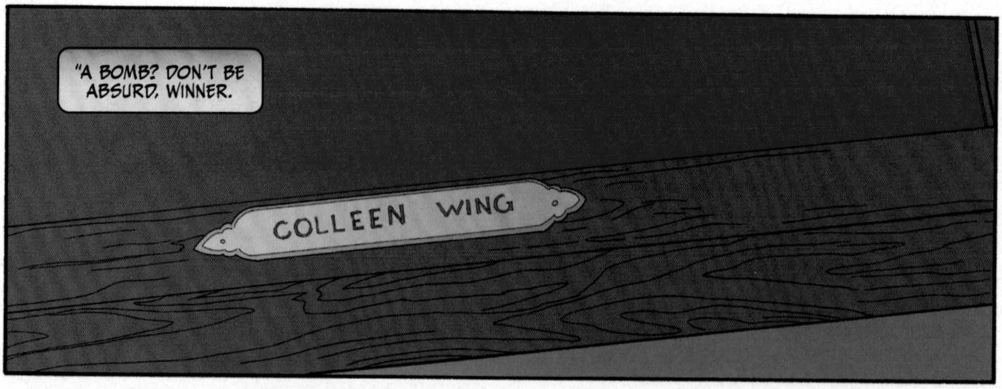
"A BOMB? DON'T BE ABSURD, WINNER.
COLLEEN WING

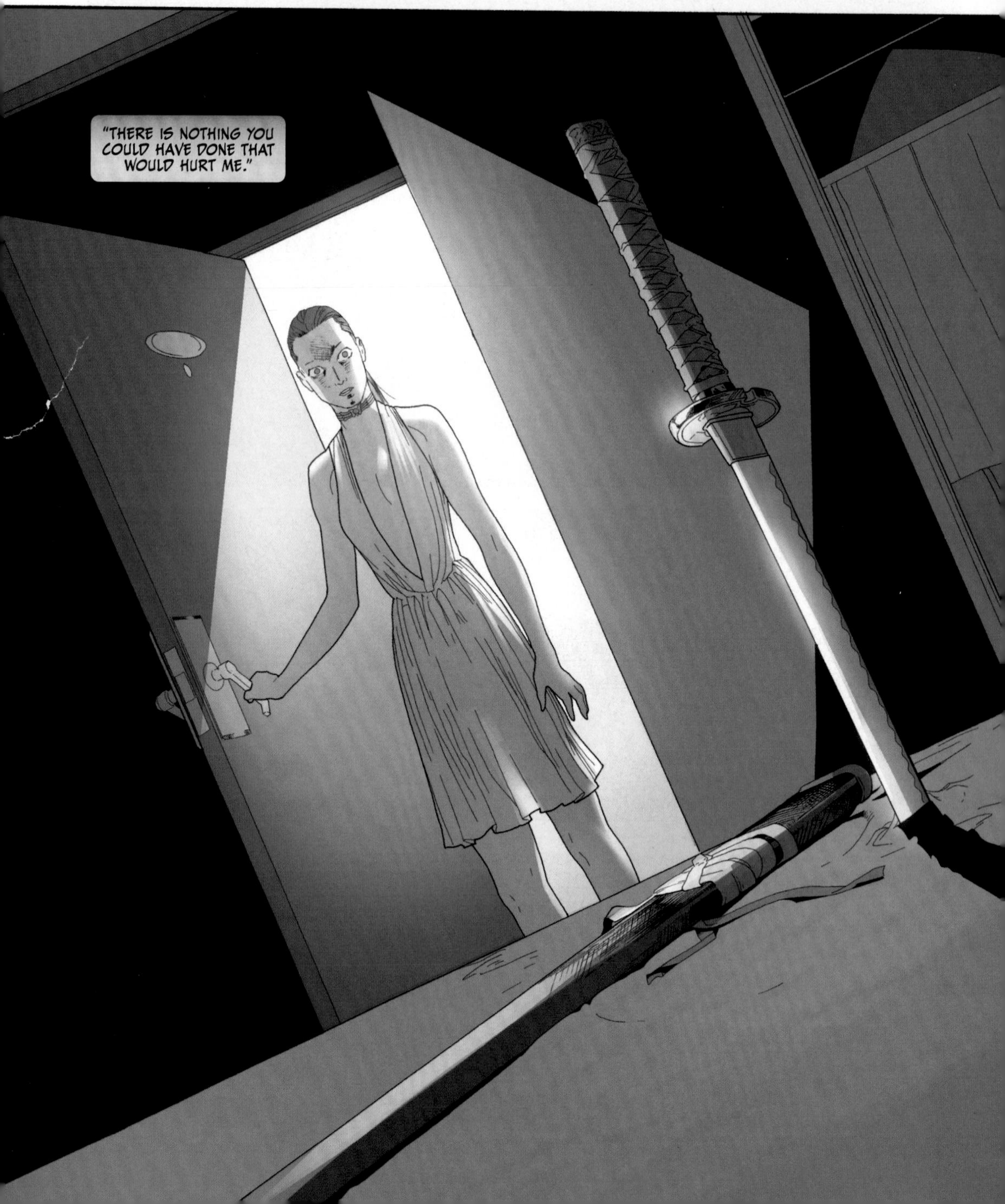
"THERE IS NOTHING YOU COULD HAVE DONE THAT WOULD HURT ME."

CHAPTER
6

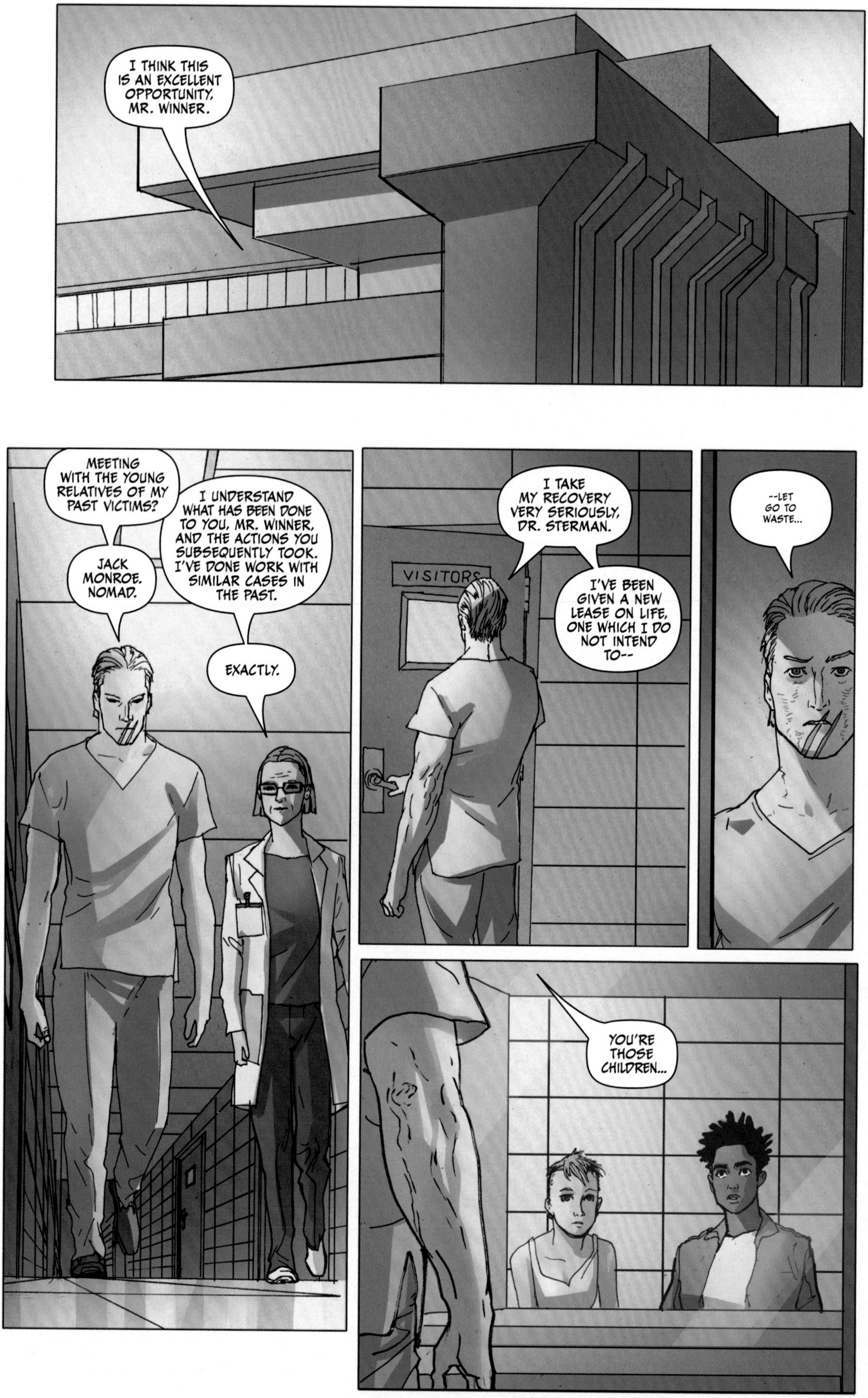
I THINK THIS IS AN EXCELLENT OPPORTUNITY, MR. WINNER.
MEETING WITH THE YOUNG RELATIVES OF MY PAST VICTIMS?
JACK MONROE. NOMAD.
I UNDERSTAND WHAT HAS BEEN DONE TO YOU, MR. WINNER, AND THE ACTIONS YOU SUBSEQUENTLY TOOK. I'VE DONE WORK WITH SIMILAR CASES IN THE PAST.
EXACTLY.
VISITORS
I TAKE MY RECOVERY VERY SERIOUSLY, DR. STERMAN.
I'VE BEEN GIVEN A NEW LEASE ON LIFE, ONE WHICH I DO NOT INTEND TO--
--LET GO TO WASTE...
YOU'RE THOSE CHILDREN...

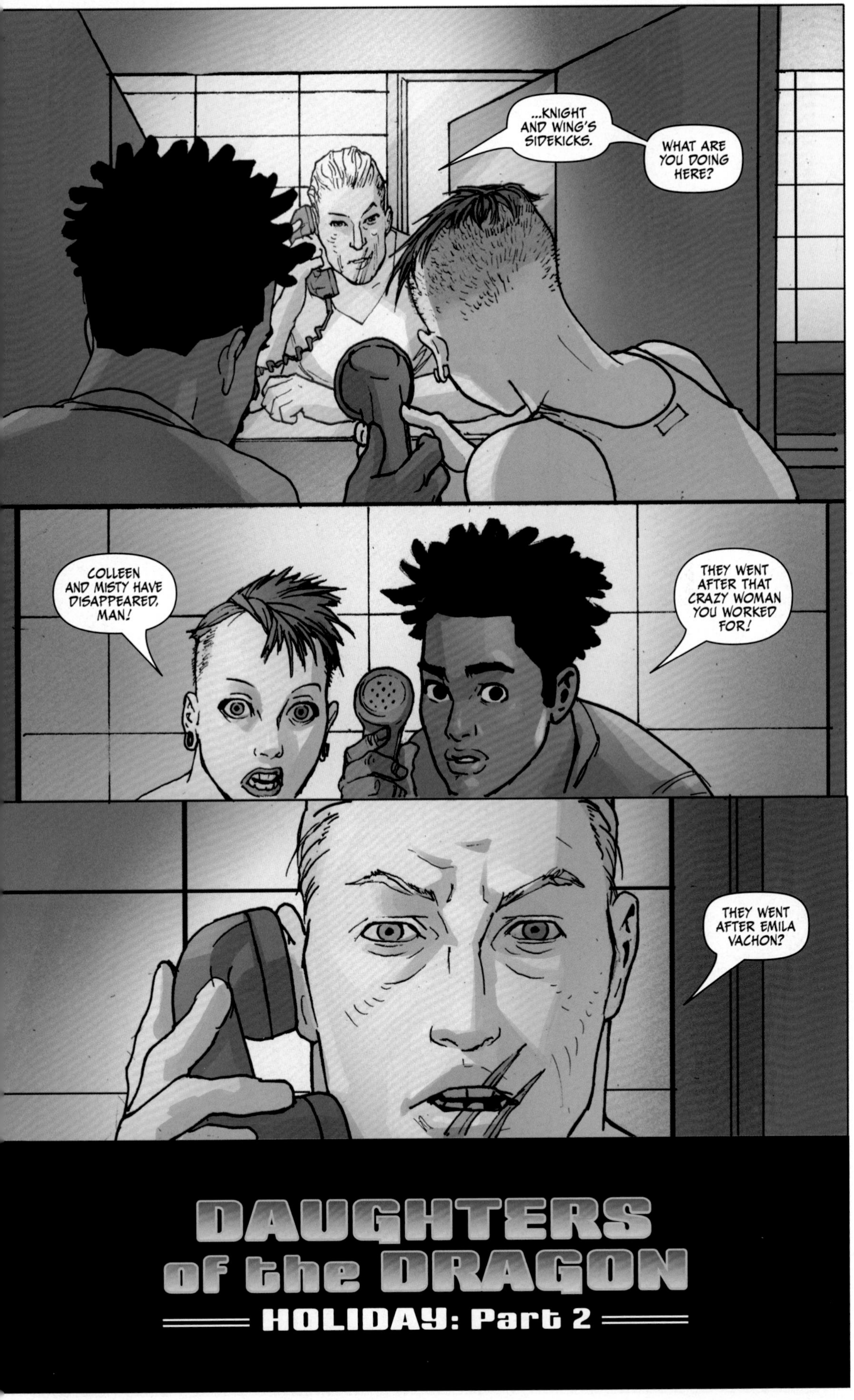
...KNIGHT AND WING'S SIDEKICKS.
WHAT ARE YOU DOING HERE?
COLLEEN AND MISTY HAVE DISAPPEARED, MAN!
THEY WENT AFTER THAT CRAZY WOMAN YOU WORKED FOR!
THEY WENT AFTER EMILA VACHON?

DAUGHTERS of the DRAGON

HOLIDAY: Part 2

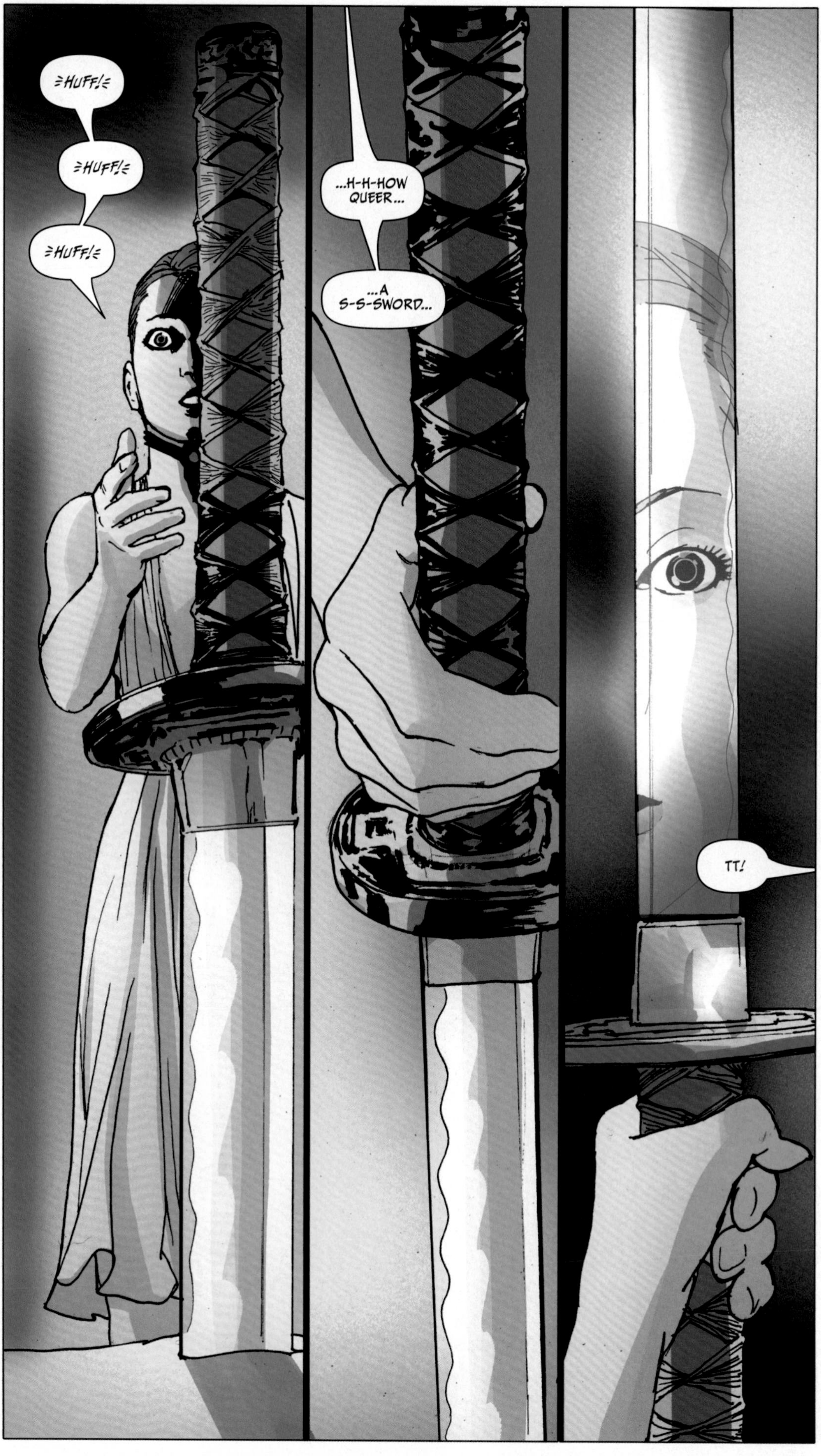

≡HUFF!≡
≡HUFF!≡
≡HUFF!≡
...H-H-HOW QUEER...
...A S-S-SWORD...
TT!

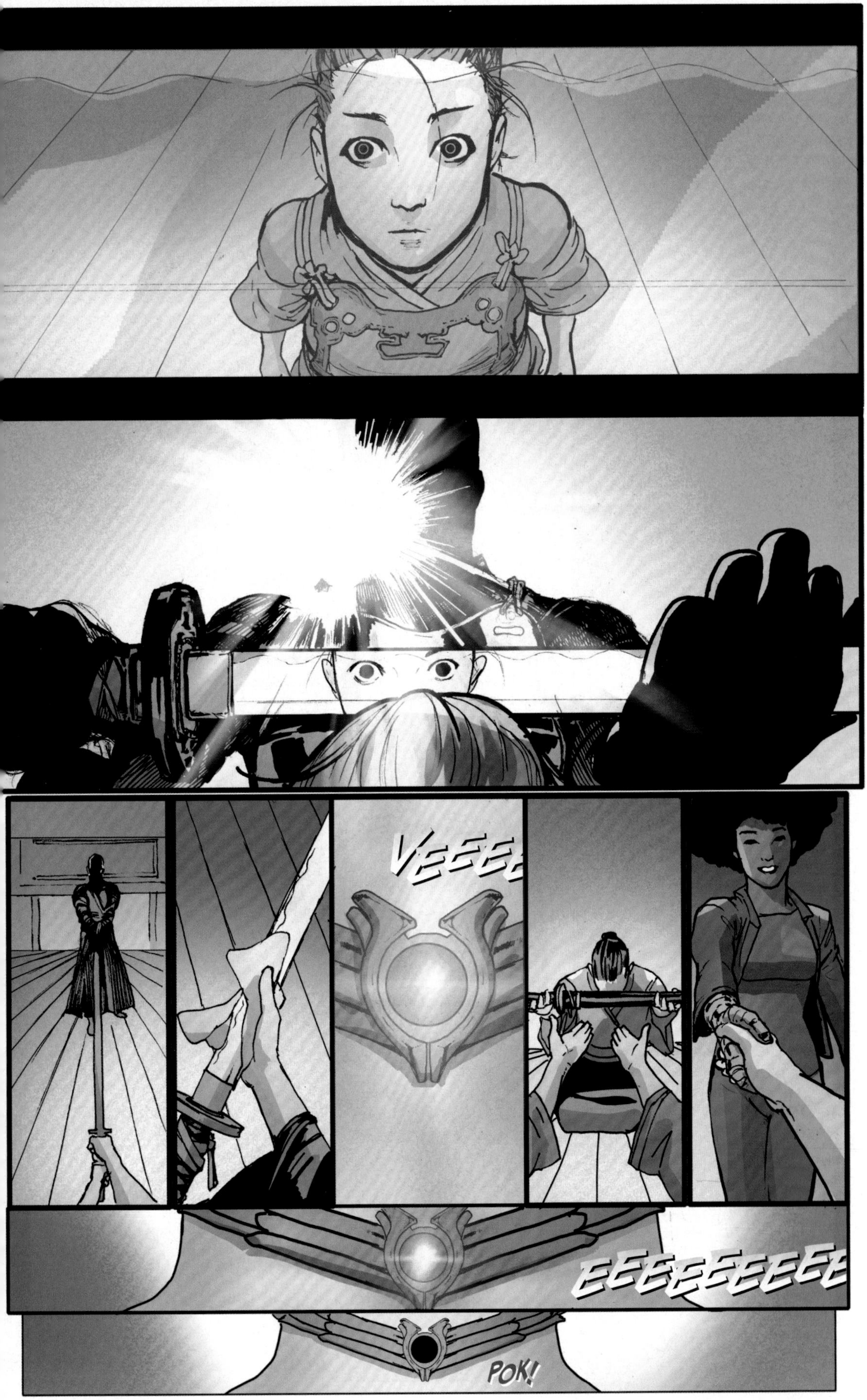
VEEEE
EEEEEEEEEE
POK!

...USING OLD PYGMALION TECHNOLOGY. THE SYNTHETIC PERSONAS, THE ELECTRO-QUANTUM INTERRUPTION OF THE BRAIN'S FUNCTIONS...

"IF YOU DO NOT CONTROL THE ENEMY, THE ENEMY WILL CONTROL YOU."

OH HEY, GIRL.

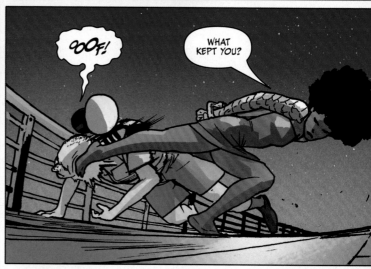

OOF!

WHAT KEPT YOU?

WHA--

TOOK A TRIP DOWN MEMORY LANE.

KUNK!

SCREW MS. PINOT AND MS. CHARDONNAY!

DAUGHTERS OF THE DRAGON ARE *BACK*, BABY!

YEAH... YOU WANT TO UNLOCK THESE CUFFS?

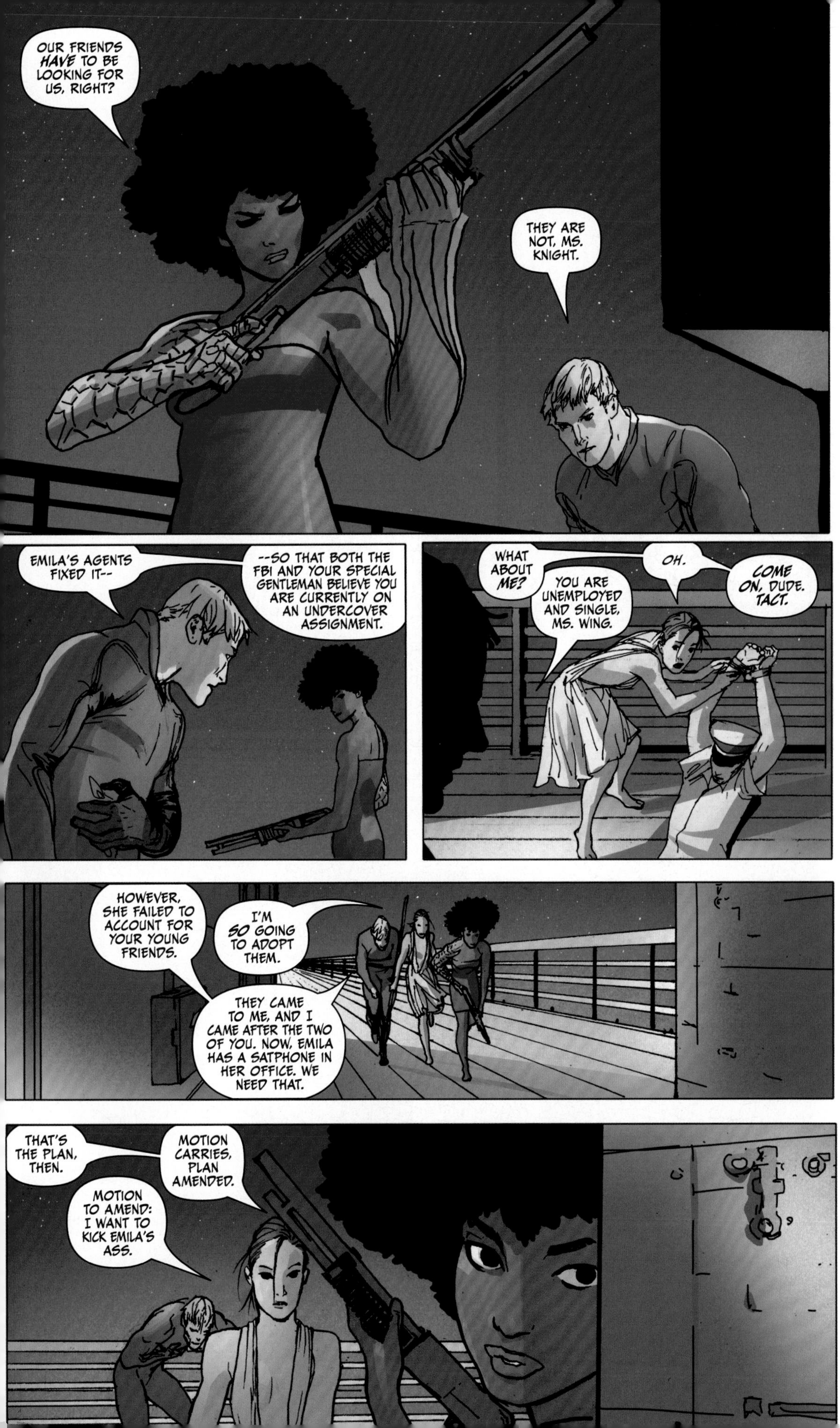
OUR FRIENDS HAVE TO BE LOOKING FOR US, RIGHT?
THEY ARE NOT, MS. KNIGHT.
EMILA'S AGENTS FIXED IT--
--SO THAT BOTH THE FBI AND YOUR SPECIAL GENTLEMAN BELIEVE YOU ARE CURRENTLY ON AN UNDERCOVER ASSIGNMENT.
WHAT ABOUT ME?
YOU ARE UNEMPLOYED AND SINGLE, MS. WING.
OH.
COME ON, DUDE. TACT.
HOWEVER, SHE FAILED TO ACCOUNT FOR YOUR YOUNG FRIENDS.
I'M SO GOING TO ADOPT THEM.
THEY CAME TO ME, AND I CAME AFTER THE TWO OF YOU. NOW, EMILA HAS A SATPHONE IN HER OFFICE. WE NEED THAT.
THAT'S THE PLAN, THEN.
MOTION TO AMEND: I WANT TO KICK EMILA'S ASS.
MOTION CARRIES, PLAN AMENDED.

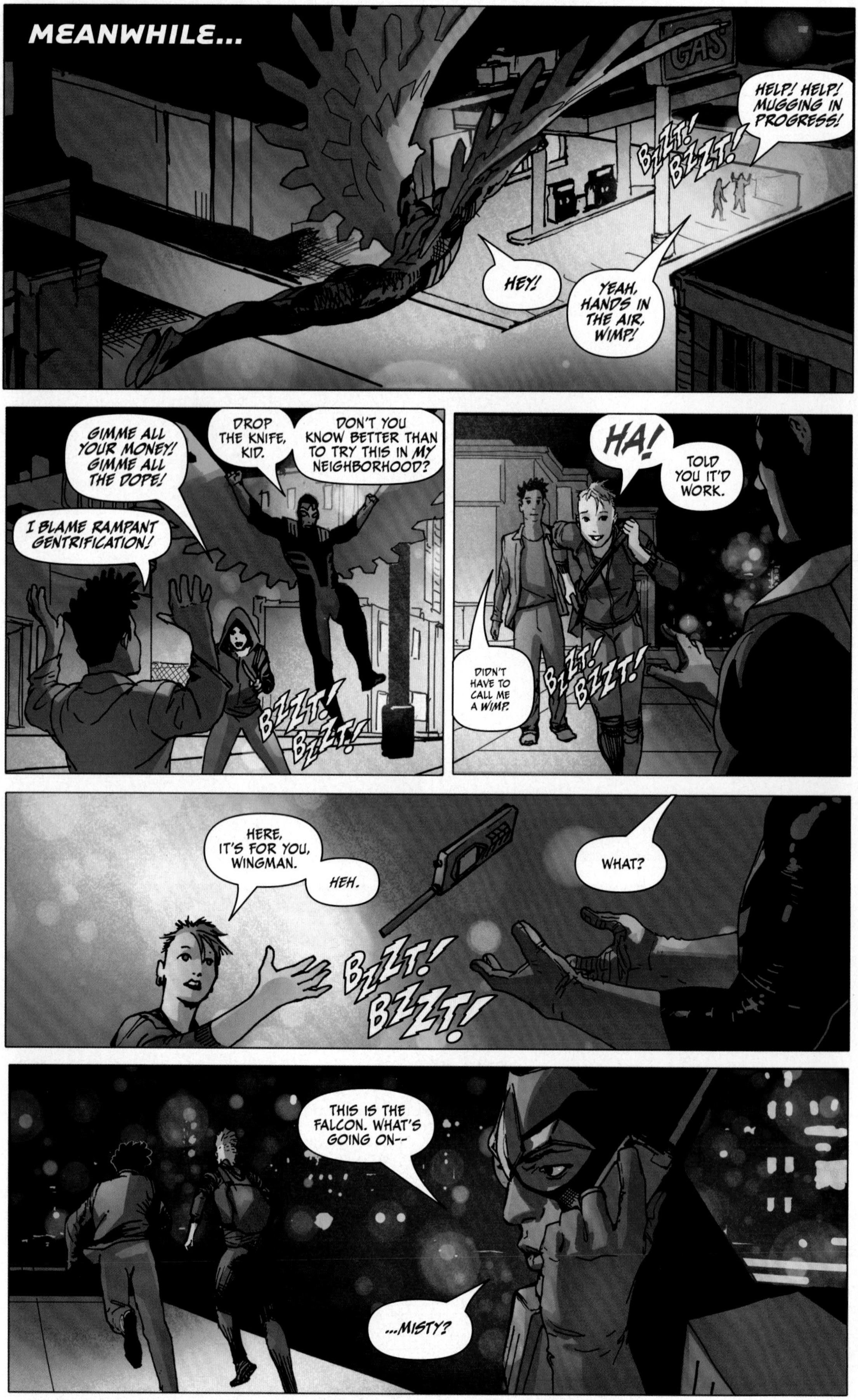
MEANWHILE...
HELP! HELP! MUGGING IN PROGRESS!
BZZT! BZZT!
HEY!
YEAH, HANDS IN THE AIR, WIMP!
GIMME ALL YOUR MONEY! GIMME ALL THE DOPE!
I BLAME RAMPANT GENTRIFICATION!
DROP THE KNIFE, KID.
DON'T YOU KNOW BETTER THAN TO TRY THIS IN MY NEIGHBORHOOD?
BZZT! BZZT!
HA!
TOLD YOU IT'D WORK.
DIDN'T HAVE TO CALL ME A WIMP.
BZZT! BZZT!
HERE, IT'S FOR YOU, WINGMAN.
HEH.
WHAT?
BZZT! BZZT!
THIS IS THE FALCON. WHAT'S GOING ON--
...MISTY?

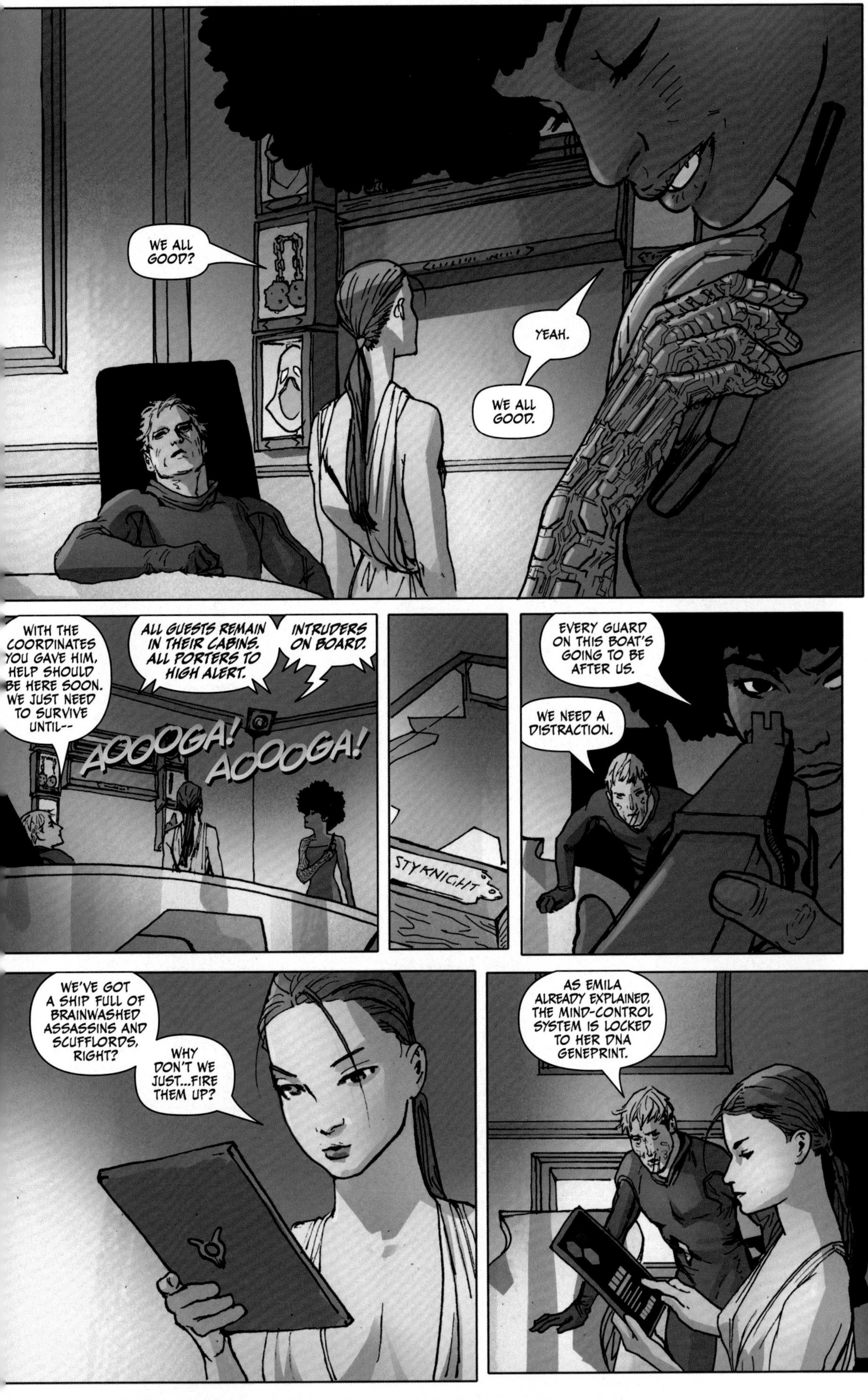
WE ALL GOOD?
YEAH.
WE ALL GOOD.
WITH THE COORDINATES YOU GAVE HIM, HELP SHOULD BE HERE SOON. WE JUST NEED TO SURVIVE UNTIL--
ALL GUESTS REMAIN IN THEIR CABINS. ALL PORTERS TO HIGH ALERT.
INTRUDERS ON BOARD.
AOOOGA! AOOOGA!
STYKNIGHT
EVERY GUARD ON THIS BOAT'S GOING TO BE AFTER US.
WE NEED A DISTRACTION.
WE'VE GOT A SHIP FULL OF BRAINWASHED ASSASSINS AND SCUFFLORDS, RIGHT?
WHY DON'T WE JUST...FIRE THEM UP?
AS EMILA ALREADY EXPLAINED, THE MIND-CONTROL SYSTEM IS LOCKED TO HER DNA GENEPRINT.

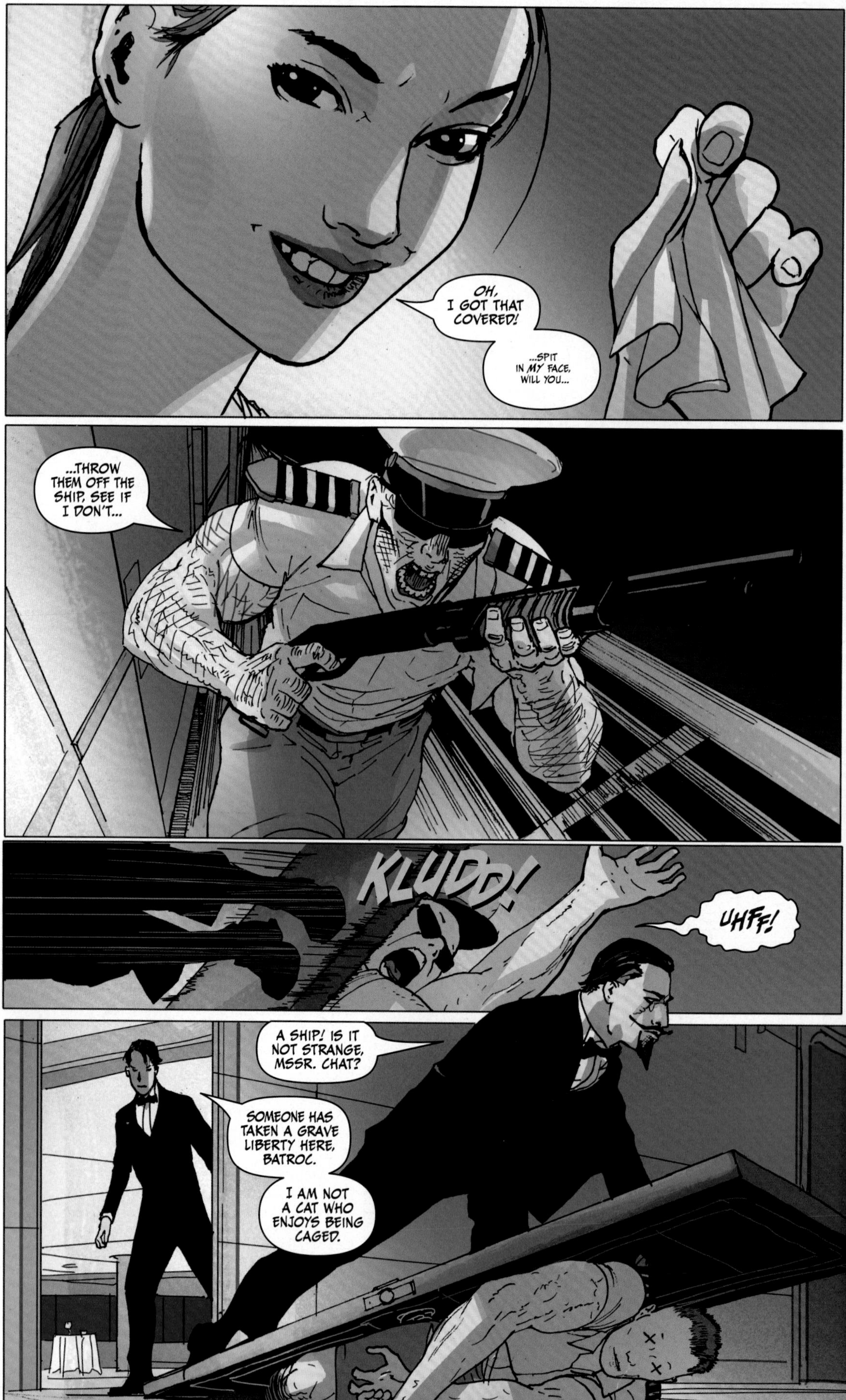
OH, I GOT THAT COVERED!
...SPIT IN MY FACE, WILL YOU...
...THROW THEM OFF THE SHIP. SEE IF I DON'T...
KLUDD!
UHFF!
A SHIP! IS IT NOT STRANGE, MSSR. CHAT?
SOMEONE HAS TAKEN A GRAVE LIBERTY HERE, BATROC.
I AM NOT A CAT WHO ENJOYS BEING CAGED.

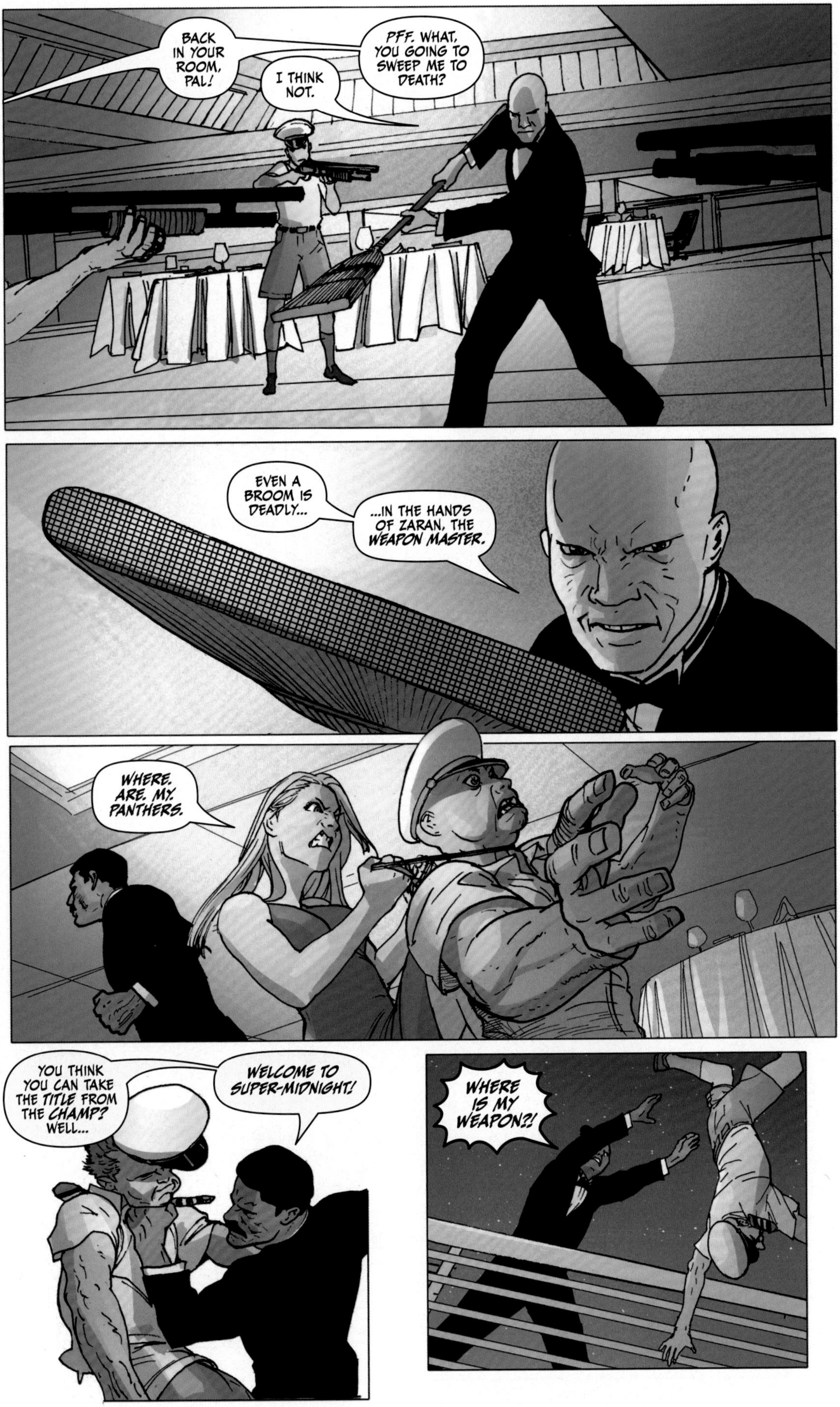
BACK IN YOUR ROOM, PAL!
I THINK NOT.
PFF. WHAT, YOU GOING TO SWEEP ME TO DEATH?
EVEN A BROOM IS DEADLY...
...IN THE HANDS OF ZARAN, THE WEAPON MASTER.
WHERE. ARE. MY. PANTHERS.
YOU THINK YOU CAN TAKE THE TITLE FROM THE CHAMP? WELL...
WELCOME TO SUPER-MIDNIGHT!
WHERE IS MY WEAPON?!

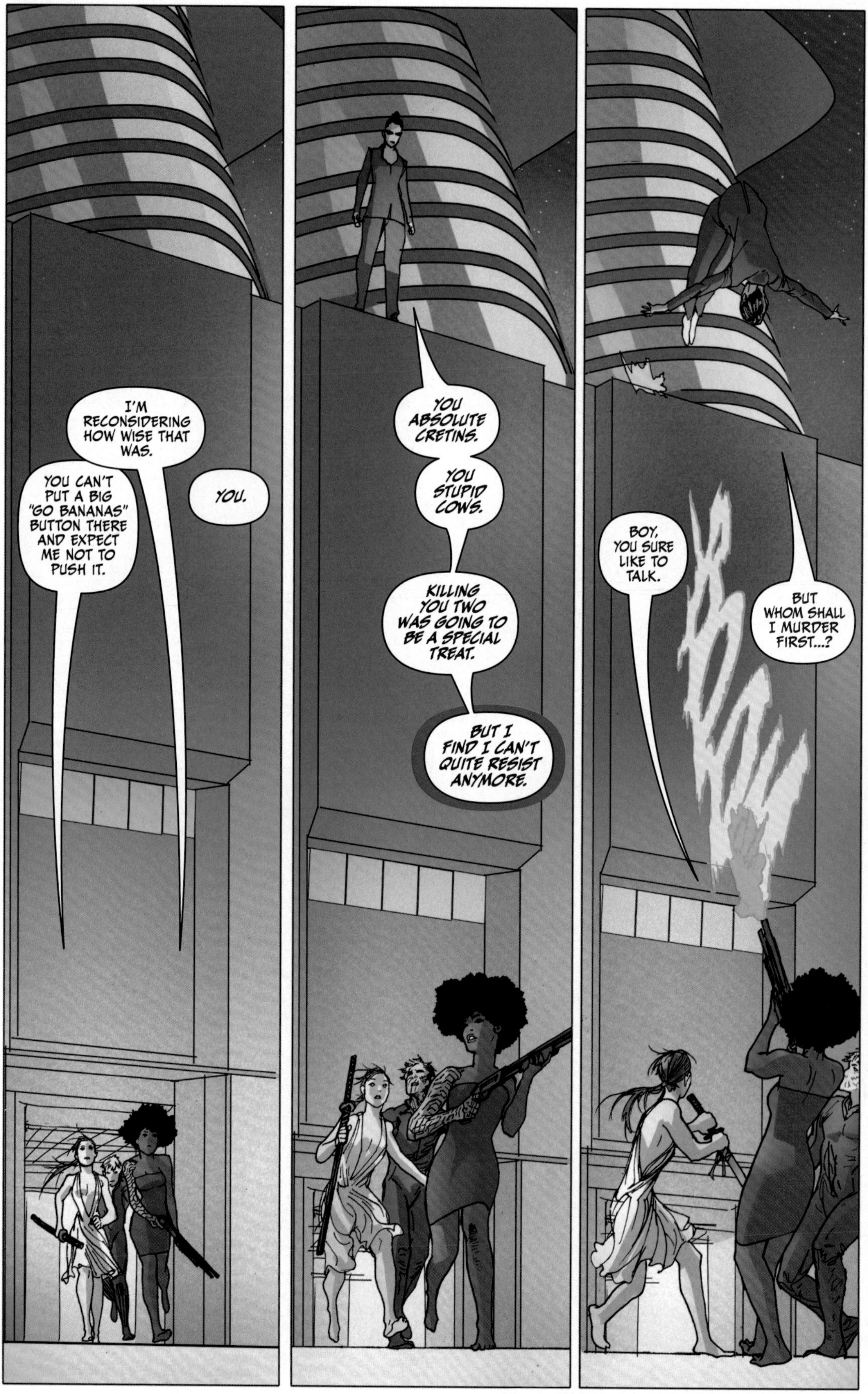
I'M RECONSIDERING HOW WISE THAT WAS.
YOU CAN'T PUT A BIG "GO BANANAS" BUTTON THERE AND EXPECT ME NOT TO PUSH IT.
YOU.
YOU ABSOLUTE CRETINS.
YOU STUPID COWS.
KILLING YOU TWO WAS GOING TO BE A SPECIAL TREAT.
BUT I FIND I CAN'T QUITE RESIST ANYMORE.
BOY, YOU SURE LIKE TO TALK.
BUT WHOM SHALL I MURDER FIRST...?

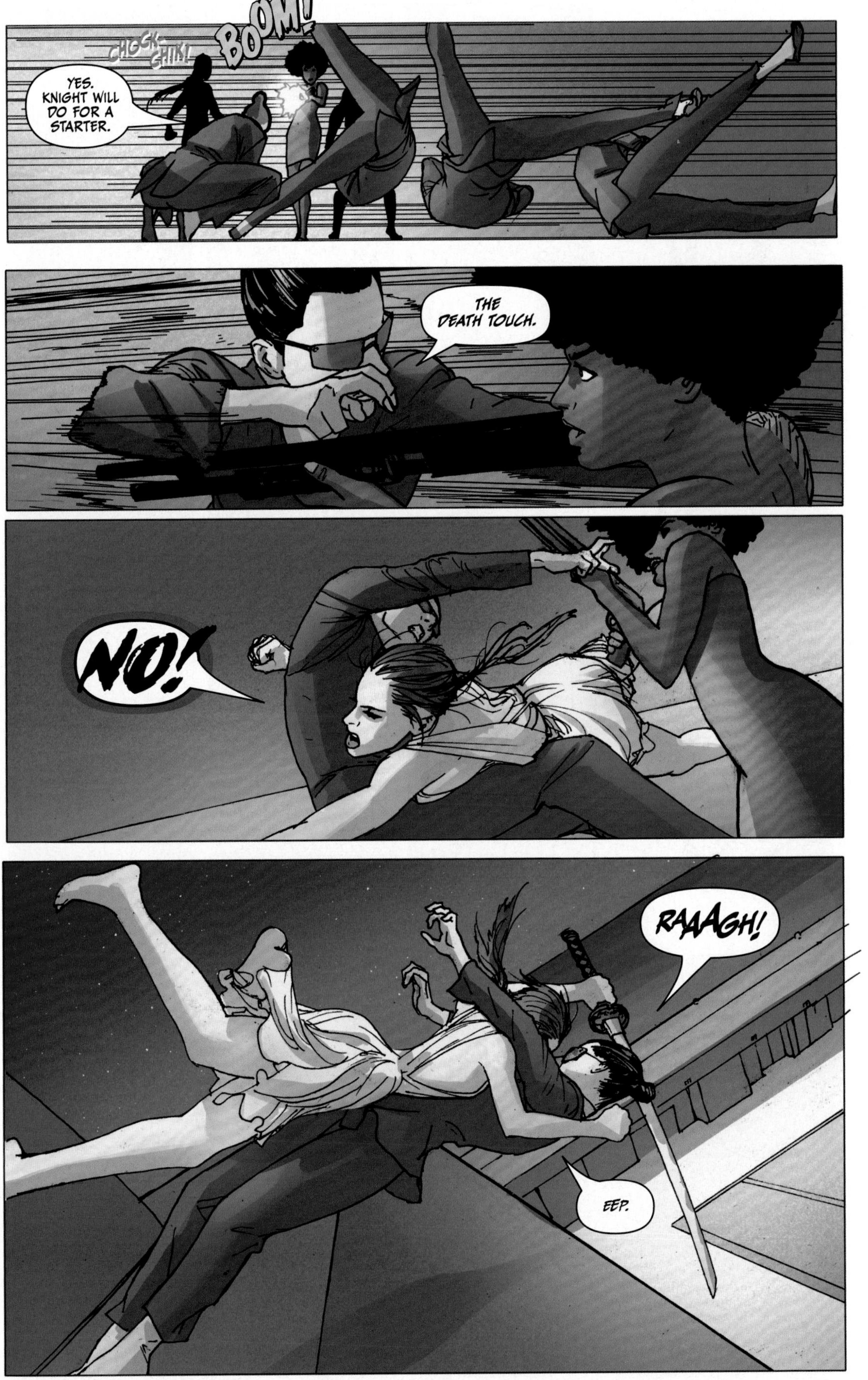
CHOCK-CHIK!
BOOM!
YES. KNIGHT WILL DO FOR A STARTER.
THE DEATH TOUCH.
NO!
RAAAGH!
EEP.

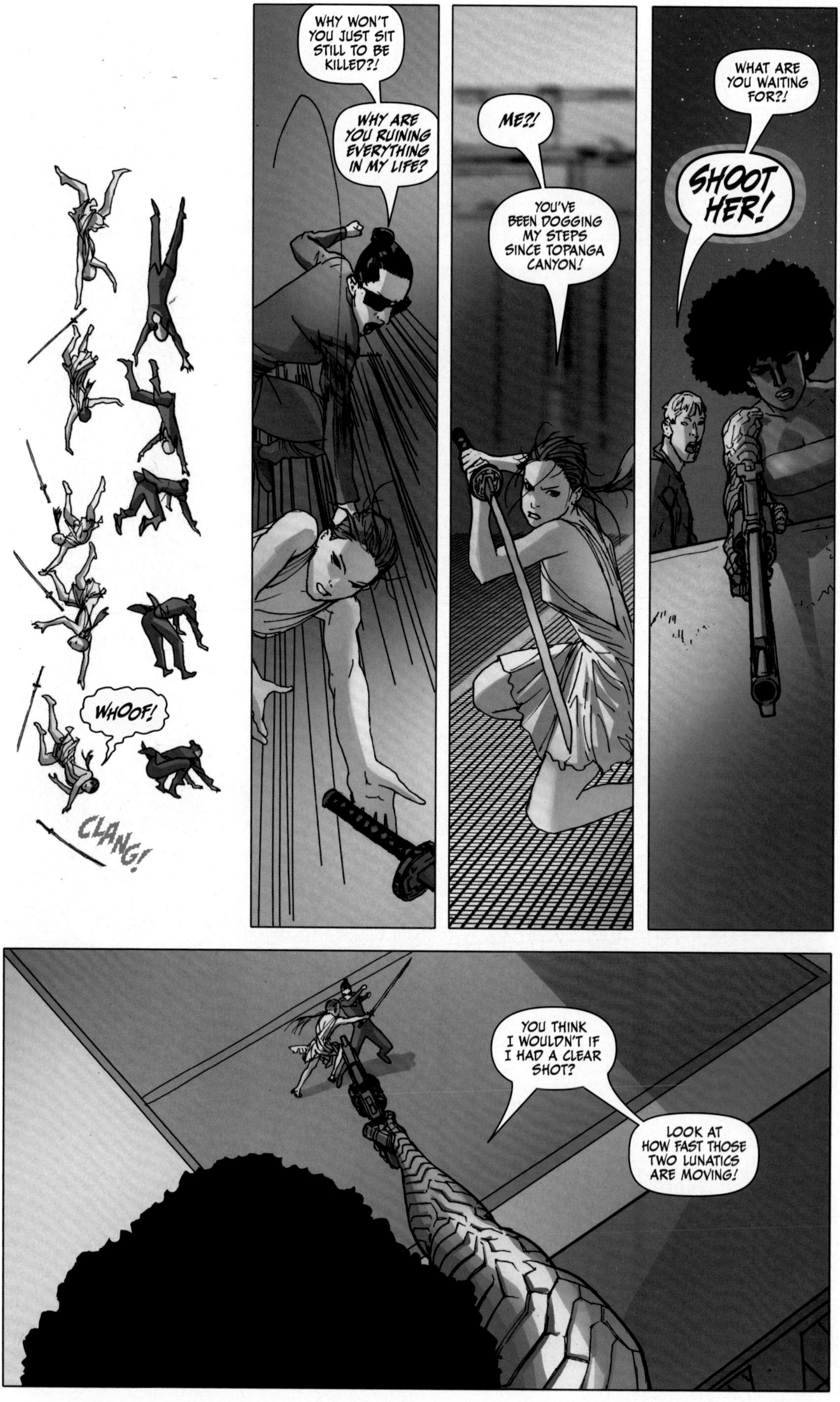
WHOOF!
CLANG!
WHY WON'T YOU JUST SIT STILL TO BE KILLED?!
WHY ARE YOU RUINING EVERYTHING IN MY LIFE?
ME?!
YOU'VE BEEN DOGGING MY STEPS SINCE TOPANGA CANYON!
WHAT ARE YOU WAITING FOR?!
SHOOT HER!
YOU THINK I WOULDN'T IF I HAD A CLEAR SHOT?
LOOK AT HOW FAST THOSE TWO LUNATICS ARE MOVING!

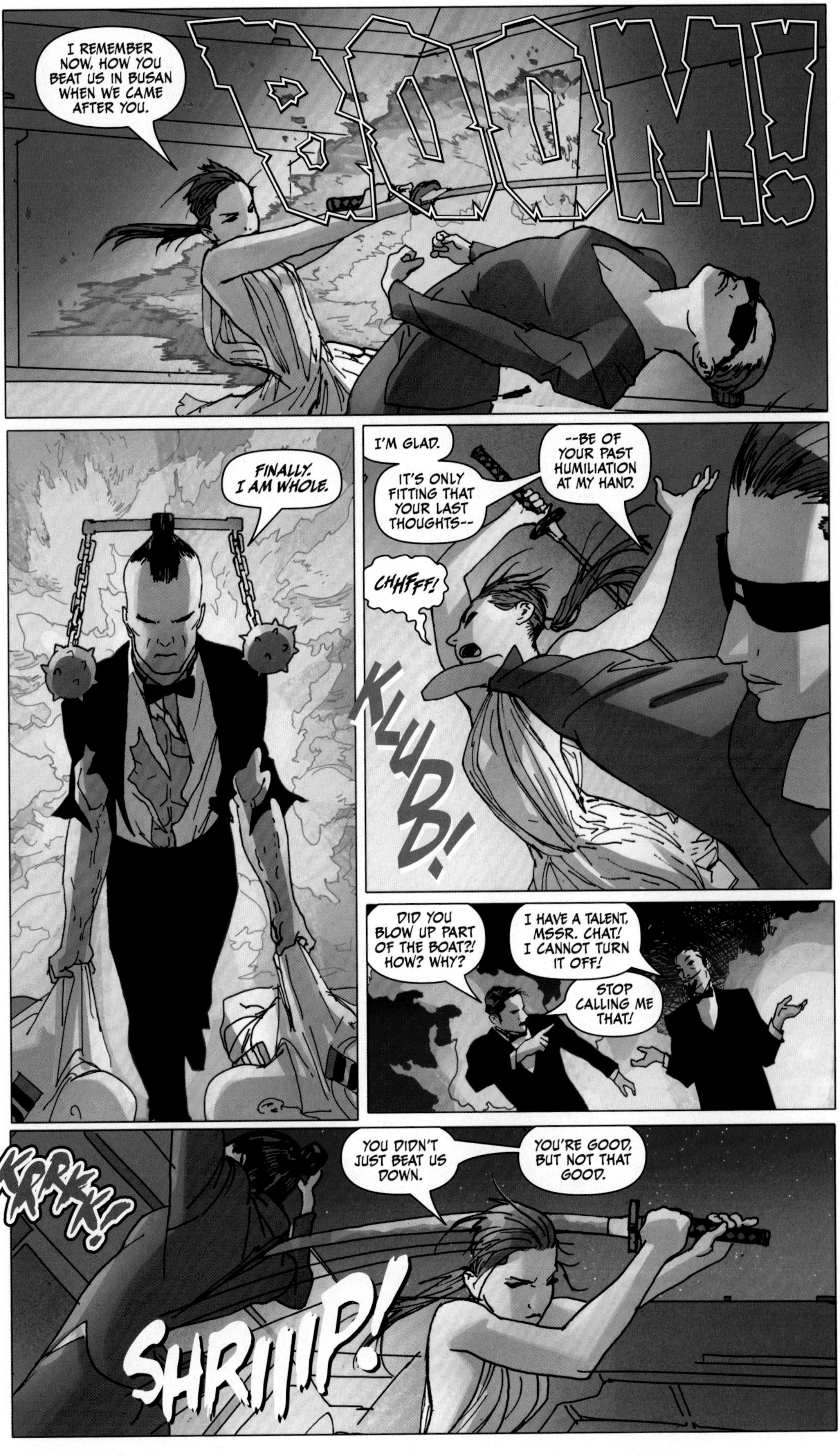
I REMEMBER NOW, HOW YOU BEAT US IN BUSAN WHEN WE CAME AFTER YOU.
BOOM!
FINALLY. I AM WHOLE.
I'M GLAD.
IT'S ONLY FITTING THAT YOUR LAST THOUGHTS--
--BE OF YOUR PAST HUMILIATION AT MY HAND.
CHHFFF!
KLUDD!
DID YOU BLOW UP PART OF THE BOAT?! HOW? WHY?
I HAVE A TALENT, MSSR. CHAT! I CANNOT TURN IT OFF!
STOP CALLING ME THAT!
KRRKK!
YOU DIDN'T JUST BEAT US DOWN.
YOU'RE GOOD, BUT NOT THAT GOOD.
SHRIIIP!

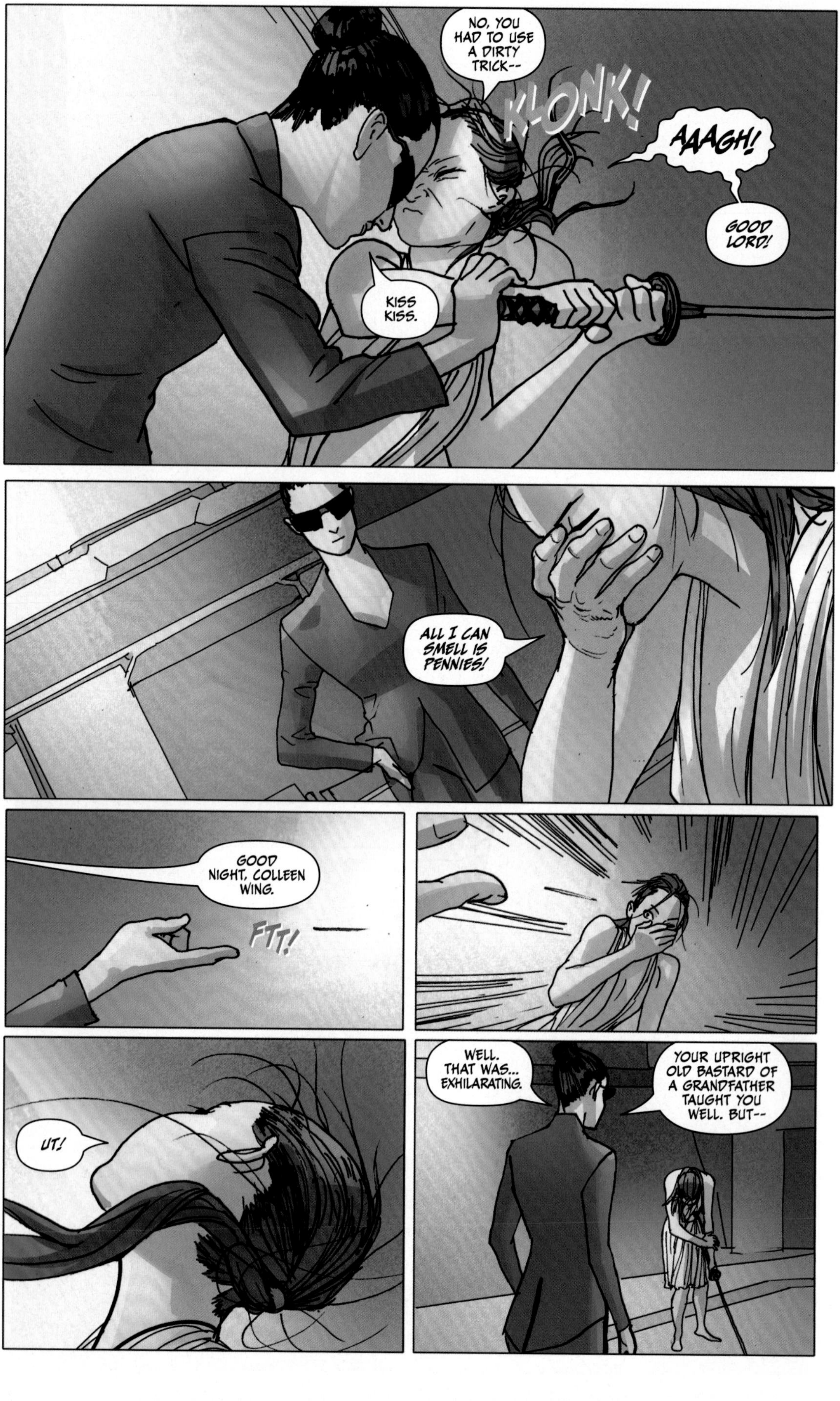
NO, YOU HAD TO USE A DIRTY TRICK--
KLONK!
AAAGH!
GOOD LORD!
KISS KISS.
ALL I CAN SMELL IS PENNIES!
GOOD NIGHT, COLLEEN WING.
FTT!
UT!
WELL. THAT WAS... EXHILARATING.
YOUR UPRIGHT OLD BASTARD OF A GRANDFATHER TAUGHT YOU WELL. BUT--

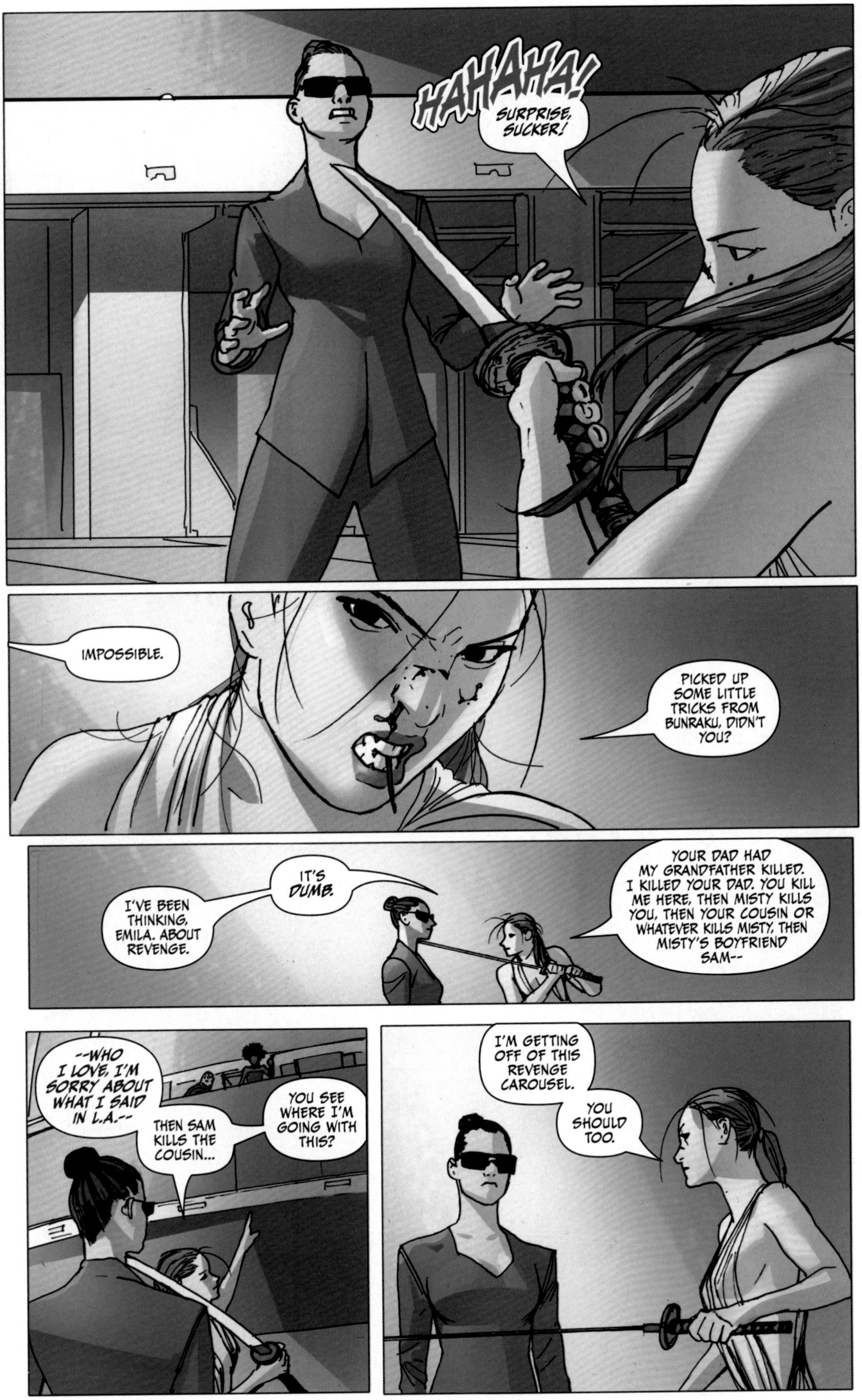
HAHAHA!
SURPRISE, SUCKER!
IMPOSSIBLE.
PICKED UP SOME LITTLE TRICKS FROM BUNRAKU, DIDN'T YOU?
I'VE BEEN THINKING, EMILA. ABOUT REVENGE.
IT'S DUMB.
YOUR DAD HAD MY GRANDFATHER KILLED. I KILLED YOUR DAD. YOU KILL ME HERE, THEN MISTY KILLS YOU, THEN YOUR COUSIN OR WHATEVER KILLS MISTY. THEN MISTY'S BOYFRIEND SAM--
--WHO I LOVE, I'M SORRY ABOUT WHAT I SAID IN L.A.--
THEN SAM KILLS THE COUSIN...
YOU SEE WHERE I'M GOING WITH THIS?
I'M GETTING OFF OF THIS REVENGE CAROUSEL.
YOU SHOULD TOO.

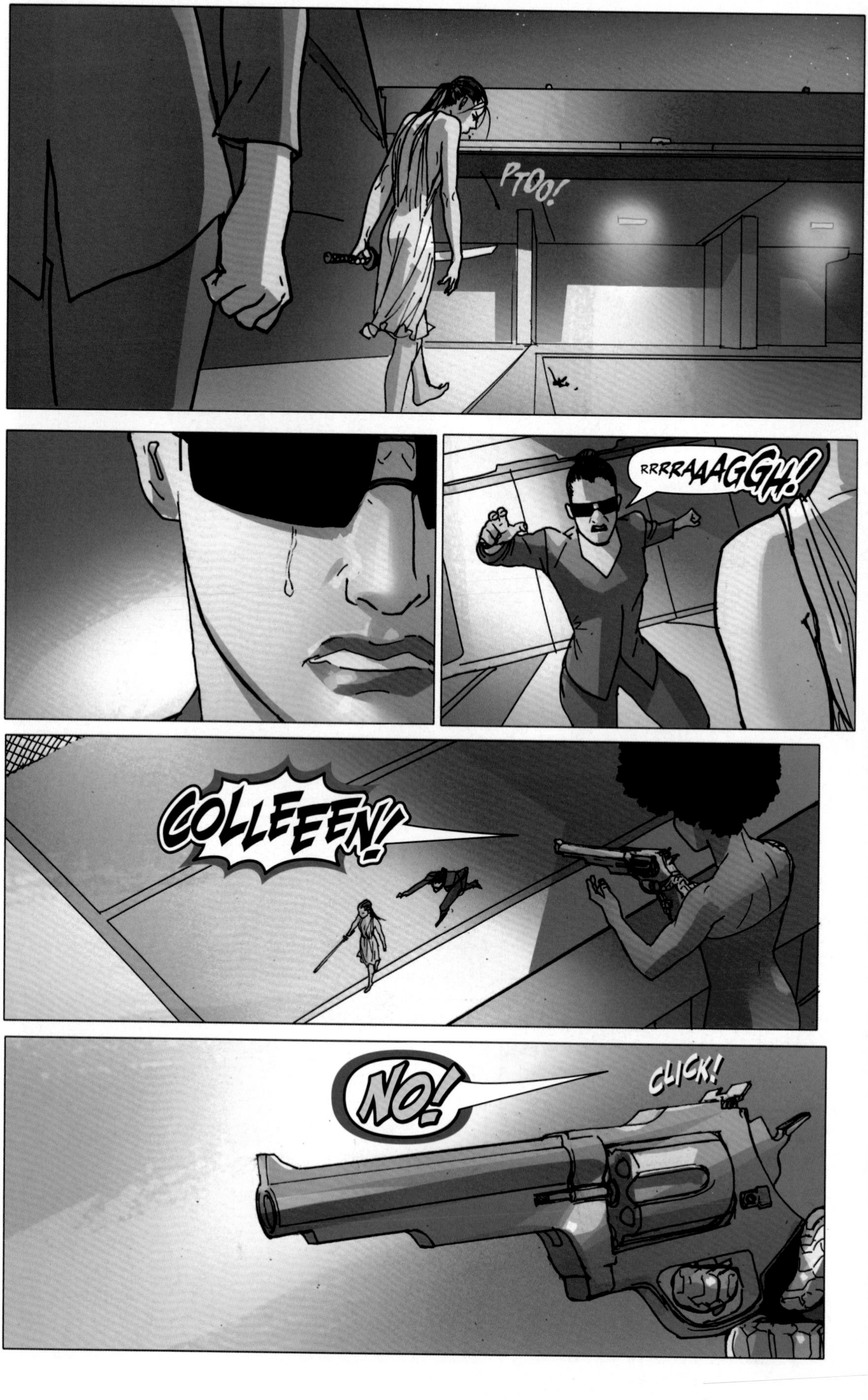
PTOO!
RRRRAAAGGH!
COLLEEEN!
NO!
CLICK!

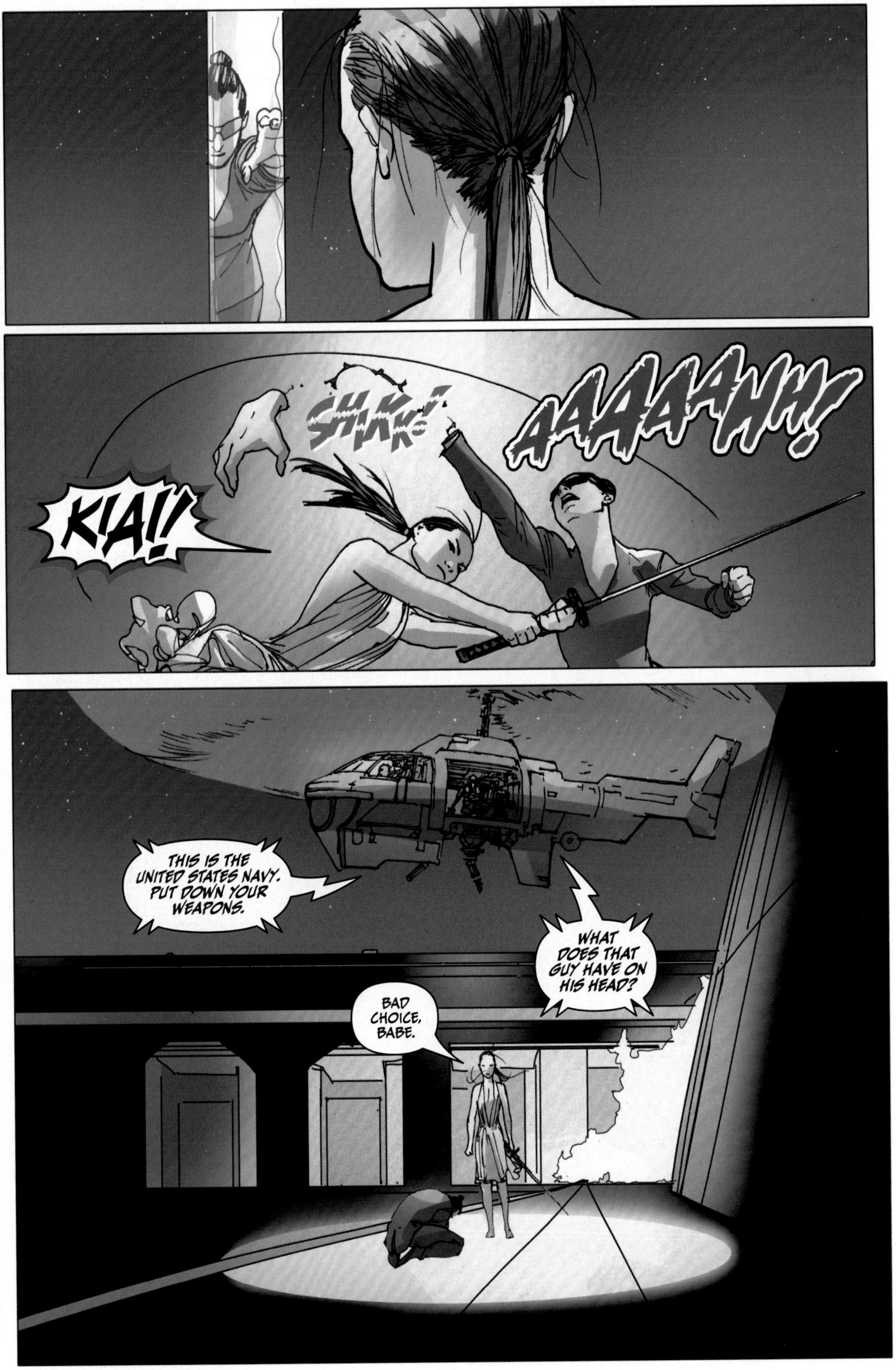
SHUKK!
AAAAAHH!
KIA!!
THIS IS THE UNITED STATES NAVY. PUT DOWN YOUR WEAPONS.
WHAT DOES THAT GUY HAVE ON HIS HEAD?
BAD CHOICE, BABE.

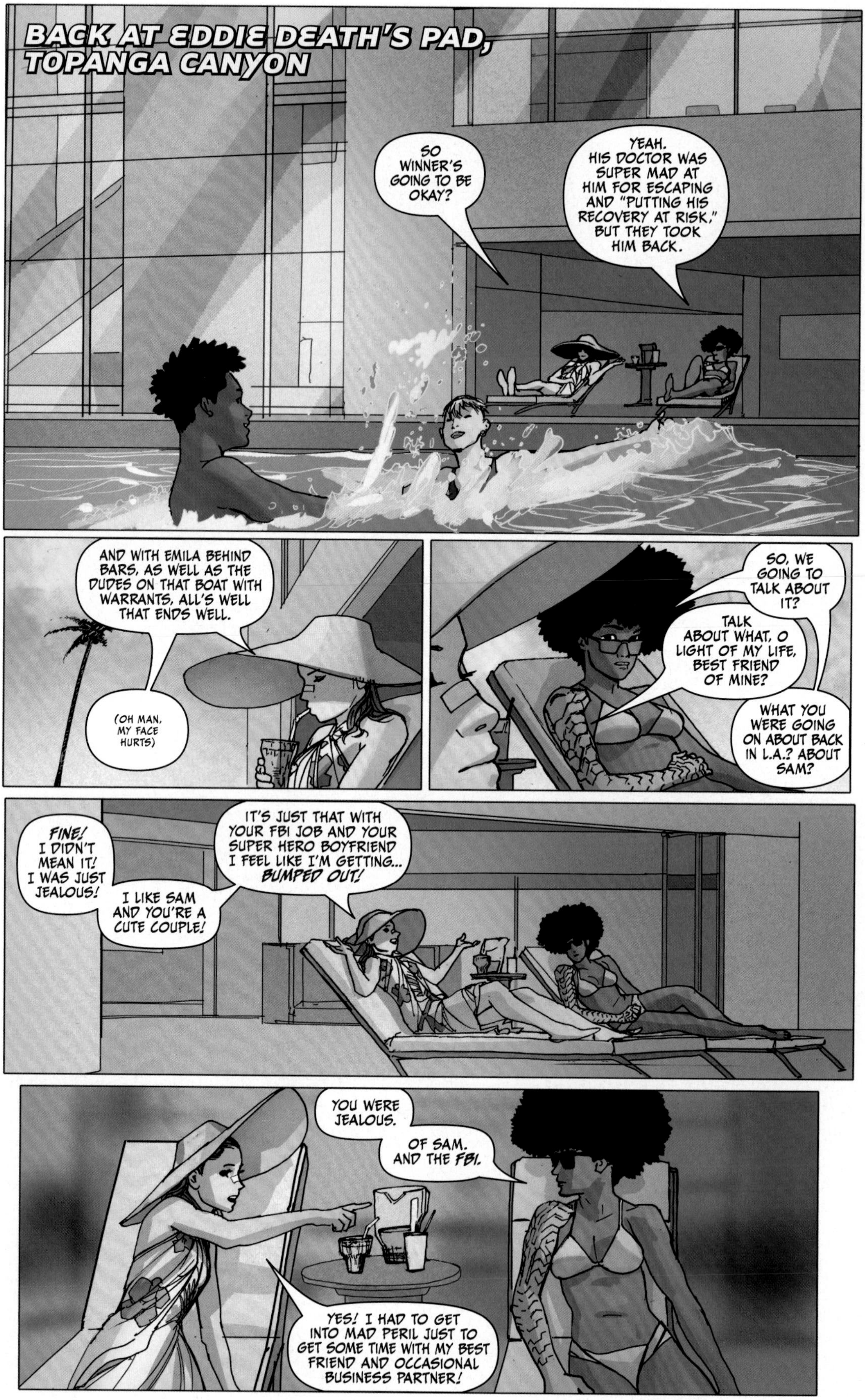
BACK AT EDDIE DEATH'S PAD, TOPANGA CANYON
SO WINNER'S GOING TO BE OKAY?
YEAH. HIS DOCTOR WAS SUPER MAD AT HIM FOR ESCAPING AND "PUTTING HIS RECOVERY AT RISK," BUT THEY TOOK HIM BACK.
AND WITH EMILA BEHIND BARS, AS WELL AS THE DUDES ON THAT BOAT WITH WARRANTS, ALL'S WELL THAT ENDS WELL.
(OH MAN, MY FACE HURTS)
SO, WE GOING TO TALK ABOUT IT?
TALK ABOUT WHAT, O LIGHT OF MY LIFE, BEST FRIEND OF MINE?
WHAT YOU WERE GOING ON ABOUT BACK IN L.A.? ABOUT SAM?
FINE! I DIDN'T MEAN IT! I WAS JUST JEALOUS!
I LIKE SAM AND YOU'RE A CUTE COUPLE!
IT'S JUST THAT WITH YOUR FBI JOB AND YOUR SUPER HERO BOYFRIEND I FEEL LIKE I'M GETTING... BUMPED OUT!
YOU WERE JEALOUS.
OF SAM. AND THE FBI.
YES! I HAD TO GET INTO MAD PERIL JUST TO GET SOME TIME WITH MY BEST FRIEND AND OCCASIONAL BUSINESS PARTNER!

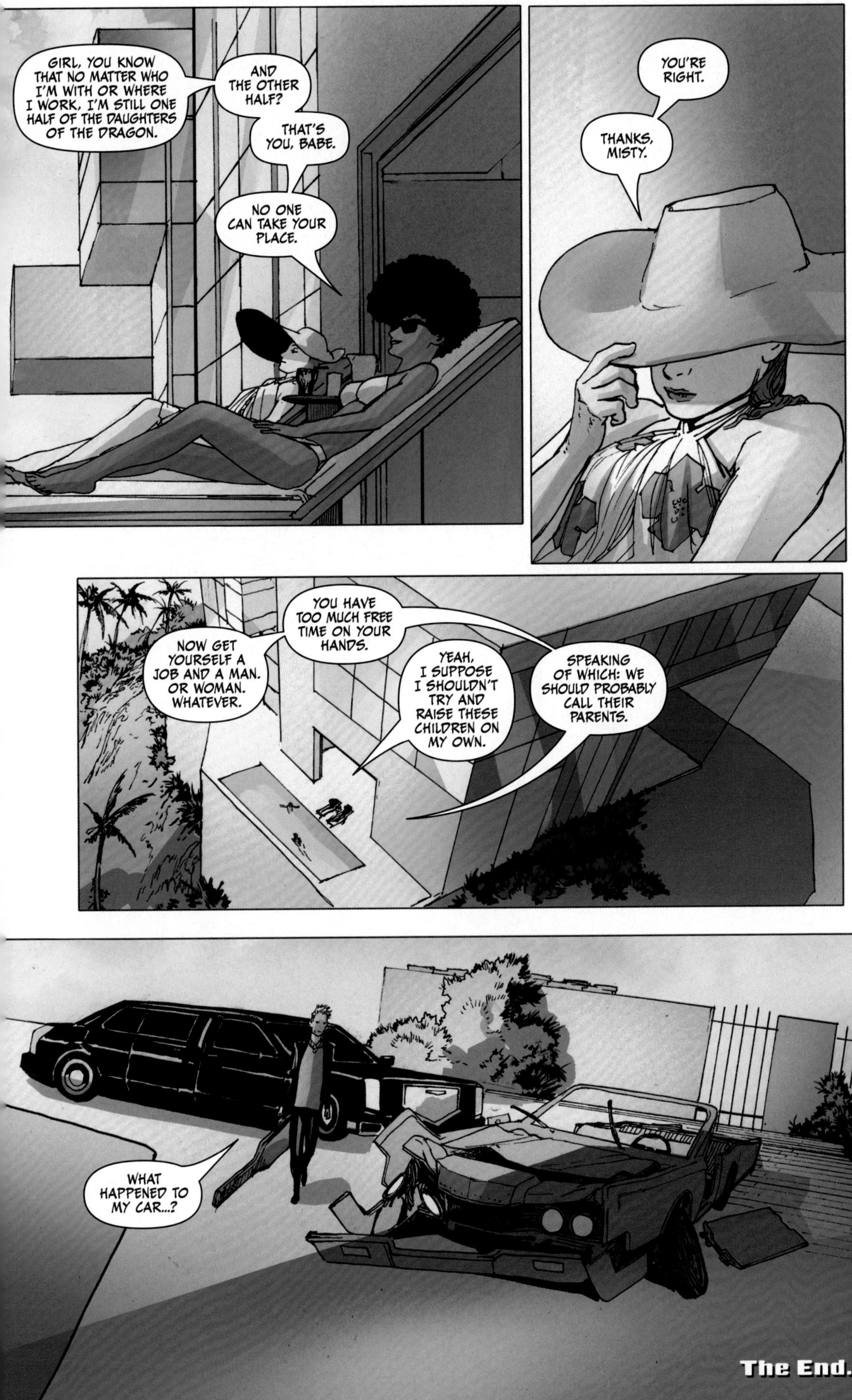
GIRL, YOU KNOW THAT NO MATTER WHO I'M WITH OR WHERE I WORK, I'M STILL ONE HALF OF THE DAUGHTERS OF THE DRAGON.
AND THE OTHER HALF?
THAT'S YOU, BABE.
NO ONE CAN TAKE YOUR PLACE.
YOU'RE RIGHT.
THANKS, MISTY.
NOW GET YOURSELF A JOB AND A MAN. OR WOMAN. WHATEVER.
YOU HAVE TOO MUCH FREE TIME ON YOUR HANDS.
YEAH, I SUPPOSE I SHOULDN'T TRY AND RAISE THESE CHILDREN ON MY OWN.
SPEAKING OF WHICH: WE SHOULD PROBABLY CALL THEIR PARENTS.
WHAT HAPPENED TO MY CAR...?
The End.

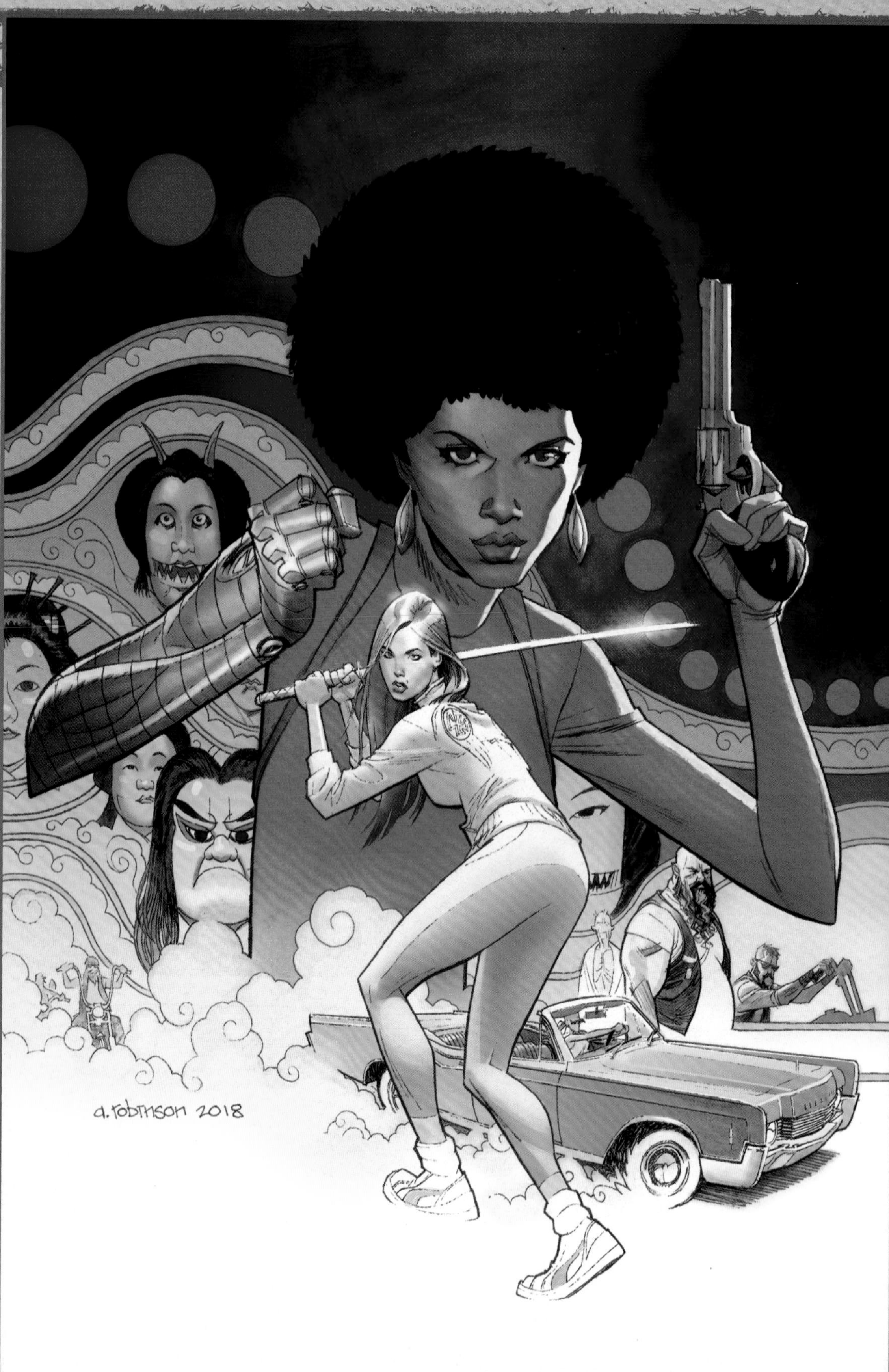
a. robinson 2018

ISSUE 1 COVER

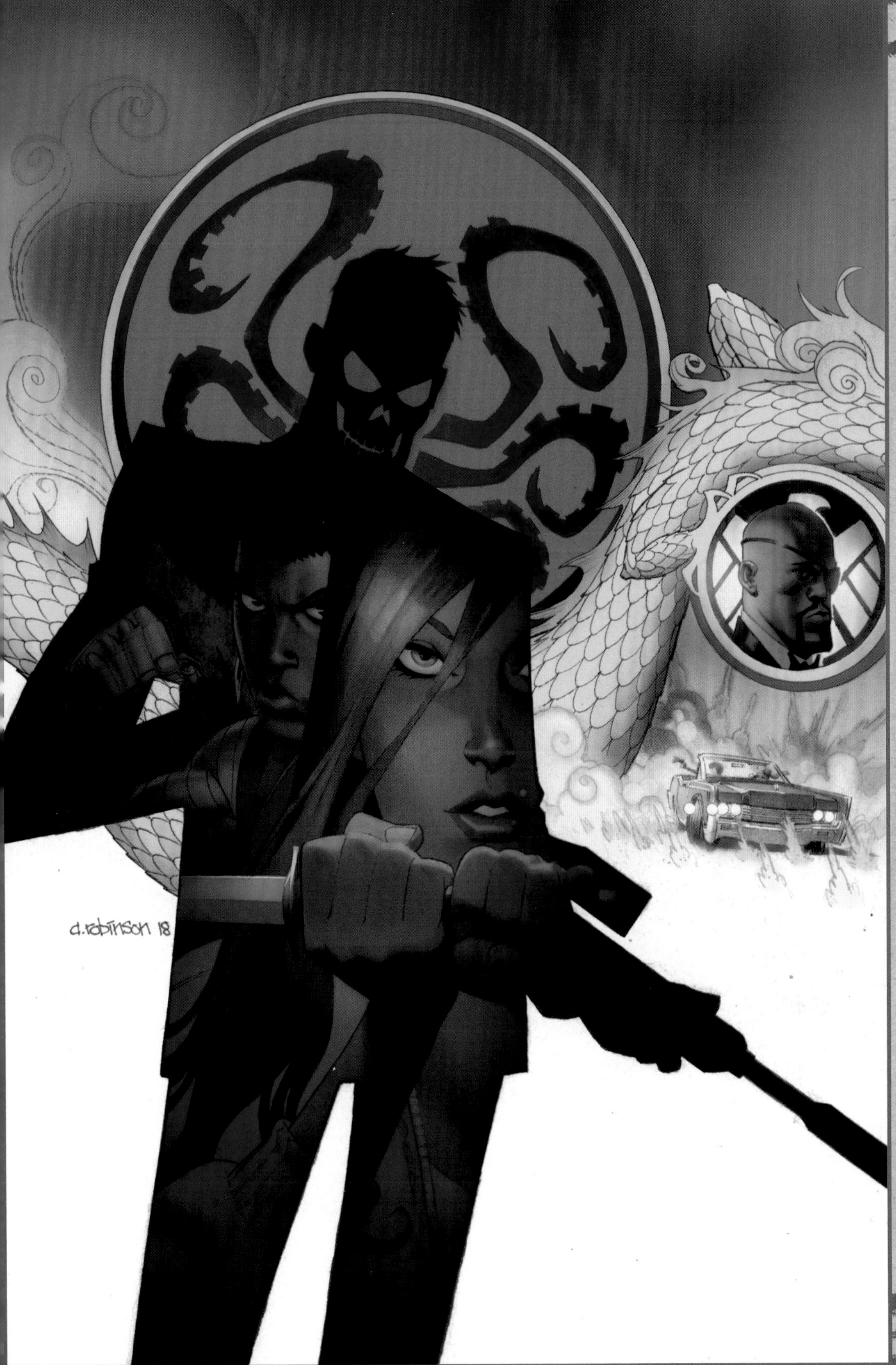
d.robinson 18

ISSUE 2 COVER

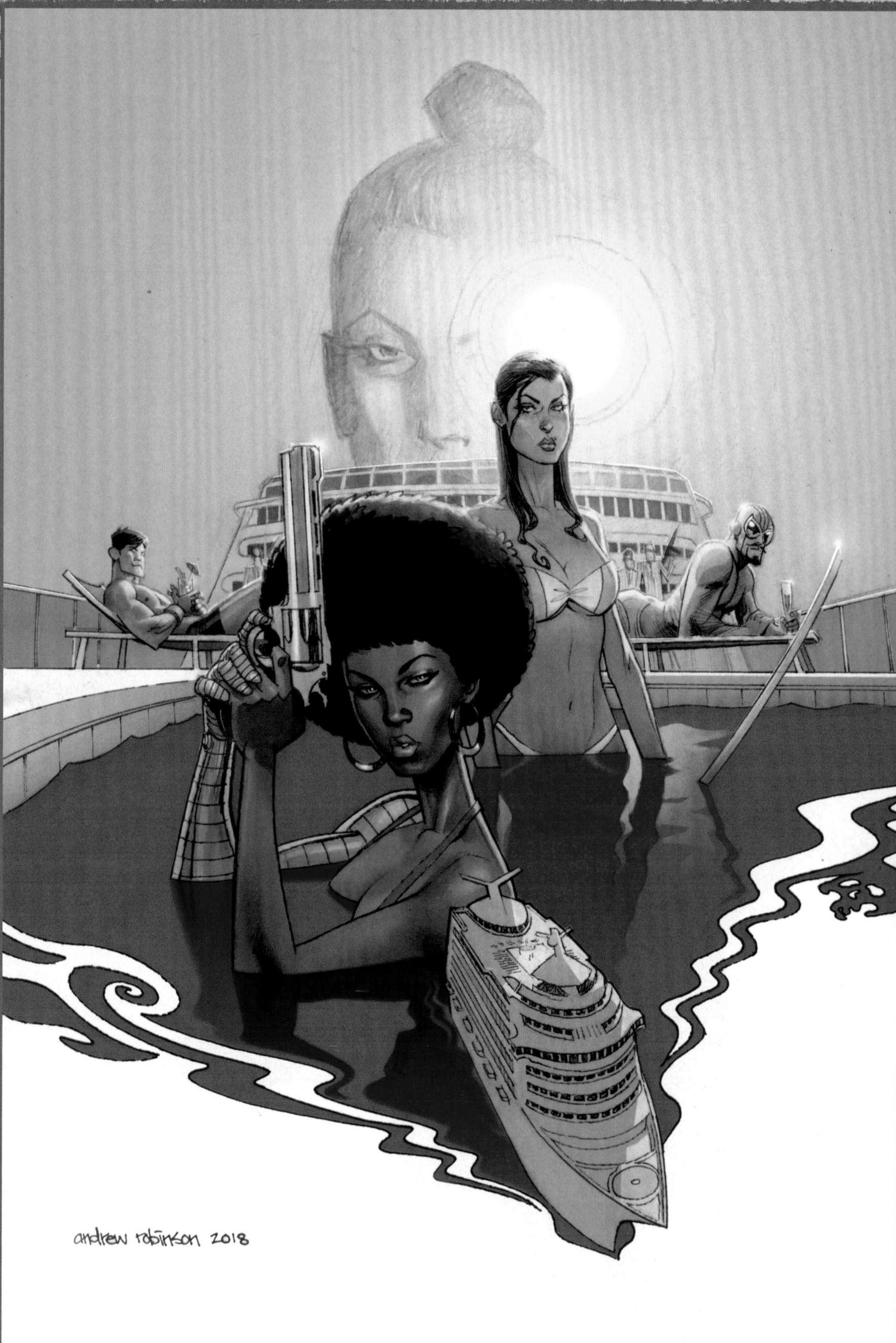
andrew robinson 2018

ISSUE 3 COVER

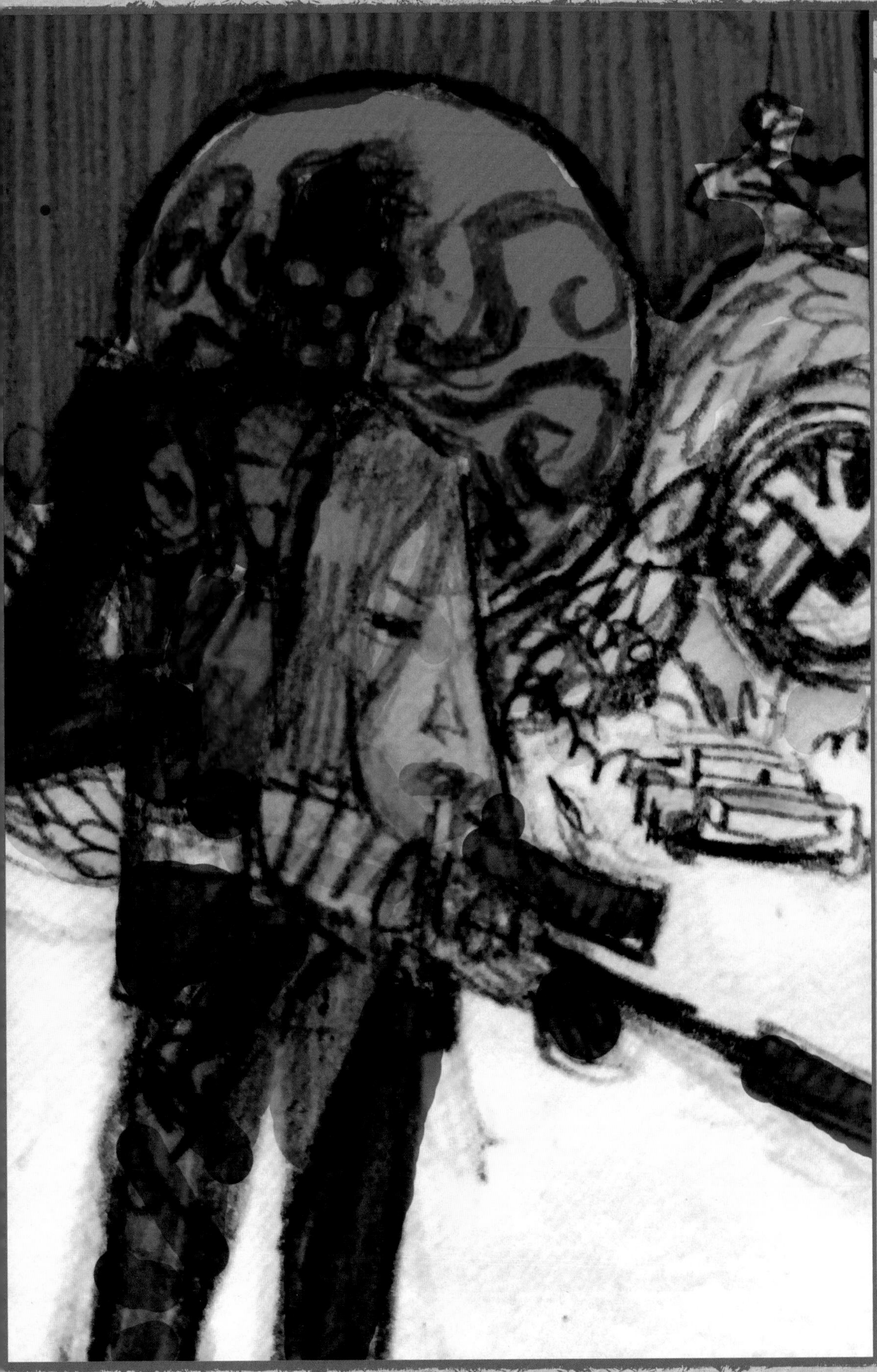

ANDREW C. ROBINSON
ISSUE 2 COVER SKETCH

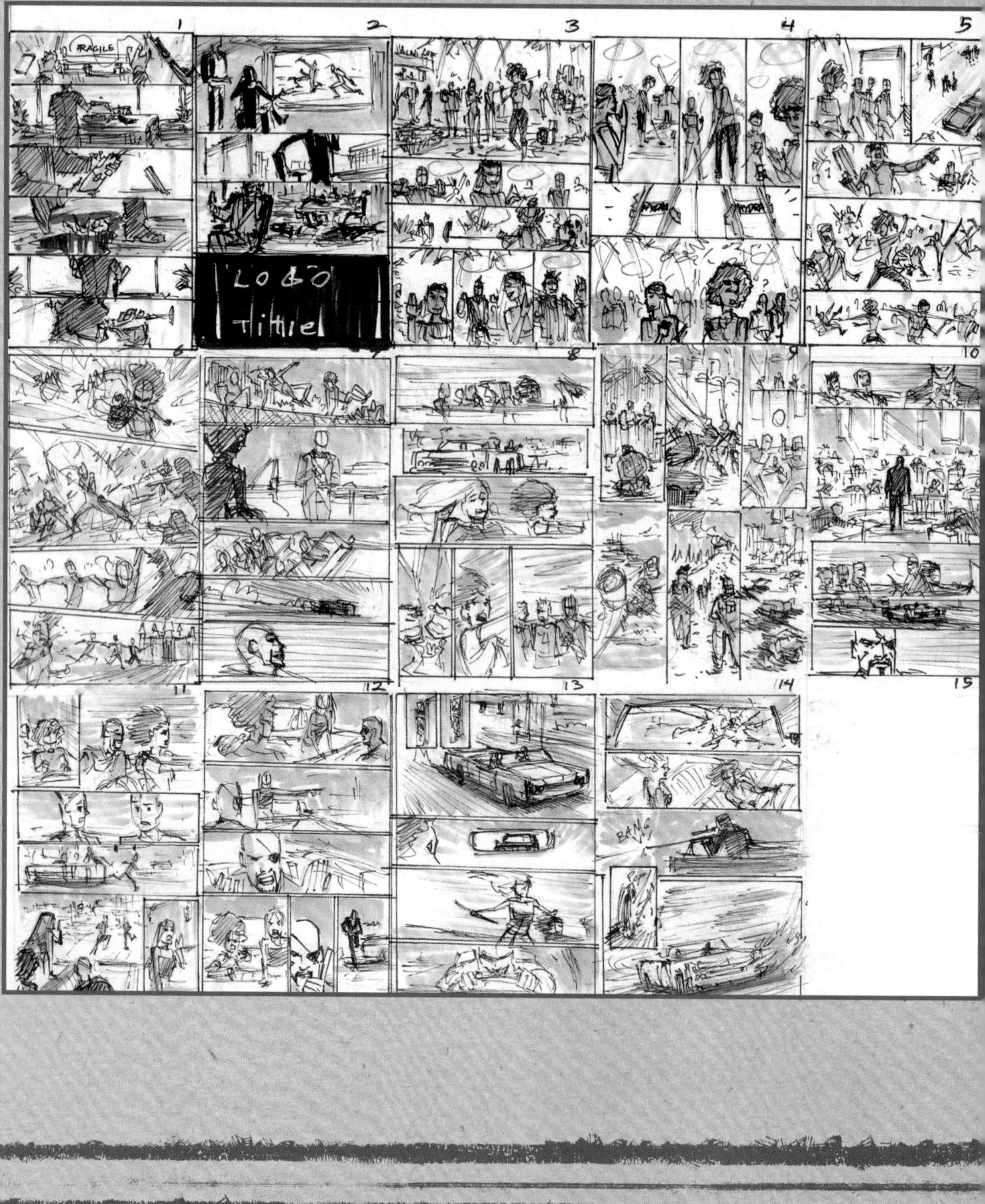
LOGO
Title
FRAGILE
BANG

JOEY VAZQUEZ
CHAPTER 3, PAGES 1-14 THUMBNAILS

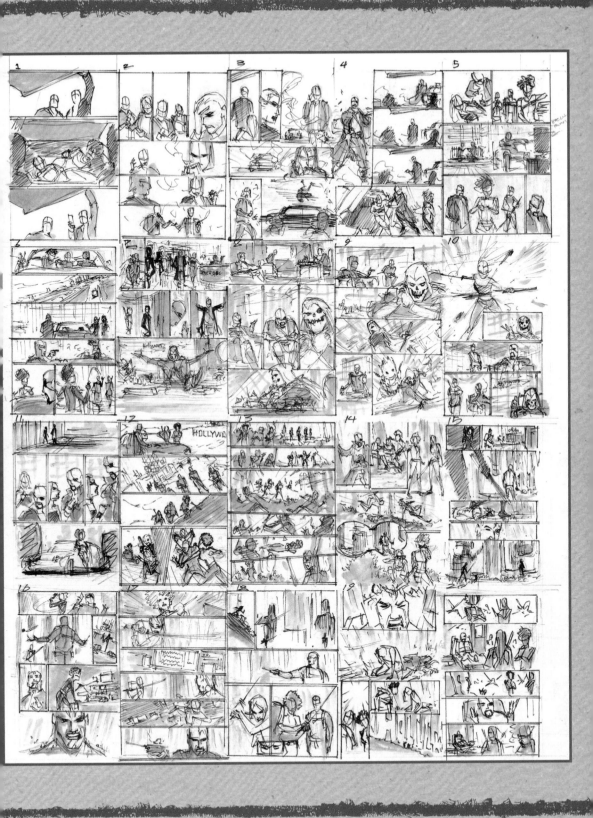

JOEY VAZQUEZ
CHAPTER 4, PAGES 1-20 THUMBNAILS

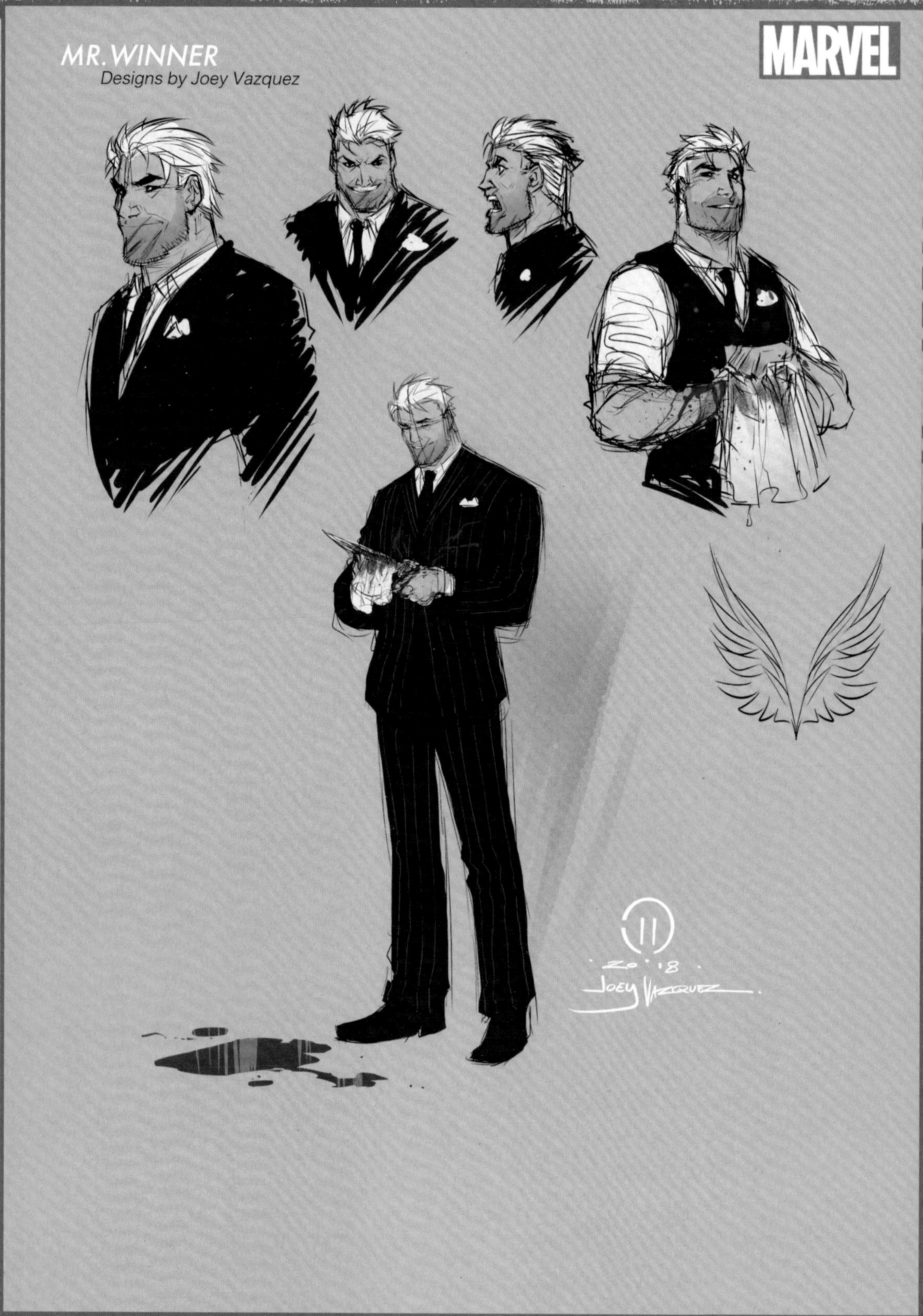
MR.WINNER
Designs by Joey Vazquez
MARVEL

JOEY VAZQUEZ
CHARACTER DESIGNS